Fame in Hollywood North

A Theoretical Guide to Celebrity

Cultures in Canada

Fame in Hollywood North

A Theoretical Guide to Celebrity Cultures in Canada

Samita Nandy, PhD

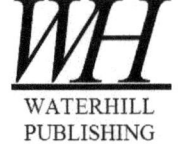

WATERHILL
PUBLISHING

The views and opinions expressed herein are those of the authors and do not necessarily reflect the positions of the publisher.

© 2015 Samita Nandy, Ph.D.

Front and back cover photographs and design:

© 2015 WaterHill Publishing, Toronto

ISBN: 978-0-9939938-3-1

DEDICATION

To Louis, Dad, and Mum.

Contents

Acknowledgments

Many institutions and individuals have offered intellectual, inspirational, and material support to conduct and complete this research. I would like to begin by acknowledging the support of Australia's Department of Education, Science and Training (DEST) and Curtin University of Technology for full-time funding of this Doctoral research. In particular, DEST's Endeavour International Postgraduate Research Scholarships (EIPRS) and Curtin University Postgraduate Scholarships (CUPS) sponsored the complete research, fieldwork, and conferences in Australia, Canada, and the United States of America.

My sincere gratitude goes to my PhD supervisors Professor Matthew Allen and Dr Helen Merrick. Their advice, constructive criticism, and encouragement supported the development and completion of the book. I am also thankful to my previous committee members Professor Jon Stratton and Dr Michele Willson. During my candidacy, their support and suggestions encouraged me to embark on my book topic and structure the chapters. After I completed the fieldwork and first drafts of writing, I received immense support and assurance from Dr John Fielder at Curtin University's Learning Centre. His suggestions strengthened the approaches and writing style of this book.

When I presented parts of my book at Curtin University's research seminar, Dr Paul Moore and Dr Ron Blaber offered invaluable comments and suggestions. Throughout the writing of this book, I carried knowledge, skills and inspiration that I received from my previous university professors and referees as well. In this respect, I am grateful to Distinguished Research Professor John O'Neil and Dr Himani Banerji from York University, Dr Anthony Wensley from University of Toronto, and Dr Bill Thompson from Macquarie University. Their drive and support from Canada encouraged me to pursue and complete this book in Australia.

The case studies presented in this book are based on an intensive fieldwork that I undertook in Canada. The fieldwork would not have been possible without the incredible support that I received from a number of media corporations and other cultural institutions in Toronto. I am indebted to Eve Goldin, Senior Librarian of the Toronto International Film Festival, for supporting my archival research. Her careful guidance and patience directed me to periodicals and media reports on Toronto International Film Festival and Canada's Walk of Fame. Marissa Soumalias, Manager of Inductee Relations, and Julianne Taskey, Manager of Special Events, Sponsorships and Marketing at Canada's Walk of Fame also supported my fieldwork. My conversations with them and their documentation offered insight into their practices and policies. I am also thankful to Scott Henderson, Vice-President of Communications at CTV television network. My discussion with him allowed me to reflect on the rise of Canada's celebrity cultures and the role of CTV in recognising the fame of Canadian celebrities.

My third chapter received constructive criticism and feedback from anonymous editors at the International Journal of Communication (IJC). On submitting a part of my third chapter as an article, the editorial board offered precise suggestions on conceptual and analytical levels of research. I am grateful to have received their suggestions and have included them in this book.

I would like to acknowledge my academic colleagues and friends who have provided me with intellectual and inspirational support while I was writing this book. For this, my thanks go to Dr Alzena McDonald from Curtin University. Her critical feedback on my initial chapters set grounds to think through the remaining chapters. I am also thankful to colleagues and friends Myles Wright, Sonia Tascon, Yaya Mori, Shaphan Cox, Betty Campbell, Liam Lynch, and Joy Scott for standing by me during critical times of research, writing, and travel. Myles' beloved mother and her passionate interests in travel, literature, and arts were deeply inspiring during my journey.

Finally, I am eternally grateful to my life partner Dr Louis Massey, Assistant Professor at Royal Military College in Kingston, Canada. His unconditional love across the world and critical feedback on my research contributed towards the successful writing, editing, and proofreading of this book. My special thanks go to Dr Jarret Ruminski for his final review of this manuscript. I am also indebted to my parents Samaresh Nandy and the late Saswati Nandy. Their ongoing love, educational support, and guidance enabled me to conduct and complete this book.

List of Acronyms

BCFC	British Columbia Film Commission
CBC	Canadian Broadcasting Corporation
CPR	Canadian Pacific Railway
CNR	Canadian National Railway
CRTC	Canadian Radio-television and Telecommunications Commission
CTV	Canadian Television Network
CWOF	Canada's Walk of Fame
FCC	Federal Communications Commission
FTA	Free Trade Agreement
NAFTA	North American Free Trade Agreement
NHL	National Hockey League
RCMP	Royal Canadian Mounted Police
TIFF	Toronto International Film Festival
TVA	Téléviseurs associés
US	United States

List of Figures

1 Introduction

Historically, Canadians have not been much good at celebrity culture. Oh, we have talent, and plenty of it, but we've never had a knack for constructing the celebrity-industrial complex that surrounds it (Gillmore, 2014).

Red carpets, limousines, TV cameras and klieg lights, movers and shakers in tuxes and evening gowns [are] somehow almost...un-Canadian. Now, I don't mean to be impolite (that would be really un-Canadian), but this is a country that tends to measure its cultural worth based on its American reception (Salem, 2002).

Fame is not a very Canadian word (Harris, 1998a).

Fame, a mildly famous Canadian once declared, is mainly the privilege of being pestered by strangers. That observation, by Montreal poet Louis Dudek, seems to sum up the Canadian attitude toward fame: a bit of nuisance, an imposition, something that is best avoided but, once acquired (usually outside the country) must be borne with forbearance (Harris, 1998a).

In television interviews, public seminars, and personal conversations, I have often been asked: what is it about fame that appeals to me as a topic of interest in cultural studies? It is neither the glamour nor the scandals: I do not even follow celebrity news. Could it be, then, the deep social impacts of fame? Could it be the creative forces underlying fame? In the context of this book, could it be the capability of fame to construct and support a nation?

Let us address these questions with positive responses, why not?

Yet, there is a negative connotation associated with fame, but such "infamy" paradoxically helps to construct fame and to maintain the social fabric. One may argue that people engage in celebrity gossip and scandals based on taboo issues. These cultural practices and narrative devices play a sociological function in integrating society on grounds of ethics and morality. But the irony is that celebrities are often consumed on unethical grounds. Celebrity gossips function as narrative devices to negotiate ideological tensions and manage social norms and behaviour. Indeed, celebrity bashing is a pleasurable practice in fame, but it shifts attention away from merit-based talent that has been characteristic of legendary heroes since historical times.

The construction of celebrities is ubiquitous and pervasive in modern culture. One can trace the historical roots of celebrity culture back to the Egyptian, Greek, and Roman eras, when hero worship was prevalent. In the wake of the Industrial Revolution and the rise of mass communication, fame has played a significant role in shaping how fans engage in pleasures and identification, how they develop para-social relations with celebrities, and the ways in which artists understand the production and representation of their own talent in popular culture. Like glamour, fame carries splendour, allure, sexual appeal, and questions of authenticity that can be partially fulfilled only when it remains an illusion. While these ongoing questions of authenticity are integral to the negotiation and maintenance of desire for celebrities, they rarely address the talent that allows some public personalities to shine and become popular in the arts and entertainment industry while most others remain anonymous.

The anonymity of talent is strongly prevalent in Canada — also called Hollywood North — and fame remains ambivalent. Academic and popular discourses indicate that English Canada does not have celebrities or a star system (Chidley, 2002; Edwardson, 2003; Ferguson & Ferguson, 2003; Francis, 1997; Hunt, 1981; Jackson, 2007; Schweitzer, 2010). This accepted dogma is generally grounded in the assumption that Canadians have a colonial mindset of experiencing dominance. From this perspective, Canadians are considered to have an inferiority complex, humility, and politeness (Govani, 2009; Kryk, 2008; Saul, 1997; Winereserva, 2009). An alternative assumption is that Canadians may be too arrogant and believe that they are better than their American counterparts, who feel compelled to celebrate their stars (Kryk, 2008). Either way, popular discourses support a myth that Canadians do not celebrate their own talent, which simplistically leads to the interpretation that Canada lacks celebrities. However, practices in popular culture show regular production and consumption of celebrities in Canada. In fact, celebrities are produced and consumed in association with national symbols and myths.

Fame in Hollywood North examines the discursive construction of celebrities in Canada. In particular, it looks at the emergence of Canadian meanings of fame within national discourses. In exploring the meanings of fame, the research is not limited to representation of Canadian celebrities. It rather considers Canadian representation of both Canadian and American celebrities and, to some extent, celebrities of other nations. *Fame in Hollywood North* draws on classical notions of Hollywood stardom that historically emerged in America. It then examines ways in which this stardom is mediated in the national context of Canada, and particularly how Canadian media construct national identity through representations of celebrities and fame.

Defining Fame and Celebrities

Fame can be defined as a set of practices and processes that distinguish public personalities as celebrities in particular social and cultural contexts. For Chris Rojek (2001), fame can be defined in four different ways: ascribed (legendary), achieved (meritocratic), attributed (based on concentration of media attention), and renown (popular recognition in closed social networks). Media texts representing celebrities sociologically function as a system of signs. Richard Dyer (1998) looks at the sociological and semiotic origins of stars in films. The sociological approach considers stars as a social phenomenon and symptomatic of the industrial organisation of films. The approach stresses that films are significant because they have stars. The semiotic approach emphasises the reverse: stars are significant because they appear in films and are culturally constructed and represented in ways films signify them. Both the sociological and semiotic views are interdependent. From these two points of view, stars do not exist outside of film or any media text. When these texts become "social facts," semiotics must draw on sociological assumptions to textually analyse them (Dyer, 1998, p. 1).

Drawing on Richard Dyer's work, I define the celebrity as a media text that is discursively constructed by communication technologies. Without this textual representation by media technologies, a celebrity cannot exist. Chris Rojek supports that media representation is "the key principle in constructing and consuming the celebrity" (2001, p. 13). Celebrities are represented in the form of media products such as visual and written texts. Graeme Turner amplifies Rojek's argument and Richard Dyer's notion of the "star text," arguing that the celebrity is not only a "media process that is coordinated by an industry" but is also a "commodity or text which is productively consumed by audiences and fans" (2004, p. 20). To this end, the media text of a celebrity can be defined as a complex interplay between media institutions, governments, celebrities, and audiences. Using this perspective, *Fame in Hollywood*

North largely focuses on the celebrity as a textual representation, a discursive effect, and an industrial production.

Semiotically speaking, a celebrity text can be defined as a system of signs. The text has various parts called signs that are both related and bound together. These signs can be defined as something that is read as meaningful and are related to other signs in texts such as those representing a nation. The signs in celebrity texts represent dominant cultural meanings within society. Texts constituting the celebrity can be visual or literary media artefacts such as television interviews, film stills, paparazzi photos, and articles or gossip columns in magazines and newspapers. These texts represent and construct the celebrity with the help of signs such as red carpets, awards, luxurious garments, close-ups in security-guarded places, and caught-unaware stills in public and private settings.

Celebrity texts articulate two kinds of contradictions: the binary difference between 'extraordinariness' and 'ordinariness' and its 'presence' and 'absence.' For example, binaries like public/private and distant/close are contradictory characteristics of celebrities (Ellis, 2007; Geraghty, 2007). Celebrity texts are thereby incoherent — they are sustained by "contrasts" between the performing 'presence' and 'absence,' i.e., what happens on-stage and off-stage (Ellis, 2007; Geraghty, 2007). Celebrity texts with contrasting conditions generate appeal. In particular, there is a question of authenticity in the tension between the "ordinary" and the "extraordinary" that creates and sustains the appeal of, and desire towards, the ideological status of a celebrity. One of the ways in which authenticity is framed is representing what can be considered natural. As Richard Dyer states, ordinariness, as well as its difference from extraordinariness, "must be embodied as true and natural" and hence, the star "image insists on her or his authenticity" (2004, p. 157). In fame, the rhetoric of authenticity in the "ordinary" is particularly questioned and legitimised as one of the most valued meanings in contemporary society.

In exploring discursive constructions of fame, I interchangeably use the terms "star," "celebrity," and "famous." Historically, stardom in North America has its origins in the classical Hollywood period of cinema, during which film played a discursive role in creating the actor as a star. Later, television actors became famous stars as well. However, Su Holmes draws on Christine Geraghty and argues that in contemporary media, the "contexts of stardom are less specific, blurring the boundaries of terms used to conceptualise fame" (2005b, p. 9). Indeed, public personalities can be constructed and celebrated in any medium. Holmes expands:

> the term 'celebrity' has gained an increasingly elastic range of meanings in contemporary culture, variously used to indicate a more fleeting conception of fame, the contemporary state of 'being famous' in which 'meaningful' distinctions between hierarchies of

importance have diminished, or when fame rests predominantly on the private life of the person as opposed to their performing presence (2005a, p. 36).

Thus, in her work, Holmes uses the general term 'celebrity' to "indicate people who enter into media representation to attain a degree of public visibility, whether this be film, television or music" (p. 36). From this perspective, celebrity culture can be defined as a shared system of meanings of fame that may or may not include stardom, and passed down from one generation to another through media technologies. I draw knowledge from the work presented by Su Holmes and Christine Geraghty and shift from using the term 'star' in an exclusive way. Any celebrity, as I defined earlier, is a text whose fame is discursively constructed by mass media. Without textual representation in media discourse, the celebrity cannot exist. Although media texts of the Hollywood studio system have primarily represented film and television stars, fans or audiences can now also become stars on reality television shows and the Internet. The shift from using the term star exclusively for films is pertinent to the Canadian situation where the film industry is not as dominant as it is in the US. In fact, as seen in Canadian practices of fame, undermining stardom as 'film exclusivity' appears to be a mode of cultural defence against America. In light of this defence, Canadian stardom has been limited to personalities in literature, journalism, and sports. These personalities are famous for direct communication or performances of media texts other than classical Hollywood's film and television acting. I consider these historical and national settings in describing public figures that are famous in Canada. Hence, I use the terms star and celebrity in interchangeable ways to refer to any Canadian public personality that is recognised as 'famous.'

The ways in which media construct ordinariness as authenticity today mark a shift from constructions of film stars in the past. Reality TV shows and online media are primary sites where this change can be observed. Scholars Sue Holmes (2004, 2005b), Graeme Turner (2004), and David Marshall (2007) have studied how reality TV shows mark shifts in fame. Their studies particularly show that reality TV celebrities differ from past constructions of film stars in two major ways. First, the exclusivity of cinematic stardom and specificity of medium are less important in constructions of reality TV and online celebrities. Second, ordinary audiences/fans can now participate in the construction of celebrities. Despite their ordinariness, they can also become a reality TV contestant or use interactive tools and construct themselves as celebrities. The past boundaries between celebrities and audiences/fans are often blurred in present constructions of fame.

David Marshall (2007) and Graeme Turner (2004) have studied new ways in which ordinary citizens are celebrated as stars in reality TV programs and their media representations. Marshall suggests that emphasis on the "individuality" of ordinary contestants and voters increasingly indicates a sense of democracy in fame. This emphasis is significant because desires of individuality and equal opportunities of self-achievements are central to developing a democratic society (Marshall, 1997). In contrast, Turner argues that although an increased visibility of ordinariness represents the democratic will of media consumers as contestants and voters, it is not an authentic representation of democracy. He thus refuses to confuse ordinariness with democracy; rather, he observes the democratic potential of diverse, ordinary people who become celebrities as a "demotic turn." The phrase "demotic turn" describes "the proliferation of the construction of the ordinary in contemporary media" whereby the "public remains perfectly capable of expressing their own desires as if the production industry simply did not exist" (Turner, 2004, p. 91). However, the diversity of contestants on reality TV shows is still in the hands of those who operate the industrial productions of the shows. In this way, the industrial production of reality TV shows and their media representation not only support manufacturing of contestants as stars, but more importantly express particular forms of ideologies that appeal to voting fans nationwide.

Representations of ideological tensions serve to authenticate celebrities as well as the nation in which celebrities are produced. The ideological tensions might serve to authenticate a star image and, more importantly, the social value that they embody (Dyer, 1991). Among the sociological functions performed by celebrity texts are resolving ideological tensions of the nation in which they are produced and supporting national values.

Social Function of Celebrities in a Nation

Fans play a role in constructing and understanding the meaning and function of fame in a nation. In some ways, critical cultural studies on celebrities overlap with fan studies. This overlap is particularly found in relation to how fans recreate and circulate media texts on celebrities. These fans are not passive "cultural dupes" (Jensen, 1992) or "hysterical fanatics" (Jensen, 1992) as earlier critics would assume. Rather, "they are active audiences and cultural producers, creating symbolic capital and meanings of what it means to be truly celebrated" (Nandy, 2011b). In his book, *Celebrity and Power: Fame in Contemporary Culture* (1997), David Marshall draws on cultural studies and behaviourist approaches to further understand how the public constructs meanings and functions of celebrities on a collective level. He particularly looks at the celebrity offering an "affective function" and expressing popular will of the public in organised and rational ways. For Marshall, the "affective power" of the mass/crowd/public lies in the rationalisation and legitimacy of feelings, sentiments, and identification. Affect is, then, an important factor to consider when identity is constructed and legitimised through celebrities.

David Marshall's theoretical standpoint on audiences and collectives is useful to understand how fans play a role in accepting or negotiating dominant expressions of national identity through affect. The way in which technology shapes the formation of the Canadian nation and the formation of identity can be particularly understood in relation to affect in fame. In Canada, technology is rhetorically used to integrate the nation through affective responses to collective memories of the North. As suggested by the bidirectional relation between form and content in Chapter 3, texts representing Canadian celebrities are specific forms of technologies that interplay with Northern content. It can be argued that the affective power of Canadian citizens mobilises Northern discourses through fame-based practices. The affective responses of fans towards these celebrity texts are often rationalised as legitimate expressions of national identity within public discourses of the North. In addition, fans can now become celebrities with the help of new media technologies within Northern discourses of Canada. Chapters 7 and 8 shed light on the ways in which audiences/fans actively take part in celebrity constructions in new media. Although broader issues of fan spectatorship, gaze, and performances of affectively adoring celebrities are beyond the scope of this book, the adoration of celebrities has been, and continues to be, a major focus in cultural studies. The cultural production of celebrities symbolises values that are meaningful for a society and offers social gratification to consumers. The adoration of celebrities also offers social gratification that is significant for a nation. The gratification occurs on two levels.

First, audiences and fans can share belief systems and media artefacts about celebrities. Here, the mode of communication among fans, as scholar James Carey (1989) argues, is ritualistic and participatory, and in turn, leads to and sustains a community. It can be conversely argued that cultural industries constructing celebrities follow what scholar John Dewey (1916) called a transmission model of communication: sending messages over distance for the purpose of control. These two kinds of communication in celebrity culture, whether for control or participation, support the formation of a community with a common belief system, which is central to constructing and sustaining national identity.

Second, celebrities can offer social gratification by offering opportunities for nationwide fans to engage in celebrity worship and develop para-social relationships (McCutcheon, Range, & Houran, 2002). A para-social relationship can be defined as an illusion of a face-to-face relationship between a spectator and a media personality (Costello, 1999; Horton & Wohl, 1997). The development of para-social relationships between celebrities and fans has been historically important due to their shared identity and social functions. Scholar Chris Rojek explains that, "celebrity culture is a significant institution in the normative achievement of social integration" (2001, p. 98). The combination of the decline of organised religion, the democratisation of society, and the commodification of society over the last two centuries provided the foundation for the rise of celebrities. Specifically, "celebrities replaced monarchy as the new symbols of recognition and belonging, and as the belief in God waned, celebrities became immortal" (p. 14). It can be argued that the institutional power of celebrities "is very limited or non-existent" (Hills, 2006, p. 113). However, their systematic media representations and shared sense of belonging have the ability to comply with the social needs of fans and produce "social cohesion" (Rojek, 2001, p. 98). For a nation, the para-social functions of celebrities based on shared national identity help to control citizens and provide conditions for national cohesion.

The way in which celebrities act as role models and strengthen national cohesion of fans is not necessarily through classical forms of heroism and merit. This kind of popularity follows Daniel Boorstin's definition of celebrities as public figures that are known for "well-knowness" (1962, p. 57). James Monaco (1978) further highlights, "Celebrities are, of course, well-known. But people have been well-known, more or less, for centuries" (1978, p. 5). Unlike heroes of the nineteenth century, celebrities now "needn't have done – needn't do – anything special. Their function isn't to act – just to be…To a large extent, celebrity has entirely superseded heroism" (Monaco, 1978, pp. 5-6). In this view, celebrities supporting their nation need not be heroic. Crucially, they only need to be 'well known' for the national values that they signify.

In scholarly literature, three studies linking celebrities with nation are those of Joshua Gamson, Mary Caudle Beltrán, and Julie Rak. For Gamson,

> [C]elebrity culture is built on major American fault lines; simultaneous pulls on the parts of producers and audiences alike to celebrate individual distinction and the equality of all, to demonstrate that success is available to all and available only to the special, to instate and to undermine a meritocratic hierarchy, to embrace and attack authority (1994, p. 12).

Here, Gamson points out how celebrities function to support American national ideologies of individuality and democratic equality. Beltrán (2002) considers stardom as a national force, yet one with conflicting modes of operation. In a Canadian context, Rak (2008) expands that the greatness of a celebrity can be ideologically linked to the greatness of a nation. The greatness of celebrities refers to them embracing cherished national values. Gamson, Beltrán, and Rak's research are significant because they indicate a link between celebrities and their nations. However, the industrial and discursive process in which authenticity of celebrities is constructed by Canadian governments, media, and businesses has not yet been studied in popular culture.

Popular representations show that authenticity of famous Canadian personalities is often established through intimacy with Northern nature. The representation of Northern nature in wild, vast spaces and cold climatic conditions is a recurring theme in Canadian popular culture and academic studies (Kaufmann & Zimmer, 1998; Millard, Riegel, & Wright, 2002; Osborne, 2006). In these representations, Mounties, maple leaf, ice/snow, ice hockey, Canucks, polar bears, and vast wilderness landscapes are popular symbols of the Canadian North. In his study of celebrity endorsements of environmental conservation, Dan Brockington states that wildlife and nature are particularly the "product of careful, calculated manipulations and editing" (2008, p. 565) in cultural practices. In Canada, selective images of Northern nature are often associated with representations of Canadian celebrities but this aspect has not yet been explored in academic studies. The selected images of Northern nature in the Canadian context serve to authenticate both celebrities and the Canadian nation. As Richard Dyer states, "[a]uthenticity is both a quality necessary to the star phenomenon to make it work, and also the quality that guarantees the authenticity of other particular values a star embodies..." (1991, p. 133). The primordial and organic qualities of Canadian nature not only serve to authenticate a star image but also the national value that the image embodies. These symbolic practices of Canadian fame have not been critically investigated in media and cultural studies.

In Canada, celebrity texts are often constructed within different national discourses. These texts address existing problems of national identity occurring due to ideological differences in the nation. Dyer argues that, "star images function crucially in relation to contradictions within and between ideologies, which they seek variously to 'manage' or 'resolve'" (1998, p. 38). Here, 'manage' does not necessarily mean to solve but rather to negotiate competing ideologies through signs. Dyer further explains that the relation of the star to the contradictions in ideologies "may be one of displacement...or the suppression of one half of the contradiction and the foregrounding of the other...or else it may be that star effects a 'magic' reconciliation" (p. 30). A sociological function of celebrities is to manage ideological values of a nation through myths in second-order signs or connotation. The signs often communicate national values through ritualistic practices of adoring and consuming celebrities in a national context. In order to facilitate this consumption, institutional apparatuses such as cultural industries engage with existing discourses of a nation.

Canadian cultural industries effectively intervene in the discourse of national identity and supply "a ready-made identity for a community at a time when it feels threatened by a lack of identity" (Sherbert, Gerin, & Petty, 2006, p. 7). When cultural industries such as media construct celebrity texts, they often emerge within existing discourses of the nation that accept, negotiate, or contest national identity and serve to authenticate the nation through various notions of fame. The layers in Canadian celebrity culture and its variations lead *Fame in Hollywood North* to identify "celebrity cultures" and not a monolithic "celebrity culture" in Canada, also symbolised as Hollywood North. Hollywood North is used as a metaphor for Canada and signifies contested relations with Hollywood in America. While a particular focus on the film history of Hollywood North is beyond the scope of this study, the cultural space of Hollywood North adds layers to the theoretical understanding of celebrity culture in Canada and is contextualised in this book.

Structure of the Book

While this chapter introduces Canadian celebrity cultures and its relation with the nation, Chapter 2 situates Canadian celebrities in existing trends of popular culture and its critical notions of national identity. The general function of celebrity culture in a nation is important to consider. From this perspective, *Fame in Hollywood North* occasionally mentions "celebrity culture" to indicate the broader fame-based culture in which Canadian celebrities are situated. The particular problem of the meaning of Canadian fame, as seen in Chapter 2, is not only present in overall popular culture but also in the academic treatment of it. This issue is historically rooted in economic and political contexts that have both facilitated and contested the crisis of national identity in Canada. Despite its ambivalence, Canadian celebrity cultures function in ways that support mythic representations of the Northern frontier.

Using the lens of technological nationalism, Chapter 3 sets the theoretical framework and identifies why the North acts as a recurring space for popular icons in Canada. The chapter argues that technological nationalism is a set of ambivalent constructions of technology and nation that is expressed in Canadian media texts and practices. In the first part of the chapter, I highlight the theorisation and rhetorical practices of technological nationalism in Canadian academic literature and in federal policies. Using this theory, I specifically describe the rationale of using Canadian national symbols of the North in the second part of the chapter. In light of a bidirectional, yet ambivalent, relationship between the form of technology and content of nationalism, the chapter suggests that technological nationalism gets expressed in popular culture through national symbols of the North. The mythical construction of the nation in Canadian media is critically studied from the theoretical perspective of technological nationalism and its bidirectional relation to media content/texts. The bidirectional relationship between technology and nationalism is important to understand the technological reproduction of Northern symbols in popular culture, particularly for the study of Hollywood North in Chapter 4 and case studies that will follow. The theorisation of Northern symbols and how they are reproduced in popular media is a recurring theme explored throughout *Fame in Hollywood North*.

While Chapter 3 offers a theoretical framework, Chapter 4 shows how Hollywood North acts as a context for media constructions of celebrities in Canada. Chapter 4 particularly explores how this cultural construct is underpinned by continental drives of the US on one hand, and technological nationalism of Canada on the other. In light of these two practices, the chapter argues that 'Hollywood North' is an expression of the competing dynamics of continentalism and technological nationalism. As an expression of both of these concepts, the idea of Hollywood North unfolds as an ambivalence that negotiates tensions of American cultural imperialism and homogenous representations of the Canadian nation-state. To negotiate these tensions, the Canadian state and cultural institutions produce artefacts that imagine Canada as a Northern frontier. The imagination of the North helps to simultaneously adapt and resist the dominant practices of Hollywood. The usage of Northern symbols in Hollywood North is thus ambivalent in relation to America's Hollywood. This ambivalent usage of the North sets the ground for interrogating underlying assumptions in homogenous representations of celebrities in Canada. These cultural representations are explored through case studies in Chapters 5, 6, 7, and 8.

Chapter 5 examines how the Toronto International Film Festival (TIFF) acts as a cultural site articulating expressions of nationality through practices of fame. For the purpose of this chapter, I use TIFF as a case study, exploring the construction of celebrities in the context of Hollywood North. The chapter uses a two-step approach in studying TIFF. First, it considers TIFF as a "media event." Second, TIFF is considered as a 'context' that is associated with Hollywood North. These two approaches help to observe how TIFF events use Hollywood stardom to support the American film industry in Canada while resisting it with national symbols of the Canadian Northern frontier. The study, while focussing on Canada and its national expressions, considers the discursive construction of American celebrities and international stars as well. The chapter finally examines how TIFF acts as a context to read Canadian nationality in cultural productions of stars. The chapter shows that the national meaning of fame produced through TIFF events is multiple, layered, and complex.

Chapter 6 examines Canada's Walk of Fame (CWOF) as a cultural site through which national discourses intersect in multiple ways. The chapter focuses on expressions of fame in CWOF and shows that Canadian national identity is a product of layers of overlapping, competing, and even contradictory, national discourses. The chapter explores the ambivalence of Canadian national identity through a set of three interrelated national myths in media discourses. First, CWOF adopts Hollywood's standard constructions of fame that have been successful in America while supporting national myths of "inferiority complex" in Canadian achievements. Second, CWOF supports a notion of "inferiority complex" while celebrating the glory of Canadian inductees as national heroes. Finally, CWOF establishes the Canadian North as a stronger frontier while, in the process, undermining America's Wild West. This chapter explains how contemporary practices of fame engage with existing national discourses of Canada. It also sheds light on the rise of Canadian celebrity cultures in ironical ways.

Chapter 7 explores national identity and fame in Canadian reality TV shows. Production and reception of Canadian reality TV shows indicate a rise of Canadian celebrity cultures while they support particular national discourses that intersect in various ways. The chapter considers two kinds of Canadian reality TV shows: homegrown and franchised. Many Canadian reality TV shows support a Northern frontier ideology through fame. Other shows appropriate local, urban, and region-based national identities. In most cases, Canadian reality TV fame is constructed in relation to the US. In this respect, hosts and contestants become famous for a mediated reality of their Canadian values. The case studies show that stardom of hosts often helps to undermine and reconstruct fame of contestants in a way that reclaims past Canadian values. At the same time, through new performances of Canadianness, there is a popular recognition of Canadian fame. This appeal for fame is ironical and constitutes a new Canadian value that was not present in the past. The appeal of rising Canadian celebrity cultures through reality TV marks both continuities and shifts in Canadian practices of fame in a national context.

Chapter 8 examines celebrities represented in Canadian online media and ways in which those representations express offline constructions of national identity. These representations include celebrities that became famous over the Internet as well as celebrities who were constructed through traditional media with the Internet supporting their fame both offline and online. As explored in previous chapters, online fame also revolves around the question of authenticity. The use of national discourses not only authenticates celebrities online but also authenticates Canada as their place of origin. The markers of these discourses, such as national flags and emblems, have origins in physical, offline settings. For the purpose of this chapter, I explore constructions of fame through online representations of three Canadian stars: Justin Bieber, Lisa Ray, and Maria Aragon. Drawing on their textual representations, I demonstrate how online texts representing Canadian celebrities and the nation intersect through notions of authenticity. The authenticity of online celebrities is significant to the nation in which they are produced and received. In particular, the chapter shows how the Canadian national identity of an online celebrity can be restored, negotiated, or subverted on the Internet.

Chapter 9 concludes the book. The chapter looks at notions of national identity expressed in Canadian celebrity cultures. In particular, it highlights the Canadian meaning of fame in national discourses. In Canada, the construction and representation of fame is largely underpinned by Canada's technological nationalism. This concluding chapter shows how the book addresses its central question through a set of three interrelated myths emerging in technological nationalism: 1.) the North, 2.) the lack, and 3.) the American better 'Other.' In Canadian constructions of fame, celebrities are mostly mediated as a discursive effect of the Northern frontier, the lack it creates, or the America it "Others." The case studies demonstrate that the construction and representation of fame both engage with and contest past Canadian myths.

This is the first book that theorises Canadian celebrity cultures through the history of Canadian communication and popular media. This focus does not entail overlooking variations that may occur in negotiating or subverting dominant ideological practices in past or contemporary representations of individual celebrities. A development of a coherent and original theoretical framework can, in fact, map the ideological relations and variables found in particular cases of celebrities such as Nell Shipman, Mary Pickford, Pierre Trudeau, Terry Fox, Don Cherry, Wayne Gretzky, Justin Bieber, and Jian Ghomeshi, among many others. This development is crucial for understanding Canadian celebrity cultures as well as individual celebrities in a larger cultural framework. The Canadian context is also used as an organised tool for expressing tropes of celebrity culture, but it has not heretofore been shown or explained in any coherent manner. In most instances, books, edited collections, chapters, and journal chapters have offered the potential to contribute to an understanding of Canadian celebrity cultures. Indeed, case studies presented in these works offer insights into the intersections of colonialism, racism, classism, sexism, and ableism. The scope and variety of case studies prohibit the development of a grounded and coherent theoretical perspective to explain the reason for specific ideological practices. Nevertheless, historical trajectories of the development of Canadian celebrity cultures shed light on it and can be cohesively presented.

Fame in Hollywood North emphasizes Canada within a broader literature on the concept of nation. It particularly focuses on English Canada and does not include French Canada. French Canada has its own star system, which is increasingly accepted across the nation. Yet there is a dominant myth that the whole of Canada does not have stars or a star system. It can be argued that Quebecois stardom provides another 'Other' against which English Canadians construct national identity in the form of an absence of integration. As Amelia Kalant explains, "an 'improper' internal cultural-national boundary separates French Canada (Quebec)/English Canada (ROC)" that makes "bodily integrity" (Kalant, 2004, p. 33) of the nation impossible. This lack of integration through the systematic Othering of Quebec, in turn, plays a role in performing national difference from the US in the South. The North, then, becomes a "metaphor or rhetorical device" that refers to "the Northern Territories, Yukon, to Northern Ontario and Quebec" (p. 54) where the 'Othering' occurs and helps to build Canada as a nation. It functions as an "essential dividing line between Canada/US and as an origin for a Canada that is both French and English" (p. 33). While Quebecois stardom exclusively focuses on French-Canadian stars, binaries with Quebec are expressed through stardom in English Canada. In Canada's English language news, for example, Celine Dion, "Quebec's biggest star" (Young, 2001, p. 652), figures both as a unifying and a separatist national force. She is represented as a Canadian while she "figuratively waved both Canadian and Quebec flags" (p. 656). The expression of Canadian national identity in contesting relations to Quebecois culture is further demonstrated in case studies conducted in chapters 6 and 7. The systematic 'Othering' of Quebec, as seen with the US, plays a role in understating national identity of celebrities in English Canada.

French-Canadian stardom thus plays a role as an 'Other' in constructing the national identity of English Canadian celebrities. In this perspective, *Fame in Hollywood North* focuses on English Canada only and does not include French Canada. This book explores the English Canadian meaning of fame and its problematic relation to the dominant English practices of America. French-Canadian stardom is beyond the scope of this book, as its complexity would require a separate study unto itself. A separate book on Quebecois national identity and fame, or a comparative analysis between English Canadian and Quebecois star systems is viable after studying historical movements of English Canada's technological nationalism and its expressions in popular culture. *Fame in Hollywood North* demonstrates the historical background of technological nationalism and its expression through fame in popular culture. An understanding of technological nationalism in popular culture will, however, provide strong grounds for studying Quebecois star system in future studies.

Although *Fame in Hollywood North* recognises that media productions take place in other Canadian cities, the scope of the case studies focuses on major media productions in Toronto. The rationale for this Toronto-based focus is that Toronto is the financial capital of Canada and is its most populated urban centre. Toronto hosts the most important film festival in Canada, the Toronto International Film Festival (TIFF), as well as Canada's Walk of Fame (CWOF). Toronto is also the centre of production for major reality TV shows and media representation of celebrities. These significant cultural sites are covered as case studies in the book. Although certain media policies are considered in relation to representations, greater emphasis has been placed on the economic and political histories that shaped these policies. Policies are dependent on these contexts that can shift, as reflected in various media representations.

The media is selected on the basis of two criteria. First, the media — public or private — should produce and maintain English content at a national or provincial level in Canada. This production includes indigenous and multicultural entertainment content in English. If content is related to a Canadian celebrity but produced outside Canada, it is used to compare with or analyse in relation to primary media texts produced in Canada. Second, most media content are selected on the basis of their production or distribution in Toronto. This location is selected because it is the largest city in Canada and its programmes would be available to most regional areas. While applying a hermeneutical analysis to the content, rhetorical analysis identifies techniques of persuasion and ways in which national identification with celebrity texts are constructed. The study of the visual rhetoric and hermeneutical analysis of celebrity texts is informed by literature in critical cultural theory and celebrity studies.

The shift and rise of fame in these media are significant to note in Canadian popular culture. Earlier stardom of Canadian artists was limited to work in Hollywood. Within Canada, film stardom was relatively absent due to a lack of economic and human resources necessary to sustain a commercial film industry and its star system. With the rise of reality TV shows and the Internet, cultural productions shifted focus away from studio-controlled practices of cinematic fame. Reality TV and Internet productions not only celebrate emerging talent and fame, but also celebrate the nation through Canadian discourses.

2 Celebrity Cultures in Canada

In popular culture, Canada is mythically known as neither having celebrities nor a star system. At the same time, Canada continues to produce and consume stars for the Hollywood studio system. Additionally, Canadian talents migrate to America to build a career, and many of them become international stars. This stardom involves a three-step process whereby most Canadian talents 1.) migrate to America, 2.) become amalgamated into Hollywood's popular culture and subjected to an erasure of their Canadianness, and 3.) are later reclaimed as Canadians through media attention when honoured at sites such as the Toronto International Film Festival (TIFF) and Canada's Walk of Fame (CWOF). These Canadian talents include Christopher Plummer, Michael J. Fox, Mike Myers, and Pamela Anderson, among others. Apart from these stars, there are local celebrities who are often known for their renown and fame in certain networks and contexts. The layers in Canadian celebrity culture and its variations reflect different ways in which talents are popularised, thus creating celebrity cultures as opposed to a monolithic celebrity culture in Canada.

In general, Hollywood readily comes to mind as a primary site of star production. Hollywood is a mystique and fantasy-based concept that can be considered to be a principal ideology of Western society: it dominates the world mass entertainment business and stands as the origin-point for the mass production of fame (Dyer, 1998; Redmond & Holmes, 2007a; Strinati, 2000). However, the term Hollywood is a misnomer because the actual production activities are not only based in Los Angeles and Southern California, but also in other areas, including New York and Canadian cities such as Vancouver, Toronto, and Montreal. Indeed, many Hollywood actors perform in American films that are actually produced in Canada.

Moreover, Canadian actors also become famous for their work in Hollywood. In both cases, Canada acts as a cultural site for articulating fame in popular culture.

There are, however, two problems underlying the organisation and practice of fame in Canadian media. First, Canadian broadcast media are "generally linked to the Americanisation process" (Filion, 1996, p. 447) and have "historically been saturated with images and fictions originating south of the border" (Leach, 2002, p. 113). As a result of this origin, Canadian fame tends to be viewed as Americanised. This view is facilitated by the linguistic and geographic proximity of Canada and America. Second, the study of celebrity cultures in a Canadian context is mostly absent from academic work in Canada. In general, as scholar Aniko Bodroghkozy notes, "theorising 'the popular' within the Canadian context has historically been thin" (2001, p. 5). Scholar David Jackson expands on this point, noting that Canadian studies analyse "the meaning of entertainment products, and while not typically asserting that the material influences the beliefs of Canadians [...], it does suggest that entertainment at least reflects the beliefs of Canadians" (2007, p. 2). These beliefs refer to the need for American entertainment while dismissing in-depth understanding of popular personalities in Canada. Audience understanding of Canadian popular culture is heavily informed by American representations, while scholarly analysis does not provide adequate understanding of popularity in the Canadian context. These problems lead to a limited understanding of fame in Canada.

National Identity in Canadian Media

Canadian content is the cornerstone of the Canadian Radio-television and Telecommunications Commission (CRTC) and Canada's *Broadcasting Act.* In defence of the cultural integrity of Canada, CRTC has established policies and regulations to meet the Parliament's objectives and develop the presence of Canadian content. To this extent, CRTC specifically defines Canadian content as "Canadian artists and Canadian stories having access to Canadian airwaves" (CRTC, 2002). It further states that private television stations and networks (e.g., CTV, Global, TVA) and ethnic television stations must achieve a yearly Canadian content level of 60% measured during the day, that is 6 am to midnight. However, on conventional Canadian television stations, only 54.1% of programming had Canadian content in 2004, which marked a decline from 56.5 % in 2003 (*Television viewing,* 2006). This decline is a result of the heavy influx of American content in Canada. The Americanisation of Canadian culture is strongly illustrated in most Canadian media that circulate texts and images of Hollywood celebrities.

In response to the cultural dominance of American Hollywood content, Stephen Waddell, National Executive Director of the Alliance of Canadian Cinema, Television and Radio Artists (ACTRA) called for CRTC to take immediate steps to "fix the imbalance" (Taverner, 2008). In this respect, Waddell specifically stated, "We need CRTC help to halt the annual Hollywood shopping spree by Canadian broadcasters, where they overspend millions of dollars on American shows" (Taverner, 2008). However, Canadian televisual practices continue to endorse Hollywood content and deny the 'priority' of Canadian programming that was defined by the CRTC regulation in 1999. This denial does not conform to the federal broadcasting policy of promoting "one Canadian identity" in opposition to the "more and more influential American popular culture" (Filion, 1996, p. 447). The problem of Canadian identity in popular culture forms the contextual framework of my research question: How do contemporary Canadian media represent celebrities in a Canadian context? In relation to this question, *Fame in Hollywood North* specifically addresses how Canadian media construct national identity through representations of celebrities in popular culture.

The origin of the Canadian identity problem is first grounded in national politics. Canadian identity has been in crisis since the beginning of Confederation in 1867. The crisis stemmed from the co-existence within the same state of the two different English and French cultures. English and French-Canadians[1] have each advocated their own nationalism. The Official Languages Act of 1969 enabled the expression of Canadian identity in official bilingualism (Hudson, 2002). However, Canada is actually multicultural rather than bicultural, and hence has "regional divergences" (Collins, 1990, p. 24). Consequently, Canadian identity can be defined as "pluralist" (Mackey, 2002, p. 13), one that is a result of "a bland bilingual, multicultural papulum" (Collins, 1990, p. 24). As a result, "culturally one may be Canadian in varying degrees" (p. 26). This variation is problematic when institutions attempt to construct and maintain a monolithic Canadian national identity. The need to establish a coherent nation is so critical that Canada is often referred to as a 'Canadian nation,' a term that I use in this book. Another aspect of the Canadian identity crisis is geopolitical. Indeed, Canada's southern border is shared with a military, economic, and cultural giant: the United States of America. As such, Canada's identity tends to be determined by inequalities with the US. This binary relation with America is a recurring theme in *Fame in Hollywood North*.

---

[1] The use of hyphen in describing French-Canadian and other language and ethnic groups signifies a hyphenated national identity as opposed to the unmarked, dominant English Canadians. This concept is discussed in Chapter 8.

Leaving the political and geopolitical aspects behind for now, another issue of interest is the problem of Canadian national identity originating from communication studies that focus on technological nationalism. Canadian communication scholar Maurice Charland describes technological nationalism as a cultural model that contributes to the development of Canadian national identity through technological mediation (Charland, 1986; Cohen, 1995). Chapter 3 considers this model and discusses how Canada is unified as a sovereign state because of the communication technologies that bind the nation. The nationalist discourse of technology is central to the Canadian imagination of uniting the vast geography of the country. As such, Canadian national identity may be partially or wholly a consequence of technological nationalism.

However, the rhetoric of technological nationalism and the federal government desire to maintain a homogeneous national culture can be problematic. The concept not only dismisses 'regional divergences' but is also technologically deterministic and denies social factors that play a key role in the "form" of media technology:

> [...] discussions of Canadian culture and its relationship to Canadian social and political values concentrate on content to the exclusion of form. These discussions fail to take into account the degree to which, at a certain base or structural level, these values are not entirely distinct from a capitalist modernity chiefly expres- sed in American society (Szeman, 2000).

In studying media representations in Canada, it is important to recognise how the technological 'form,' and not just 'content,' can influence national identity. Often, a dismissal of the form in favour of nationalistic content can fail to address the economic inequality and profits that frame cultural production and reception in Canadian popular culture. For example, it must be noted that the form of the free-to-air television medium requires advertising for sustenance. In this respect, Canadian television broadcasting has needed the support of government institutions. However, the government has often been associated with "'high' rather than 'popular' cultural traditions" (Leach, 2002, p. 113). This lack of attention to popular culture has driven television stations to cut production costs and import Hollywood content. Although Canada's private broadcasters have larger funding and "increased their revenues in 2007, they cut their spending on Canadian programming" (Taverner, 2008) and are unable to reflect Canadian mass culture. In fact,

> CRTC's industry report confirms that Canada's private broadcasters spent $616 million on Canadian programming in 2007

compared to $624 million the year before. In contrast, they increased their non-Canadian spending by 5%, up to $722 million in 2007 (Taverner, 2008).

Such "overspending on U.S. programming" and failure to "produce homegrown shows" (Taverner, 2008) explains the predominance of American content and how 63% of Canadian television viewing is "of foreign-programs, the vast majority of these American" (Boberg, 2010, p. 31).

In light of the problem of American cultural imperialism, the federal government proposed to prioritise Canadian content in television (CRTC, 1985). In this situation, an overemphasis on content, rather than the technological form, can lead to what scholar Brian Bow characterises as the "production of a narrow, overdetermined definition of Canadianness" (2008, p. 1) that is ideologically constructed against American identity. As Bow further states, "one of the most distinctive features of the Canadian nation-building project is the way that it has tended to define itself in terms of separation from, and opposition to, the United States" (2008, p. 1). However, if the government fails to address the economic requirements to sustain the medium or form of television, it will not effectively address the diverse needs of citizens across the nation. It will instead support the development of Canadian media content that can resist American cultural imperialism.

This cultural difference with America is a simplistic construction to define Canadian national identity. It does not allow for an authentic expression of locally diverse experiences of citizens across the nation. Yet, authenticity is central to identifying with, and supporting, the nation-state. As scholars Eric Kaufmann and Oliver Zimmer argue, "the key concept with regard to national identity is authenticity" (1998, p. 3). They expand that the "authentication of a national culture entails two processes: the construction of continuity with a nation's alleged ethno-historical past (historicism) on the one hand, and the creation of a sense of naturalness (naturalization) on the other" (Kaufmann & Zimmer, 1998, p. 3). As discussed in Chapter 3, media representation of an authentic Canada is mostly limited to an English Canadian ethnic culture that historically dominated the Northern frontier nature. This domination, in the process, is imagined to resist American cultural content that is paradoxically imported and sustained in Canada. The representation of a dominant English Canadian national identity helps to maintain an authentic and coherent image of the nation that can both manage diverse cultural issues and values as well as the opposition to the US in a much simpler way. In media, this maintenance of Canadian nationality is observed in celebrity cultures, whereby the production and consumption of celebrities support existing national discourses and values that are meaningful to the Canadian nation-state.

Study and Meaning of Fame in Canada

The study of celebrity as a genre of representation, discursive effect, and industrial production is nearly absent from research in Canadian cultural and media studies. *Fame in Hollywood North* addresses a compelling question raised by scholar Marlis Schweitzer: "What is it about Canada that we are so unwilling to support a star system? [...] Why don't we respect our stars?" (2010, p. 6). Schweitzer indicates the need to explore "the extent to which Canadian celebrity culture differs from celebrity culture elsewhere" (p. 6). In particularly focussing on Canadian national identity and representations of the nation, it is also important to consider David Jackson's question: "The most interesting question remains the one of effect: do [Canadian] celebrities influence the political beliefs of their audiences through political expressions in their art or public statements?" (2007). This book sets theoretical grounds to understand the politics of the Canadian state and how its ideological beliefs are reproduced in the performance and representation of celebrities. Celebrities, in turn, may influence the views audiences have of the nation.

These understandings fill a major gap that scholar Graeme Turner identifies in studies of celebrity culture. Turner points out that most academics have focused on celebrities as a genre of representation and discursive effect. In this respect, there has been a major focus on individual celebrities as texts and details of their media representation, but not their industrial production at a structural level. Turner calls for a base for studying industrial production of celebrities and integrating modes of analysis that are not limited to textual and discourse analysis. The study of industrial production is important because it contributes ways of understanding the celebrity as a commodity that supports political and economic developments of national and transnational brands. For this purpose, Turner specifically states that it is important to build awareness of, and response to, "local and national production environments" (2010, p. 15). Scholars need to particularly identify "organisational and corporate connections between the media, business, and government" (p. 16) in national and local contexts. In his study of transnationalism, Jo Littler further suggests that cultural "texts can be read differently according to the national cultures they are part of, and celebrity is subject to similar cultural reframing" (2011, p. 1). While Littler considers celebrities in national cultures to be beyond the territorial boundaries of a nation, *Fame in Hollywood North* looks at national identities of celebrities that overlap or contradict *within* a nation. Furthermore, it looks at both Canadian and international (mostly American) celebrities in Canada. This international approach offers opportunities to explore Canadian meanings of fame rather than simply studying the media representation of individual Canadian celebrities and their national identity.

In light of Canada's national identity crisis, there are three problems underlying the interpretation of the Canadian meaning of fame. First, Canadian celebrities are media productions that, as noted earlier, are associated with Americanisation and saturated with images and fictions originating in Hollywood (Filion, 1996; Leach, 2002). The Americanisation of Canadian popular culture is strongly illustrated in most Canadian broadcast and print media that circulate texts and images of Hollywood celebrities. As scholar David Jackson observes, "English-speaking Canadians embrace US celebrities to a large degree" (2007, p. 2). Guy Mayson, President of the Canadian Film and Television Production Association specifies, "entertainment magazine shows carry a lot of news about the personal lives and appearances of Beyoncé and George Clooney, raising the question of whether they should be considered Canadian" (CBC, 2006). Even though many Hollywood celebrities are Canadian, they are often known and celebrated in an American context. For example, the 2006 edition of the *Canadian Business* magazine revealed its annual Celebrity Power List, a ranking of Canadian actors who demonstrate "serious clout in La-La land" (Mlynek & Pulfer, 2006). The report then specifically notes "The top 15 Canadians in Hollywood" and lists actors such as Jim Carrey, Keanu Reeves, and Pamela Anderson. These actors may be Canadian citizens, but their national identities as Canadians are generally revealed only when they are celebrated in Hollywood.

In contrast, celebrities who are well known for their work in Canada were not listed. This representation further shows the cultural imbalance between representations of celebrities in America and Canada in a Canadian context. The pervasiveness of Hollywood celebrities in Canadian media is regularly illustrated in the opening headlines of entertainment news segments. For example, opening lines of Canada's prime-time entertainment news magazine *eTalk* on CTV once stated "Hollywood Goes North!" (CTV, 2009b). Another CTV report stated that, "Hollywood touches down for TIFF and we're with the stars every step of the way!" (CTV, 2008d). The symbolic notion of "Hollywood in Canada" situates Canadian celebrities in standardised and homogenous cultural constructs of America on one hand, and in a Northern cultural construct that overlooks local/regional differences in Canada on the other.

The second problem in understanding Canadian fame is the lack of critical attention to popular culture in Canada. Fame occupies a central area of attention within popular culture. In cultural studies, research on popular culture considers analysis of texts that are produced and consumed by a mass audience in everyday life. As opposed to high culture, popular culture constitutes these texts as a site where meanings of popularity for the mass can be articulated. Fame is one of the types of popularity that is meaningful for a mass culture. Since fame is rich in texts and in the effects of existing discourses, scholars in cultural studies are interested in its process and practices. In the case of Canada, however, cultural institutions such as academia and media heavily emphasise high culture instead of popular culture. Due to a lack of Canadian content productions and celebrity texts in popular culture and the heavy import of Hollywood content and stars, media practices and academic studies offer a limited understanding of celebrities in Canada.

Whether Canadian celebrities are famous for their work in Hollywood or not, there is a limited study about them in Canadian academia. Research in Canadian media and popular culture is either limited to the heavy influx of American content or, to a lesser extent, artefacts of high culture compared to cultural studies in America and abroad. Otherwise, there are very few studies on popular culture in Canada. Gaile McGregor (1995) contends that this situation is partly due to the way labour is divided in Canadian cultural research. The political attitudes of Canadian research, particularly in the humanities and social sciences, are grounded in Leftism rather than in egalitarianism, and they support a class-based theory of intellectual attitudes (Nakhaie & Brym, 1999). From this perspective, official high culture, often dismissed as "irrelevant and elitist" (McGregor, 1995) and considered to be a bipolar opposite to coexistent capitalist interests of Americanised content in media, does not appeal to Canadian faculty.

As a consequence, studies of Canadian popular culture and its media texts are nearly absent in the research conducted within Canadian cultural studies. Although Brock University started a program in popular culture, there is a lack of university departments and professional societies specialising in Canadian popular culture (Flaherty & Manning, 1993). Publications such as *Pop Can: Popular Culture in Canada* (Luven & Walton, 1999), *Mondo Canuck: A Canadian Pop Culture Odyssey* (Pevere & Dymond, 1996), and *The Beaver Bites Back? American Popular Culture in Canada* (Flaherty & Manning, 1993) have attempted to illustrate selected case studies of popular culture in Canada. However, there are limited historical and theoretical studies and methodological approaches that act as a body of evidence, a process of inquiry, and an analytical framework for interpreting celebrity cultures in Canada. This limited academic interest in Canadian celebrity cultures impacts the way we think about Canadian celebrities and constrains the way a critic would write about and interpret the system of fame. It thereby creates a limited understanding of celebrities in Canada.

The limited attention to celebrities in Canadian media and academic studies does not mean that Canada is short of public figures that can be celebrated. In fact, some media reports and academic research have focussed on celebrities, but they are limited to Canadian literary, media, political or sports personalities. These celebrities often rise to fame through work performance rather than media texts. Most of the research focuses on individual case studies rather than the sociological and semiotic constructions of celebrity texts in Canadian media. I identify this limited focus on certain types of celebrities, and the lack of sociological and semiotic analysis, as the third problem in interpreting the Canadian system of fame. Hence, we are lacking a comprehensive historical and theoretical study of celebrities and of the cultural meaning of fame in Canada.

Existing research in cultural studies offers critical tools of analysis that can be applied and extended to the study of all celebrities in Canada. It sets grounds to explore contextual frameworks for interpreting the media construction of fame in Canadian popular culture. Yet, research in Canada often overlooks the technological, political, and economical intents of commercial media texts that usually construct and sustain celebrities. The ideological challenges in interpreting fame call for a rigorous research agenda in studies of Canadian culture. Does the reason to examine Canada lie in the fact that we, as authors, are Canadians and speak from situated experiences? Or does the Canadian context really matter to the in-depth understanding of celebrity cultures in Canada and abroad? Perhaps there is a bit of both. In any case, what is exactly unique about Canadian celebrity phenomenon that can add to understanding existing paradigms of celebrity studies? The question of nation can be irrelevant in a global framework of transnational practices. Nevertheless, nations do continue to play a fundamental role in shaping celebrity cultures on local and international levels of production, circulation, and distribution of celebrity texts.

For Lorraine York, Canadian cultural icons do not engage in fame in a global sense. In previous studies, York examined the fame of authors such as Margaret Atwood, Michael Ondaatje, and Carol Shields who are popular in Canada. York's essays and her book *Literary Celebrities in Canada* critically focus on the tensions and conflicts in negotiating the identity of Canadian celebrity authors. In her book chapter "Large Ceremonies: Literary Celebrity of Carol Shields" (2007), York shows how Canadian authors Carol Shields and Alice Munro are ambivalent about their celebrity status and, in some ways, negate fame. She also explores how the career of Margaret Atwood is managed and maintained in *Margaret Atwood and the Labour of Literary Celebrity* (2013). York traces a variety of responses to literary fame and highlights that the responses are ambiguous and, at times, even contradictory. One of her essays sheds light on the contradictory nature of stardom experienced by many other Canadian authors:

They did not *really* become celebrities, at least not in the globalized sense of stardom that we have inherited from Hollywood culture, because, somehow, it is not in the nature of Canadian cultural icons, those wide-eyed innocents, to become worldly, to be changed by fame (York, 2002).

In general, as Joe Moran (2000) argues, literary celebrities are different from most celebrities that are primarily constructed by commercial media such as tabloid press, entertainment television shows, and the Internet. Moran explains that the difference occurs because the

encroachment of market values on to literary production [...] forms part of a complicated process in which various legitimating bodies compete for cultural authority and commercial success, and regulate the formation of a literary star system and the shifting hierarchy of stars (2000, pp. 3-4).

Although literary celebrities are subject to the same competition for space in print and broadcast media, they, Graeme Turner suggests, are "partly produced by their own writing" (2004, p. 18). The distinction of literary celebrities is especially seen when they are traditionally considered to reside in what Wenche Ommundsen identifies as a "high cultural order" (2004, p. 45). The presence of literary celebrities in high culture is expressed by the anxiety of literary celebrities who lose "high-minded pursuits" or who experience the "dumbing down" of their "serious art" (Ommundsen, 2004, p. 52). The apparent "contamination" of literary celebrities in popular culture leads Ommundsen to claim that, "writers, like their textual products, find themselves involved in the competing economies of "crass commercialism" and "high art" (2004, p. 53) in the public sphere. At the same time, literary celebrities are partly produced through the performance of their written texts, as Turner suggests, and thus do not need to be subjected to commercial media. The celebrity status of writers is therefore constructed in ways that are markedly different from dominant practices of commercial media.

In Canada, representations and studies of literary fame do not show how celebrities are constructed in commercial media, nor do they show the social values celebrities represent. Hence, studies of literary fame generally overlook Canadian celebrity cultures and lack an in-depth understanding of sociological and semiotic processes through which Canadian cultural productions limit literary celebrities and celebrity cultures.

A parallel can be drawn between Canadian academia and celebrity cultures; the elitism of the former disdains the latter in a hierarchy of values. Celebrity culture, as a whole, does not exclude celebrity academic and non-academic writers. In fact, as Sean Redmond and Su Holmes (2006) suggest, "the process of interpretation, and the construction, selection and processing of evidence" (p. 127) is integral to understanding fame and guides textual productions within it. Redmond and Holmes explain that writing the history of fame and explaining its changes demand reflection on the celebrity culture in which that history is steeped, both textually and visually. In the process, the writing, like drawing portraits, reflects and reinforces fame in a way that is not static and objective, but *subjective*. As "celebrity only exists within representation," (p. 128), it is necessary to draw on stories written about celebrities as well as their photographs and performances in mapping the history of fame. Gary Boire notes that,

> Because of institutional conditions, political compromises, and the interpellated ideologies that constitute and sustain a still predominantly White, male, heterosexist, middle-class academic elite, we have a professoriate that – whatever it claims to the contrary – replicates and perpetuates the class values of a capitalist nation-state. Research is commodified within a celebrity star system (i.e., the Canada Research Chair Program, Ontario's Premiere's Excellence Award, the Polyani Prizes; [...] and pedagogy is so commercialized that we now celebrate super-classes of thousands [...] (2004, pp.230-231).

In general, previous research on selected Canadian celebrities can be relevant to celebrity studies, which is an emerging and promising area of scholarship. Previous research can be expanded using new perspectives on Canadian celebrities. Crucially, however, this existing research needs to establish a critical and coherent theory explaining celebrity culture, as well as its 'lack' in Canadian social sciences and humanities. That said, the need for a critical and coherent theory of celebrity culture must not lose sight of already established perspectives. *Fame in Hollywood North* largely considers the theoretical framework and historical trajectories through which individual celebrities can be examined — an area that has been insufficiently examined in Canadian research and practice. The mythic tradition of a "lack" or an "absence" of celebrities, as well as an artistic tradition perceived to be inferior to that of the United States has, in general, defined the discourse of Canadian nationalism. This Canadian context offers a critical space for understanding celebrity cultures. The governmental bureaucracy of education, arts, cultural heritage, legal administration, and labour dynamics, coupled with a bilingual culture, play a critical role in Canada. The privileged role of a White-male ableist figure in the bureaucracy of arts specifically plays a dominant role in understanding Canadian celebrity cultures. The discussions of these roles are consistent themes that need to be tied together through a coherent theoretical framework. This focus will create a vibrant dialogue and open opportunities for change in what appears to be uniquely problematic in Canadian celebrity cultures. The cultural meaning of fame is problematic, however, because it is the purview of both Canadian popular culture *and* academic studies. The notion of celebrity, if there is any, is limited to academic and non-academic communities in Canada.

Like literary figures, journalists are also "partly produced by their own writing" (Turner, 2004, p. 18) and celebrated as celebrities in Canada. It can be argued that the celebration of journalists is observed in other nations as well. However, the status of celebrity is often limited to literary figures and journalists while excluding other talents in Canada. As writer Ryan Porter observes:

> In Toronto, film stars and wealthy tycoons can remain virtual unknowns next to a roster of household names that are published daily across Canada. Journalists like Wendy Mesley and William Thorsell, their profiles boosted by Toronto's strong media industry, can end up with reputations more familiar than those of Canada's entertainment personalities [...] the stature of Toronto's media equals that of conventional celebrity roles, such as the screen stars, TV personalities and singers that the American star system thrives on (2003).

In Canada, journalists are particularly represented as famous public personalities. Their representations are systematically organised and ritually celebrated on grounds of their routine and familiar performances through writing and anchoring. The central characteristic of Canadian journalists is the illusion of 'familiarity' that is established through direct communication by media technologies. As David Marshall (1997) explains, television, in particular, is able to construct public personalities in a way that is not distanced by aura but more familiar through modes of direct address. Canadian national television networks, for example, promote broadcast news anchors as well-known public personalities. Their representations are observed in regular previews and advertisements of their "live" news as well as off-screen archival and distribution of their images. Larger-than-life images and names of broadcast anchors in Canada are widely disseminated by television, radio, magazines, and billboard advertisements. They thus become iconic figures sought by Canadian viewers. CTV's news anchor Lloyd Robertson, who started his broadcasting career with 1240 AM radio in 1952 and the Canadian Broadcasting Corporation (CBC) in 1954, is known as one of the earliest public personalities and was the first journalist inducted into Canada's Walk of Fame. Similarly, Peter Mansbridge has been celebrated as Canada's trusted news anchor. Since he started his broadcasting career at CBC in 1968, he received twelve Gemini Awards[2] for his excellence in English-language television. Cultural critics Geoff Pevere and Greig Dymond (1996) note that these iconic broadcasters gained so much popularity that they were not only sought by multiple Canadian networks, but American networks as well.

Print journalists are also celebrated for their direct communication and familiarity through regular performances of their writing skills in Canada. Shinan Govani is a classic example of a Canadian print journalist who constructs Canadian celebrities and, in the process, has constructed himself as a celebrity. A columnist for the Canadian newspaper *National Post,* Govani is known for celebrating the names of twenty-five Canadian journalists between September 6 and December 6, 2002. In a report, Ryan Porter highlights Govani's observation: "we don't have an awareness of who makes our movies...But there is a heightened awareness of who our media personalities are" (Porter, 2003). Govani's observation was confirmed when he was treated as a red-carpet star during the Toronto International Film Festival (TIFF) in September 2009. He became instantly famous for *Boldface Names* (Govani, 2009), a Canadian novel about celebrities. Govani (2009) and Porter (2003) shed light on how Canadian fame is often constructed in ways that are different from standard forms of film stardom in America and elsewhere. Instead of Canadian media constructing talented individuals as celebrities, the fame of media personalities is constructed by direct performance of their own texts and their familiarity. This familiar performance of media personalities parallels the popularity of literary figures. While academic studies briefly discussed media and literary celebrities, they neither addressed the rationale for using direct performance of media texts nor the meaning of fame in Canadian popular culture.

The use of direct performance and familiarity in Canadian fame is not only observed in literary figures and journalists, but sports celebrities as well. In general, Canadian sports personalities appear to rise by virtue of their own performance, and are not wholly determined by commercial media practices. David Giles argues that sport is "one of the few areas of public life that is truly meritocratic," and sports celebrities can "prove they are the best" (2000, p. 107). Graeme Turner further states that the cultural prominence of sports celebrities "can be regarded as deserved" (2004, p. 19). He draws on Andrews and Jackson (2001) and notes that sports celebrities, as opposed to film and television performers who adopt a

---

[2] National awards for English Canadian television programs

fictive identity, offer a "spectacle of real individuals participating in unpredictable contests" (2004, p. 19). As a consequence, a drop in their real life performance can lead to a decline of public interest in them as well as their commercial and professional potential (Andrews & Jackson, 2001; Turner, 2004). In Canada, media institutions and various marketing brands draw on the symbolic value of familiarity in the live performance of sports players and endorse them as celebrities. Particularly, media and marketing brands celebrate ice hockey players as stars in Canada. Scholars Steven J. Jackson (2001), Lloyd L. Wong (2002), and Ricardo Trumper (2002) have studied the cultural construction of, and fan identification with, Canadian hockey star Wayne Gretzky. Their studies set grounds for understanding Canadian fame as it relates to hockey.

Although ice hockey stars are celebrated by virtue of their live performance and familiarity, they also help perpetuating the Canadian national myth that ice is a national symbol of Canada. In doing so, the nationwide understanding of hockey stars, attached to the romantic image of ice, helps to celebrate Canada as a Northern nation. As columnist Scott Russell observes, the "ice (rink ice, lake ice, river ice, pond ice, even the frozen surface of the Arctic Ocean) is clearly the star" (2009). These mythic representations of the Northern frontier are played out in various ways within Canadian celebrity cultures and need to be critically examined in studies of popular culture and media.

An understanding on how we think about Canada as a Northern nation helps to situate the uniqueness of Canadian fame. In his book *Places on the Margin* (1992), Shields sheds light on how marginal standpoints of regional areas are crucial to the construction of dominant meanings of the nation. His book is especially useful in exploring regions that receive minimal attention in Canada yet function to support dominant myths. For example, cultural productions rarely focus on indigenous areas in Canada's geographical north. Yet, these areas are imagined and romanticised as the North in building the Canadian nation. For Shields, the Canadian North forms "the mythic 'heartland' of Canada but remains a zone of Otherness in the spatial system of Canadian culture" (1992, p. 4).

While the romanticisation of the North is stable, its construction is an ongoing process in defining Canadian national identity. The inherent ambivalence in the stability and ongoing need to construct national identity makes Canada unique in defining what it means to be a nation. According to Canadian thinker Pierre Berton, "One of the unifying forces of Canada is the long debate about who we are. No other country debates the way we do" ("Culture and National Identity,"1998). John Ralston Saul further states that Canada's lack of a monolithic mythology is a "revolutionary reversal of the standard nation-state myth" and makes Canada "out of step with most other nations" (1997, p. 8). Yet, Canada's failure to conform is its greatest success as a nation (Ibid.). Canada's unique position in exemplifying a nation's ambivalence is significant to consider within a broader theoretical context. The instability in the ambivalent positions particularly exemplifies the ironical need for predictable texts that perform and maintain a single and coherent definition of Canada as a Northern nation in popular culture.

3 Technological Nationalism -
The North in Canadian Popular Culture

Communication scholars such as Maurice Charland (1986) and Robert Babe (1990) point out how technological nationalism is used as a central rhetoric of Canadian policy. Their studies explain how the rhetorical use of technology determines constructions of the Canadian nation. The way in which technological nationalism has been studied so far has considered what it means as a discourse. These studies consider the relationship between technology and nation within that discourse. In both cases, there has been a significant focus on policies and technology infrastructures in Canadian media. The greater emphasis on the role of media and technology has led critics to respond with the perspective of technological determinism. Others have attempted to distinguish between hard and soft determinism. A third way was also developed: the mutual shaping of technology and society. In this respect, scholars have recognised that technology and culture are inseparable, hence the uptake of the terms "cultural technologies" (Berland, 2009) and "technological imagination" (Lauretis, Huyssen, & Woodward, 1980).

The current literature on communication technology and culture has progressed beyond earlier technologically determinist positions. Indeed, most recent studies open up new possibilities to look at how content in popular culture can be an expression or a product of technological nationalism, both materially and symbolically. They also set new grounds to examine what causes or prompts technological nationalism that, in turn, is reflected in Canadian media content. It is important to not simply emphasise the form or infrastructure of technology over its content, as seen in some past studies. Such an emphasis limits attention to how and why technological nationalism gets expressed in Canadian popular culture. Rather, it is useful to consider historical and socio-cultural contexts of producing and receiving content as well as the implications of technological nationalism in media practices. In her work, Jody Berland (2009) argues against overly deterministic views of technology and suggests ways in which technology emerges within, and is shaped by, discursive practices and narratives. These discourses allow us to explore the complex and often ambivalent socio-cultural foundation of technology, and they need to be further addressed in current research. Indeed, there is need for research on how the mythic qualities of technological nationalism can play a role in the use of media technology and its production of cultural texts in popular culture. This chapter emphasises the value of reading popular texts in light of technological nationalism and reduces the risk of oversimplifying the complex ways in which national identities are articulated in Canada.

In doing so, *Fame in Hollywood North* fills the gaps in existing research by examining how the mythical use of technological nationalism informs the production and theorisation of cultural texts and practices in Canada. In particular, it focuses on Canadian national symbols of nature and shows how their usage in cultural texts is rooted in the rhetoric of technological nationalism. This usage demonstrates how technological nationalism functions in relation to the dual crisis of Canadian nature that will be discussed later in this chapter. Drawing on the theoretical perspectives of Arthur Kroker (1984) and Marco Adria (2010), I argue that technological nationalism is a set of ambivalent constructions of Canadian media technology and nation that is expressed in Canadian cultural texts and practices. This chapter incorporates rhetorical, political, economic, narrative, and cultural studies approaches for the study. Using these approaches, the chapter particularly addresses how national identity is understood in relation to technological nationalism. It also explains how national identity is expressed through symbols of nature in popular media. I will thus argue that national symbols of nature in media are grounded in mythic qualities of technological nationalism.

In the first part of the chapter, I highlight the theorisation and rhetorical practices of technological nationalism in academic literature and Canadian federal policies. Using this theory, the second part of the chapter will then specifically describe the rationale of using Canadian symbols of nature in cultural texts of popular culture. In light of a bidirectional, yet ambivalent relationship between technological nationalism and cultural productions, I show how and why the nation is expressed, albeit unnoticeably, through symbols of Northern nature in Canadian popular culture. The second part of this chapter explores these symbols further and is central to *Fame in Hollywood North*. Popular art of the Group of Seven, the historiography of the Laurentian School, the work of pianist Glenn Gould, as well as television series such as *Ice Pilots NWT* and *Ice Road Truckers* are examples that illustrate the symbolic expressions. These expressions will be further illustrated by celebrity representations in the book.

Technological Nationalism

In this section, I explore the rise of Canada as a nation in a historical context by focusing on the emergence of Canadian national identity. The literature review highlights the significant role that technology plays in constructing and maintaining the Canadian nation via nationalist movements. As further discussed in this section, the role of technology has led scholars to conceptualise technological nationalism as both a theory and a rhetoric of Canadian communication, particularly media practices. There are complex and ambivalent ways in which the rhetorical use of technological nationalism is represented in popular culture. A review of the scholarly work of Arthur Kroker, George Grant, Marshall McLuhan, and Harold Innis sets the theoretical grounds to explore these popular representations in the next section.

Canada as a Nation, Nationalism, and National Identity

Canada is defined as a technological nation (Charland, 1986; Kalant, 2004). A glimpse into Canadian history shows how the use of technology played a significant role in unifying the nation. The Treaty of Paris of 1763 marked the creation of British North America and the end of French domination in what is now Canada. At that time, British North America also included the British colonies that are now the Eastern states of the USA. The British Loyalists settled in Canada after the American Revolution (1775-83), at which point North America was divided into the USA to the south, and what is now Canada to the north. The Confederation of 1867 was both an attempt to unify the northern part of North America in face of American expansionism and a framework to unify French and English Canadians. The use of technology played a significant role in unifying Canada.

Canadians developed and implemented technology in Canada on two different levels. First, they integrated the territorial land on economic and political grounds and established it as a nation-state with use of technology. This integration was necessary due to the large land mass and sparse population. The construction and implementation of technologies specifically refer to the Canadian Pacific Railway (CPR) and to the public broadcasting system. Second, on a cultural level, the use of technologies helped to mitigate tensions among existing local and regional groups across the nation.

The ideal of a monolithic Canadian national culture has been threatened due to the inability to locate a shared, unique culture among diverse groups. In political and economic practices, the use of technologies gives the impression of developing and integrating the nation across cultural differences. Despite calls for a single and coherent definition of the nation, the efforts of federal policies, and the use of technology, the construction of an Anglo-centric Canadian nation is unstable. The instability is rooted in the settlement of English Canadian colonials. Historically, English Canadian colonials were British Loyalists fleeing the American Revolution and earlier colonisers, both often invading the indigenous land. Drawing on the work of Homi Bhabha (1990), Cynthia Conchita Sugars (2004), and Laura Frances Errington Moss (2003), it is clear that Canadian colonialists were in an ambivalent and hybrid position when constructing the nation. The ambivalence resulted from the tenuous positions of English Canadian settlers who were colonisers of an Indigenous land but also the colonised 'Other' in a colony of the British Empire.

Yet, English Canadian invaders/settlers identified with a hybrid of British and European cultures in Canada, and an older sense of British English (Sugars, 2004). On one hand, English and French Canada separately advocated old, classical ideals of nations that have been historically in conflict with each other. The two separate Canadian nations that thus emerged created a mutually dependent relationship between federal politics and language, expressed in official bilingualism (Collins, 1990). The federal policy of bilingualism, however, does not necessarily express bicultural differences. On the other hand, Canada is a multicultural community with diverse ethnicities and "regional divergences" (Collins, 1990, p. 24). In theory, the Canadian nation can be defined as "pluralist" (Mackey, 2002, p. 13) that is a result of "a bland bilingual, multicultural papulum" (Crean and Rioux, 1983, p.12 as cited in Collins, 1990, p. 24). That said, multiculturalism, like bilingualism, is not equally manifested in popular practices. Canadian multiculturalism is marginal in the sense that it is organised around a core Anglocentric culture marked by federal bilingualism, which does not admit/recognise other languages used by Canadian citizens (such as aboriginal languages). It is instead based on the ambivalence of ethnic cultures that originated outside of the territory of the settled Canadian nation.

The instability in the ambivalent positions consequently requires predictable texts to perform and maintain a single and coherent definition of the nation. Benedict Anderson (1991) and Homi Bhabha (1990) thus define a nation as a community that is imagined with narratives. In these narratives, both literary and visual texts constitute symbols and values that construct and legitimise the nation. The cultural texts particularly consist of signs that persistently manufacture and sustain a mythic origin that is contingent on central ideologies of a nation. These texts intersect with other texts to support shared ideologies, such as those on authenticity. In Anderson's work on nationalism, the nation is constructed as an imaginary community because most inhabitants will never meet. It is imagined because the "members of even the smallest nation will never know most of their fellow-members, meet them, or even hear of them" (1991, p. 6). Hence, we invent "nations where they do not exist" (p. 6). Given that most citizens will never meet, the narration of a nation through texts helps to express central ideologies and unite the nation.

Often, the discourse of nationalism operates around ideals of a nation having a monocultural and monolingual identity (Druik, 2006). When the political principle of 'one state, one culture' is violated, an invented nationalism emerges. Indeed, nationalism can be defined as a social and political "invented tradition" that seeks to align the nation and state (Adria, 2010; Bhabha, 1990; O'Leary, 1998). The social movement of nationalism often involves the use of myths and symbols that imagine the nation and align it with the state. In nationalism, Michael Billig (1995) argues that these symbols are routinely "flagged" or unconsciously reinforced in the daily life of citizens. To understand the daily yet unnoticed rhetoric of the nation, Billig introduces the concept of "banal nationalism." For Billig, the "metonymic image of banal nationalism is," for example, "not a flag which is being consciously waved with fervent passion" (1995, p. 8). Rather, "it is the flag hanging unnoticed" (Ibid.) on a public building and often operates mindlessly, beyond the level of conscious awareness. Billig questions the orthodox understanding of nationalism as a movement that is aggressively extraordinary, politically charged, and emotionally driven. He rather considers the unnoticed and banal ways of reproducing national symbols that are important to consider in studies of Canadian popular culture.

In examining Canadian national identity, cultural productions of writers such as Northrop Frye and Margaret Atwood are instructive. Northrop Frye is the first writer to question and represent Canadian national identity in the context of place. As Zoe Druik comments, Frye suggests that Canadian identity is about "where is here" as opposed to "who am I" (2006, p. 87). Margaret Atwood similarly represents Canadian identity as "lost," an identity that needs to map its territory to locate itself mythically. The construction of such national identity is not a luxury but a necessity for culturally diverse groups of Canada (Atwood, 2004, pp. 18-19 cited in Druik, 2006, p. 87).

In an effort to mitigate tensions of cultural groups, narratives often represent and identify Canadians by a coherent ideal of what it 'is not' rather than what 'it is.' Canada is marked by cultural and regional differences that destabilise and challenge the monocultural and monolingual idea of the nation. For each local and regional group in Canada, as observed in history lessons in schools, there are stable but different definitions of the nation. No single definition equally speaks to or is meaningful for all groups across Canada. In light of this perspective, Amelia Kalant argues that in Canada,

> The metanarrative of 'failure of place' (territory/land) or body has been the condition of imagining the nation, and it has been tremendously productive: Uncertainty of place and failure to approximate the norms of nation have been constitutive of national myths (2004, p. 33).

In Canada, Kalant argues, the 'failure of place' is a coherent idea of nation that circulates around a myth of 'lack.' In this respect, the 'lack of place' or 'placelessness' is a monolithic ideal that may speak to all cultural groups across the Canadian nation.

The ambivalence of place in this myth is particularly constructed in, and supported by, policies of the Canadian state. Carolyn J. Tuohy (1992) calls this ambivalence an "institutionalised ambivalence." This ambivalence arises from opposition between America's free market philosophy and Canada's public subsidies that support protectionist measures for cultural productions. In cultural productions, the ambivalence of Canada is expressed in terms of how it is "not" the place of the American Dream and thereby identified as an American 'Other' (Bow, 2008; Kalant, 2004). In Canadian nationalism, this myth is located in the uncertainty of a single place that might be meaningful to all cultural groups. Cultural productions, as Kalant indicates, have supported the "myth of lack" in a way that may erase regional and cultural differences and imagine a conflict-free nation. The "myth of lack" provides imaginary conditions for negotiation of conflicting cultures across Canada. They also help negotiating tensions between the ambivalent subject positions of Anglo-Canadian invaders/settlers in search of a monocultural nation. It is in light of this myth that Canadians have developed technologies and "provided the conditions for the possibility of the nation" (Jones-Imhotep, 2004, p. 6).

The Theory of Technological Nationalism

The theory of technological nationalism suggests that Canada is historically unified and exists as a sovereign state because of communication technologies that integrate the nation (Adria, 2010; Charland, 1986; Kroker, 1984). It is a set of cultural attitudes that reflect and reinforce predominant ideologies around the use of technologies in binding the nation of Canada. The use of communication technology in Canada can be traced to the "classical origins of the technological dynamo in European history," and the economic and technological development of America (Kroker, 1984, p. 7). Canadians viewed America as a threat to the sovereignty of their nation, and this led to a coast-to-coast communication system that would unite the vast, empty land and act as a cultural defence of Canada. The development of the Canadian Pacific Railway (CPR) between 1881 and 1885 is historically understood as a deliberate political and economic attempt by Canadians to unite all regions from the east to west coasts. The transcontinental railway has facilitated the movement of goods and information across a vast northern wilderness.

Since 1919, another railway company, the government-owned Canadian National Railway (CNR), played a key role in the nationwide telegraph network (McPhail & McPhail, 1990; Murray, 2004). In addition to developing railways and telegraph, CNR offered a platform to deploy another significant technology at the time: radio. As a broadcasting system, radio aimed to increase Canada's prosperity and unity. In this respect, Sir Henry Thornton, the President of CNR, equipped some of the parlour cars of CNR with radio sets and established a network of radio stations in 1923. He believed that the radio would be a significant unifying force for the nation and presented the rail service as more appealing and attractive to tourists and settlers in Canada (McPhail & McPhail, 1990). In 1933, the broadcasting network that CNR founded formed the basis of the Canadian Broadcasting Corporation (CBC) system to facilitate national unity.

Based on the combined efforts of transportation and communication technologies, Canada came to exist as an economic and political unit. Since then, Canada has been imagined as a sovereign nation that has been integrated by communication technologies (Babe, 1990; Berland, 1988; Charland, 1986; Fremeth, 2006; Hillmer & Chapnick, 2007; Jones-Imhotep, 2004; Kalant, 2004; Lorimar & Gasher, 2001; McPhail & McPhail, 1990; Schafer, 1995; Vipond, 2000). This imagination leads Maurice Charland to argue that Canadian national identity may be, to a large extent, both mythically and rhetorically, a consequence of what he called "technological nationalism."

Maurice Charland (1986) identifies the dominant expression of "technological nationalism" in Canadian media content and communication policy documents. His work offers a significant insight into the rhetorical use of technology in Canadian nationalism. It has allowed for the examination of the ideological use and deterministic effects of technology in shaping the Canadian nation. Charland argues that if radio, for example, "were to bring forth a nation by providing common national experience, that experience would be one of communication, of sheer mediation" (1986, p. 206). This mediation, Charland argues, is the collective, national identity of Canada that is based on the shared experience of communication technologies. In his interpretation, the process of communication (form) is privileged over the substance (content) to be communicated. Therefore, "the content of the Canadian identity would be but technological nationalism itself" (p. 206) and is rhetorically expressed in Canadian media institutions and policy.

Charland took a rhetorical approach to technological nationalism while Robert Babe (1990) took a political economy approach. For Charland, the idea of Canada depends on the rhetoric of technology. In this respect, technology is integral to Canadian consciousness. For Babe, telecommunication is an instrument of continental economic integration so that Canada, as a nation, persists despite communication media. The material and ideological bases of technological nationalism is well indicated by Darin Barney (2005). Barney's angle is political and he is interested in the crisis of democracy. In this context, Barney writes that, "technological nationalism is easily co-opted to industrial and commercial strategies that primarily benefit private interests and, moreover, obscures the authenticity and diversity of Canadian national experience" (2005, p. 76). This chapter uses these approaches to examine the way in which technological nationalism is expressed in Canadian popular culture and the way it mediates authenticity. In particular, it focuses on the relationship between form and content in the rhetoric of technological nationalism. It is also important to note the representation of its relations with cultural productions and the conditions in which these productions occur.

Conditions of the Rhetoric of Technological Nationalism

Canada is a "political and economic entity for pragmatic and imperial rather than nationalistic reasons" (Vipond, 2000, p. 3). The myths of nationalism help the government to integrate Canada as a coherent unit and administer the country in a way that is politically and economically viable. In this context, Maurice Charland and other scholars have stated that the rhetorical expressions of technological nationalism is a discourse of the state (Babe, 1990; Szeman, 2000). However, Charland and others need to further recognise that technological nationalism has also been constructed and sustained by private media corporations (Hillmer & Chapnick, 2007). Their rationale is that media are technologies that are instituted and regulated by the government (Berland, 1988; Lorimar & Gasher, 2001; McPhail & McPhail, 1990). For example, the Canadian Radio, Television and Telecommunications Commission (CRTC), a federal regulating agency, requires a minimum of sixty percent Canadian content in television (CRTC, 1985). Media corporations usually meet this requirement through adopting rhetorical strategies of expressing Canadianness. In fact, media corporations, both public and private, reproduce the rhetoric of "technological nationalism" in a social and cultural context to unite Canada on economic and political grounds.

In order to recognise rhetorical constructions of the nation, it is important to study the conditions and variables that influence the constructions. The study of these variables shows how technology impacts both media texts and the expression of Canadian national identity in cultural productions. Thomas and Brenda McPhail (1990), Rowland Lorimar (2001), and Mike Gasher (2001) studied variables that influence the role of technology in the Canadian nation. Based on their work, six variables can be identified that explain the reasons for policies and productions to employ the rhetoric of technological nationalism in Canada.

First, the Canadian land is so vast that the eastern and western parts of the nation need to be connected through technology. Second, Canada has a low population. There are few human resources in production and a sparse market in reception. Lorimar states that these two variables influence the government of Canada to a third condition: to "invest in expensive per capita transmission systems so that Canadians can stay in touch with each other" (2001, p. 65). However, heavy investments in technology in a sparse market lead to limited revenue and severe cutbacks in Canadian programming. For these reasons, the Canadian government deregulates the heavy import of American productions for cost-effective programmes.

The heavy import of American content into Canada is reflective of a continentalism that depends on a fourth variable that originates from US Federal Communications Commission (FCC) policymaking. Indeed, the FCC facilitates the import of US media content by defining the continental boundaries of Canada and the USA within a technological infrastructure. The continental border of Canada and the USA is thus defined in terms of a technological network, rather than on geopolitical grounds. The changing definition of national boundaries is contingent on economic contexts. Sandra Braman expands:

> When forced to do so in 1943, the FCC chose to delineate the U.S. border in terms of the technological network rather than geopolitically. Communication within the forty-eight contiguous states — and Canada and Mexico — was defined as domestic, because the same network technologies were used throughout that space, even though that space included the territories of two other sovereign governments (2006, p. 243).

Clearly, the fluid continental boundaries turn the Canadian market into a part of the US market, with a consequently heavy export of American productions to Canada. US producers can then recoup expenses of their media products. They not only reach their profit targets on US domestic sales alone, but also export programs to Canada at a fraction of the production costs (Flaherty & Manning, 1993). This process allows Canadian media to offer cost-effective programming.

The condition of 'continentalism' in cost-effective programming is not only driven by economic and political intent but also by a fifth condition: the lack of a language barrier between the United States and Canada. The lack of a language barrier prompts media corporations to adopt the rhetoric of technological nationalism and construct Canada as powerful like America — yet distinct from it. The lack of a barrier in English language facilitates imports of American cultural productions in Canada. This strengthens the existing hegemony of American cultural values and calls for resistance through a distinctive cultural sovereignty in Canada. Liss Jeffrey explains that the initiatives of public and private broadcasting — unifying the nation — are a form of technological nationalism that realises "distinctive English Canadian" (1996, p. 215) vision and pragmatism. The way in which broadcasting adopts the rhetoric of technological nationalism leads to a sixth condition: regionalism in Canada. Canada is a vast country with different regional cultures. Although each region needs its own technological infrastructure and internal communication, the Confederation needs to be uniformly administered across the regions. On the basis of these variable conditions, the Canadian government has emphasised the development of technological infrastructures instead of media content (Babe, 1990; Charland, 1986; McPhail & McPhail, 1990; Schafer, 1995; Vipond, 2000). To develop Canada as an economic and political unit — and to uniformly administer it across regions — the government has significantly invested in communications infrastructure.

In implementing a standard rhetoric of technological nationalism across the nation, there is limited attention to experiences and needs that are specific to diverse regions in Canada. This leads Lorimar and Gasher (2001) to argue that Canada's commitment to current technology and effective, rapid transmission has not necessarily served the cultural needs of Canadians. The limited attention to the cultural needs of Canadians has been previously highlighted by Canadian thinker George Grant in the *Lament for the Nation: the Defeat of Canadian Nationalism* (1965). Grant indicates that there has been loss of human, regional, and cultural experiences in Canada. But Grant, like Charland, does not discuss the complexity of the erasure of regional and cultural differences through content in popular culture. Canadian identity is popularly represented in terms of a mythic "lack," focussing on the absence of regional and cultural differences and how it is not America (Bow, 2008; Kalant, 2004; Sherbert, et al., 2006). However, this description of nationalism is simplistic. It dismisses the ambivalent positions in the myth of the 'lack' and the complex ways in which popular texts reflect and reinforce the rhetoric of technological nationalism. The ambivalence exists on two levels. First, there is a paradoxical 'presence' of a mythic 'absence.' Second, the presence of heavily imported US media content creates a sense of American cultural imperialism that, ironically, needs to be resisted in Canadian popular culture. In this respect, there is a systematic and mythical representation of how Canada is not America, feeding back into the notion of 'lack.' Canadian popular culture is then reflective of an "institutionalised ambivalence" (Tuohy, 1992). The "institutionalised ambivalence" also exists between competing policies of America's open cultural market and Canada's protectionist views of cultural productions.

The Ambivalence of the Canadian Nation

There are complex and ambivalent ways in which "lack" is represented in the rhetorical use of technological nationalism in popular culture. These representations can be studied from Arthur Kroker's understanding of technology and nation as ambivalent constructions. Kroker writes that, "[t]echnological nationalism has always been the essence of the Canadian state and, most certainly, the locus of Canadian identity" (1984. p. 10). From this viewpoint, he explores the experience and representation of technology in cultural texts. Kroker illustrates how Toronto's CN Tower, for example, reflects and reinforces the role of communication in the nation, just as the railway track is represented in Canadian discourses. The representations of these forms of technology, however, are not specific to regional and cultural experiences of the nation.

In Canadian popular culture, there is a 'lack' or 'absence' of regional and cultural experiences in national representations of technology. Canadian metanarratives reflect and reinforce a 'presence' of an ideal of 'absence' or 'lack' in relation to America. Instead of emphasising multiple regional cultures, or even acknowledging their absence, most representations establish the presence of a homogeneous, coherent, and sovereign image of Canada. There is, therefore, an underlying ambivalent position of 'absence' and 'presence' in these images. To compare and understand how the rhetoric of technological nationalism figures in popular culture, I further draw on Arthur Kroker's theoretical understanding of technology and nation. The way Kroker understands constructions of technology and nation is based on competing views on technology in the Toronto School of Communication. He locates the ambivalence of these constructions in the intersecting thoughts of Canadian scholars Marshall McLuhan, George Grant, and Harold Innis. The comparative thoughts particularly help to map the form in relation to the content of media technology and the relation between the two in popular representations.

Marshall McLuhan (1964) contends that we live in an environment that involves innovations of technology. These innovations are extensions of human biology. In this respect, technology is an extension or "amplification" of the central nervous system of human biology. Human needs and stimuli from the environment trigger a response or "counter-irritation" in the central nervous system. The effect of this counter-irritation of biological nerves is the reorganisation of organic electrons and evolution of bodily "techniques" that can process and interpret necessary signification of the content. McLuhan's classical study of the medium as the message offers further insight into the form and content of technology and how they influence different types of societies within a nation. He argues that even media content, a social consequence or effect of technology, is just a technique in itself and is, therefore, irrelevant. As Jakub Vémola interprets McLuhan, "it is the psychic and social consequences of the media which constitute its primary message. Thus, it is not the content which is important; "it is the character of the medium that is its potency or effect - its message" (2009, p. 6). In other words, for McLuhan, the form of media technology influences its content.

McLuhan illustrates the relation between form and content with an example of a light bulb. He says that a light bulb is a medium without content, yet it sends information with its light and impacts the environment by virtue of its presence. Metaphorically, the specific element that characterises content is whether the form of technology or medium is 'hot' or 'cool.' For McLuhan, a medium such as a movie is hot if it has high definition and demands a relatively lower viewer participation. Compared to this, a medium is cool if it has low definition and requires higher viewer participation. The use and impact of hot or cold media are not neutral. From McLuhan's perspective, a hot medium such as radio segregates and detribalises society, while a cool medium re-tribalises society and "will restore the structure because of intense involvement" (1964, p. 38).

McLuhan's work indicates why and how the Canadian nation, both environmentally and socially, is contingent on particular forms of technology. The forms of technology used have particular impacts on the Canadian nation. In general, technological innovations maintain an ecological balance between the changed conditions of the environment and adaptation of the human body. The relationship between biological environment and technology explains why the harsh conditions of nature, particularly wilderness and cold climate, have prompted development of sophisticated technologies in Canada. These technologies, in turn, provide conditions for survival and the possibility of the nation (Jones-Imhotep, 2004). Although McLuhan does not specify the relationship between the biological extension of technology and Canadian national movements, his argumentative position can be applied to media constructions of Canada as a nation. For example, McLuhan states that the uniform, standardisation of vernacular languages by print technology has "demanded both personal fragmentation and social uniformity, the natural expression of which was the nation-state" (1989, p. 112). Consequently, the construction and representation of a certain kind of national society are influenced by the characteristics of a given technology, and it is possible that different technologies will give rise to different expressions of the nation. Furthermore, these multiple expressions of the nation are not only contingent upon different forms of technology, but also grounded within human agency or 'human will.' It is 'human will,' via biological reactions that shape the form of technology, that makes different conditions possible for the Canadian nation. For Arthur Kroker (1984), the freedom in the 'human will' can be expressed as 'technological humanism.'

Arthur Kroker contrasts Marshall McLuhan's perspective of 'technological humanism' with George Grant's conception of 'technological dependency.' While McLuhan perceives freedom in the use of technology, Grant focuses on technology in a dominating relation to nationalism. He argues that the Canadian nation is a technological society and depends on technology for its order. Technology determines the construction of the Canadian nation in a way that is not subject to the free will of different individuals. The constructions of, and representations by, technology do not cover individual differences across the Canadian nation. In *Lament for the Nation* (1965), he uses the word 'lament' as a literary and philosophical tool that indicates the loss of human experiences in response to technology. Kroker specifies that the dominant task of technology — organising the nation — carries an "abiding sense of lack" and "emptiness of being" (2004, p. 58).

In Canadian popular culture, the 'lack' is symbolically expressed through representations of the vast, empty lands of the wild North that overlook local and cultural differences in the northern region and across the nation. The lack of representation of locally and culturally diverse people is a homogenous expression of Canadianness, which is itself a myth. The regional and cultural differences among First Nation, French-Canadian, and ethnic minority citizens are often dismissed in homogenous depictions of Anglo-Canadians in popular media. Grant (2005) indicates that the impact of technology on the homogenisation of the nation is indicative of an economic and political move towards "continentalism," a concept I return to in Chapter 4. Under the deterministic power of technology in the continental progress of North America, Grant contends that Canada's "disappearance" and "loss" of regional and cultural differences was "inevitable" (1965, p. xxvii). Here, technology is thought of as an inevitable force that is independent of social factors and which creates social conditions that are directly determined by technology. The economic and political impact of technology facilitates a dissolution of regional and cultural differences among Canadians and the "disappearance of

Canadians" (2005, p. 346) as an effect of the ideological uses of technology. Grant's identification of this inevitable, independent force behind the Canadian national condition can be interpreted as "technological dependency" (Kroker, 1984).

In Kroker's view, Harold Innis holds a 'third perspective' that mediates the oppositional stances of Grant's 'technological dependency' and McLuhan's 'technological humanism.' This perspective is 'technological realism' (Kroker, 1984). Innis recognises the tensions of freedom and domination involved in the role of technology in constructing the Canadian nation. For example, the fur trade along water routes and the CPR may have extended the influence of European civilisation across the empty space of the Canadian Prairies all the way to the west coast. At the same time, the power of the West was set against the economic interests of the Ontario bourgeoisie in the East (Kroker, 1984). As a result, the regional and cultural experiences in Canada are segregated. Yet, the segregated regional cultures are not wholly represented in favour of a coherent and stable federal image of Canada. Hence, there are competing dynamics of regions, and the federal state constantly attempts to reconcile these differences to integrate the Canadian nation. In Kroker's view, Innis indicates the presence of a 'technological realism.'

Compared to Marshall McLuhan and George Grant, Arthur Kroker writes that Innis' approach is one of a rational and pragmatic position of 'balance' and 'proportion,' located among the competing forces of any given technological innovation (1984). This perspective allows for the assessment of technology in a way that balances optimistic and pessimistic assumptions of other scholars. It sheds light on competing claims and on paradoxical tendencies to freedom and domination in the use of technology in Canada. It also offers a less deterministic view of technology in relation to the nation. While Innis views how the nation is constituted through means of communication, McLuhan observes that media technologies should be understood in relation to society and its changes. At the same time, Kroker acknowledges the perspectives of McLuhan and Grant. In doing so, he neither exclusively follows their ideas, nor Innis' 'third perspective' of balance and proportion. In light of all perspectives, Kroker rather identifies the Canadian nation facing an "ambivalent fate" (1984, p. 15). In other words, Kroker understands the Canadian nation in terms of 'ambivalence.' This critical perspective helps to investigate how rhetorical movements of the nation are expressed as a myth in media texts. In particular, it sets the theoretical background to explain the process in which the rhetoric of 'technological nationalism' is expressed as a myth in popular narratives. This is what I now embark on in the second part of the chapter.

Canadian Symbols of Nature in Popular Culture

In this section, I show the rationale for using Canadian national symbols of nature in cultural texts. In particular, I focus on how and why technological nationalism gets expressed through symbols of the North in popular culture. Finally, I identify a bidirectional, yet ambivalent, relationship between technological nationalism (form) and representations related to the North in cultural productions (content). This relationship forms the basis for understanding why national symbols, particularly those related to the North, are often reproduced in Canadian popular culture.

Technological Nationalism in Popular Culture

In Canadian popular culture, media texts are often both a cause and effect of the rhetoric of technological nationalism that serves to integrate the nation. There are two pragmatic ways in which media texts are an effect of technological nationalism. First, representations of Canada contain selective images in relation to technology. Pierre Burton's documentary *National Dream* (1974) was the first production to depict and idealise the technological construction of the Canadian nation. Produced by the CBC, Canada's public broadcasting service, the documentary establishes the railroad as a space-binding technology that travels across the wilderness of Canada. The documentary particularly imagines and articulates that the railroad uniting the country is a 'national dream' (Charland, 1986). Although the effects of the railroad could be measured in terms of its end products, such as transportation, industrialisation, and urbanisation, its representation as a 'national dream' is an effect of the rhetoric of technological nationalism and has informed media productions (Charland, 1986). The expression is rhetorical in the sense that it persuades Canadian citizens to romanticise technology as a primary force that binds the nation of Canada together. Yet, concurrently, the images are decoupled from the regional and local differences of Canada in favour of a coherent and stable idea of a united nation. Similar to the documentary, public speeches have promoted technologies such as Canada's railway and long distance telephone services as a nation builder and nation binder (Hillmer & Chapnick, 2007). These rhetorical devices reinforce the use of technology as a legitimate, state-enforced tool that imagines the Canadian nation (Charland, 1986).

Second, policy documents emphasise the predominant role technology plays in nation-building. The central role of broadcast technology in imagining the nation, for example, is specified in the *White Paper on Broadcasting*, a 1966 memorandum of the federal government. The *White Paper* clearly emphasised the determination to develop and maintain a national system of radio and television broadcasting across Canada. The

White Paper on Broadcasting stated: "In future, broadcasting may well be regarded as the central nervous system of Canadian nationhood" (Raboy, 1990, p. 175). Broadcasting technology from coast to coast has been seen as an essential component of Canadian identity through unity. This sense of unity has led to heavy investments in technological infrastructure in Canada. However, the lack of economic capital and the small market have resulted in a failure to produce adequate media content that can be meaningful to all citizens in Canada. The tension between the rhetoric of technological nationalism and failure to deliver Canadian content is reflected in the predominance of American content in Canadian media. At the same time, it is important for the state to institute a coherent image of the nation that can authenticate economic and political intents and defend against American cultural imperialism while constructing the Canadian nation.

National Representations of Nature – The North

A primary way in which technological nationalism reflects and reinforces a coherent and stable image of Canada is through national representations of nature. In this respect, cultural productions depict selective images of northern Canada. These images focus on snow, ice, cold climate, polar bears, maple leaves, and a vast, empty wilderness in the northern parts of Canada. These representations, in turn, call for the nation to be politically and economically integrated through infrastructures of railways, telecommunications, and media technologies.

Technological nationalism originates from the relationship between technology and nature in the colonial period of Canada. Historically, the Canadian nation has been economically and politically integrated by technology, developed across challenging natural conditions. Starting with the CPR in 1889 and the subsequent radio broadcasting system, media technologies have played a crucial role in constructing Canada as a nation (Kalant, 2004). Media technologies particularly helped to represent the mythical qualities of technologies to support the ideological construction of the nation. Here, media acts both as a technology and as a representation of technology. These technologies are required to homogenise regional areas that are distinctive in both their cultural and natural environment, but which need to be integrated into a single nation. The settlement of Native territories, the harsh wilderness conditions, and cold weather challenged colonial development and called for the mechanisation and development of technologies. In the end, colonial settlers confronted Native inhabitants and overcame the hindrances of nature. The conquest of nature can be seen in the establishment of trade and communications technology that cut across the wilderness and challenged the harsh conditions of the Canadian environment. These technological developments created the framework for integrating the nation as an economic and political unit. This leads Edward Jones-Imhotep (2004) to state that Canadian scientists and politicians have historically linked 'nature' and 'technology' with a view to secure the nation.

The relationship between nature and technology has been understood in two different ways: nature is harsh; it opposes human conquest, but it is also a creative force. On one hand, Jones-Imhotep notes that most scholars and artists have treated the relationship between nature and technology in Canada as oppositional:

> [...] hostile climate or impossible terrain—has opposed technology; and technology, for its part—whether realised in railways or telegraphs, shortwave radios or communications satellites—has enabled the tentative conquests of a harsh, unforgiving, and expansive northern nature. In doing so, technology has provided the conditions for the possibility of the nation (2004, p. 6).

On the other hand, the relationship between nature and technology in Canada has been seen as one of harmony, not conflict. For example, Jones–Imhotep notes how high frequency and short-wave radio communications in Canada have been made possible through scientific studies of ionised regions of the upper atmosphere in the northern regions. He specifies that the reliable radio paths "required a scientific excursion through the geophysics of high northern latitudes" (p. 8). The way in which the hostile environment of the Arctic region has provided grounds for the development of technology leads to an understanding of the harmonious relationship between nature and technology in the colonisation of Canada. Michael Ames (1993) also highlights how nature facilitated the development of technology in Canada. Ames states that, "man's increasing ability to work in hostile environments has led to the development of sophisticated remote manipulating devices, which are the latest generation of robotic technology" (1993, p. 241).

Although the relationship between nature and technology has been understood in two different ways, I argue that there is no real distinction between the two. The use of technology is dominating when nature is harsh but marks freedom when nature is sublime. There are indeed paradoxical tendencies with regard to freedom and domination in the use of technology — in both content and form — in relation to Canadian nature. However, when it comes to the actual use of technology, the function of enabling the nation remains constant regardless of whether nature is harsh or sublime. Hence, there is neither an absolute domination, nor untrammelled freedom. Instead, an inherent ambivalence characterises the uses of technologies in building the Canadian nation.

In light of an economic and political drive for technological development, popular narratives produce ideological representations of Canadian nature. In particular, narratives represent Canadian nature in terms of wilderness of the 'North.' Here, the North does not refer to the absolute geographical north (such as the North Pole or sixty degrees of latitude and above, which is often used to delineate the northern territories of Canada). Rather, the North is a rhetorical device that imagines the whole of Canada as 'northern' through selective literary and visual representations in texts (Grace, 2001; Hulan, 2003; Kalant, 2004; Katerberg, 2003). The ideology of Canada as a Northern nation took coherent form during the 1870s via the Canada First movement (Katerberg, 2003). In this respect, official and unofficial depictions of maple leaves, Mounties (the federal police force), snow, cold weather, ice, ice hockey, lumberjacks, beavers, and polar bears are primary examples of Northern iconography in Canadian popular culture (Edwardson, 2008). These icons express how, as Renee Hulan indicates, the North of Canada has been mythologised to become "Canada-as-the North" (2003, p. 11). These representations are, in Michael Billig's words, so "routinely flagged" (1995, p. 8) that they become unconscious, yet iconic, ways of accepting the Canadian nation as the North. These banal and mundane ways of representing Northern national symbols legitimise economic and political investments in technology.

Among the Northern icons, the maple leaf has been officially adopted and routinely represented as Canada's national emblem. The maple leaf is indicative of the cold Canadian winter. As the maple leaf changes colours in autumn, it responds to climatic conditions and marks the arrival of the cold winter that is central to the Northern mythology. Marco Adria (2010) notes that since the nineteenth century, the maple leaf has been used in various provincial and federal emblems such as army badges, war-grave markers, and provincial flags. The maple leaf was officially adopted as a part of the national flag in 1965. Since then, its cultural use has become an "invented tradition" (Adria, 2010, p. 44) and has symbolically represented Canadian national identity.

Similarly, images of the Royal Canadian Mounted Police (RCMP), commonly called the Mounties, have served to reinforce the imaginary of the North in Canadian metanarratives. The RCMP, the federal police force, originated with the North-West Mounted Police in 1873. During the governance of then Prime Minister John A. McDonald, the mounted police force was sent to secure Canada's newly acquired Northwest Territories for settlement. The southern part of these Northern Territories (south of sixty degrees of latitude) was to become the present day Canadian Prairie provinces. The representation of the mounted police, then, reflects and reinforces the metaphorical nature of the North.

The North was the main focus of scientific and technological exploitation to allow for the settlement of new immigrants and the development of English Canadian nationalism (Dawson, 1998). The mounted police force played a decisive role in protecting the technological development of the Canadian Pacific Railway. It confronted the opposition of low paid, dissatisfied labourers of the CPR and Natives who were already settled in the region. In 1874, the North-West Mounted Police cleared "the Plains Indians out of the way, making room for 'white settlement'" (Dawson, 1998, p. 13) while guarding the development of technologies across the Northern regions. In this position, the police force was the primary instrument through which the federal government controlled and eliminated rebellious Natives, Metis, and labourers in the northern regions of Manitoba, Alberta, and Saskatchewan (Caragata, 1979; Dawson, 1998; Francis, 1997). In effect, Canadian national representations of the RCMP reinforce a colonialist and frontier ideology of the North, whereby the Canadian police facilitated the implementation of technologies and, in the process, 'civilised' the northern wilderness frontier. A frontier is a free land where the savage and the civilised meet; it is characterised by the strength, self-reliance, adventure, and discovery of the colonisers who built their nation-state (Heald, 2007). This representation of the RCMP in an imagined frontier is central to the movement of technological nationalism. The image of the RCMP symbolises both the North and technological nationalism in popular culture.

In contemporary popular culture, the rhetorical use of technological nationalism is reflected in the celebration of the RCMP officer as a mythic hero called the 'Mountie.' The centennial celebrations of the RCMP in 1973 started federally funded commemorations of the Mountie, symbolising the heroic formation of the North-West Mounted Police in the service of 'white settlement' one-hundred years earlier (Dawson, 1998). Since then, the Canadian federal government has actively assisted service industries in using the image of the Mountie in souvenirs and live exhibitions for the tourism and entertainment markets. The Mountie image has also been used in a number of historical narratives, autobiographies, novels, and Hollywood films (Allan, 2002; Dawson, 1998; Francis, 1997; Gittings, 1998). In popular metanarratives, the RCMP is mythologised as the Mountie and serves to commodify peaceful relations of harmony, goodwill, civic order, and deference. In doing so, the myth of the Mountie overlooks the actions of the North-West Mounted Police, who crushed peaceful protests in the name of "controlling, eliminating, and killing its opposition" (Dawson, 1998, p. 13). These protests included the Red River Rebellion, which involved the Metis and the eventual hanging of their leader, Louis Riel. Like other Northern images, the mythic image of the Mountie instead acts as a colonialist tool that enforces the frontier ideology of the North in the rhetorical use of technological nationalism. The mythic image carries a romantic representation of a Northern iconography that undermines the social, economic, and political impacts of technology on people across regions in Canada.

Romanticism and Authenticity of the North

A major impact of the rhetoric of technological nationalism can be seen in the romanticism of the North in national representations of nature. These representations have served to negotiate tensions of colonialist–colonised relations in technological nationalism. The rhetorical movements and representations, in turn, have helped to integrate and authenticate the Canadian nation. In general, representations of nature symbolise a shared environment that is timeless, universal, and historically persistent (Kaufmann & Zimmer, 1998). In Canada, the romanticism of Northern images has helped to define authentic Canadian nationalism (Katerberg, 2003; Kaufmann, 1998; Kaufmann & Zimmer, 1998).

The need to construct the authenticity of the Canadian nation can be traced back to nineteenth-century Romanticism. Following the Enlightenment and the Industrial Revolution, Charles Guignon (2004) notes, Romanticism was a reaction to the twin impacts of rationality and the mechanisation of technology on nature. Guignon specifies the impact of technology on nature in the following three ways. First, a sense of wholeness appears to have been lost with the rise of modernity and mechanisation. Second, truth is "discovered with total immersion in one's deepest and most intense feelings" (p. 51). However, the primordial source of nature in self and environment, at large, is lost in rational reflection and the scientific methods. Third, the self is the highest and most encompassing form of originality, but it is undermined by standardised practices of technology. In the Canadian context, the political economy of staples (the use and trade of fur, cod, timber, pulp, and paper) and the development of railways and broadcasting are central to understanding the way in which technology mechanised nature. Particularly, in the mid-twentieth century, uranium was a staple that Canada exported to the United States for the manufacture of atomic bombs. This signified the potential destruction of nature. Until recently, uranium mining was part of the largely unknown history of Canada's North. The increasing use of technologies prompted a restoration of nature through national representations of the North that can authenticate Canada.

The increasing use of technology in unifying and defining the Canadian nation called for a renewed interest in romantic nature. The role of representing romantic images of Northern nature in building the Canadian nation has been studied by a number of cultural scholars, such as Brian Osborne (2006), Edward Jones-Imhotep (2004), Amelia Kalant

(2004), Eric Manning (2000), and Eric Kaufman (1998). Their work suggests that the Canadian nation and national identity are located in selective representations of nature — particularly the North. For instance, Eric Kaufmann (1998) suggests that literary and visual expressions of the Canadian North and its landscape have been inspired by romantic ideas that were common in mid-nineteenth century Britain and United States. At the same time, he notes that Canadian national sentiment needed to be set free from British and American imperial powers. In this context, "the new nationalism looked to Canada's northern climate and location for inspiration" (Kaufmann, 1998, p. 682). Romanticism was further revived via the Group of Seven, the historiography of the Laurentian School, and the work of pianist Glenn Gould. These famous works located Canadian national identity in Northern wilderness landscapes. Popular paintings by the Group of Seven and by Thompson — among several visual and performative arts of the past four hundred years — depict the vast Northern wilderness as both terrifying and beautiful, and rarely with any human subject. But unlike the Romantic traditions of Britain and the United States, these Canadian expressions mostly "treated nature as a challenge to be overcome" through the use of technology, and they depicted the natural landscape as untamed, wild, harsh, and barbaric (Kaufmann, 1998, p. 680).

The romanticism of the Canadian North is reproduced in contemporary television shows such as *Ice Pilots NWT* and *Ice Road Truckers*. Media representations of *Ice Pilots NWT* depict "a classic frontier story," whereby pilots have "frostbitten ramp hands as they struggle to keep vintage warbirds flying despite blizzards, breakdowns and impossible jobs" ("Ice Pilots NWT Heads To Global," 2010). A news article on *Ice Pilots NWT* similarly portrays the Canadian North as a "merciless place" where pilots confront "bone-chilling temperatures to fly cargo and passengers through blizzards, breakdowns, and transatlantic journeys [...]" ("Ice Pilots to Film Episode in Oshkosh," 2011). Again, a report from Northern News Services states that the show offers "a real good look at the North and a real good look at how the young fellows operate the airplanes in extreme cold weather conditions like we have" (Bickford & Letts, 2009). In addition to romanticising the North, the program shows how technology is used to overcome the harsh challenges of life the Canadian North.

Representations of the Canadian North can also be observed in the US production *Ice Road Truckers*. The show depicts truck drivers who make dangerous journeys 250 miles north of the Arctic Circle, in the Northwest Territories. Their struggle involves "hauling loads of up to 200,000 pounds over icy roads and frozen lakes, carrying everything from explosives to toilet paper out to remote mines" (Carlisle, 2010). In this show, the rhetoric of technological nationalism is expressed in cultural and economic contexts. Culturally, the show reproduces the rhetoric of technological nationalism, whereby vast and disparate frozen lands reflect and reinforce the need to be settled with trade and transportation. Ironically, it is a US production that is exported to Canada at a fraction of the production costs to offer cost-effective programming to Canadian media. This cost-effective programming is significant because, as mentioned before, the Canadian government makes heavy investments into technological infrastructure with limited resources to produce domestic content. Yet, the content narrates ideological themes with which Canadian audiences can relate. The dominant narrative in both *Ice Pilots NWT* and *Ice Road Truckers* reproduces technological nationalism, whereby technology overcomes harsh Northern wilderness conditions and fosters national integration. Kaufmann draws on William New (1989) and states that, "the narrative of Canada is one of nationalisation, stressing the advance of civilisation against nature" (1998, p. 680).

In technological nationalism, popular representations of the North express contrasting yet ambivalent relations between Canadian nature and nation. Popular Canadian narratives represent technologies that overcome natural challenges and mythically integrate the nation. Here, nature and the technological nation contrast. At the same time, the relationship between nature and nation is also ambivalent. There are indeed paradoxical tendencies regarding the freedom and domination inherent in the technology/nature binary. Yet, at the same time, there is no real distinction between the uses of technologies when it comes to ideologically constructing the nation. This ambivalence partly becomes an enabler of the Canadian nation. The way Eric Kaufmann (1998) relates the Canadian nation and nature can be further understood in terms of this ambivalence. Kaufmann describes the relationship between the Canadian nation and nature in the following two ways: the 'naturalisation of nation' and the 'nationalisation of nature.' The 'naturalisation of nation' refers to a nation that happens to perceive itself as the "offspring of its natural landscape" (Kaufmann, 1998, p. 690). Here, landscape is not a part of the natural environment, but a cultural construct of representations in narratives (Osborne, 2001). In the 'naturalisation of nation,' Kaufmann particularly emphasises a direction of causation from environmental nature to a national culture, whereby a nation is imagined in terms of selected representations of nature in narratives. The "nationalisation of nature" reverses the process in which national culture influences the understanding of nature. Through this process, the Canadian nation invents a 'homeland' through settlement, the inscription of names, and the creation of mnemonic aids in historical relations to geographical territory (Osborne, 2001, 2006).

While these relationships between nature and nation help to understand the cultural constructions of the North, they overlook the production of popular natural symbols for colonial intents within technological nationalism. Bruce Willem-Braun (1997) indicates the colonial context of producing Canadian nature and nation:

> The production of nature (rhetorically and materially) has played in the colonization of particular social environments, how natural scientists (including geographers) made visible and available to colonial administration a discrete realm called 'nature' that could be seen as separate from colonised peoples, or, perhaps more important, how what counts as 'nature' today is often constituted within, and informed by, the legacies of colonialism (p. 5).

In her study, Jody Berland (2006) further examines natural resources as specific examples of colonial exploitation of nature. In particular, she uses the example of trees to indicate the colonialist relationship between nature and technology. She states that it is not the mere presence of trees in nature, but the *trade* of trees that creates colonialist grounds for building the Canadian nation. Berland argues that the Canadian development of technology has resulted in the "sacrilegious plundering" (2006, p. 73) of nature and of natural resources in the name of economic, political, and technological pursuits. Similarly, global warming and the technological exploitation of natural resources (oiling and mining) exist in the northern region even though 'Canada-as-the-North' is represented as a vast, empty, untouched landscape to be united by technologies, per the intent of nation-building colonialists.

Based on these observations, I conclude that a crisis of Canadian nature exists on two levels. One is the material level, where technological developments deplete natural resources to build the Canadian nation. The second is the symbolic level, where selected, romantic representations of nature in narratives create the conditions for national integration through technology, thereby causing a crisis of nature. Nonetheless, romantic representations may restore a sense of wholeness and truth that is lost in standardised and mechanised productions of technology. The dominant representations of nature may represent authenticity and mitigate the tensions that are created by the crisis. The representations of Canadian nature are a response to the crisis of nature that technology created. From this perspective, popular representations of the Canadian North are an effect of technological nationalism. But the vast and empty lands in the representations also create the conditions for national integration through technology. Popular representations of natural resources in narratives call for economic, political, and technological interventions that have supported the nation since the colonial period. Natural resources are exploited to such an extent that "high technology sectors" are "needed to compensate for anticipated crises in the export of the resources" (Berland, 2006, p. 73).

The material and symbolic crisis of nature creates a tension of authenticity that is negotiated by romantic representations of the North in popular culture. Such representations, in turn, facilitate the technological integration and sustenance of the nation. This crisis of nature demonstrates that popular representations of the North cause, or create the conditions for, technological nationalism in Canada. Cultural productions then have a bidirectional relationship with technological nationalism, as technological nationalism is both the cause and effect of popular representations of the Canadian North. I will explain this relationship in the final subsection of this chapter and illustrate it using popular representations of the North throughout this book.

In a way, the material and symbolic crisis of nature paradoxically sustains the Canadian nation. Both levels of crisis can be thought of as geocultural dimensions that span Canadian territory, national consciousness, and identity. One could argue, for instance, that geography created the conditions for national integration through transportation and communication technology. In addition, there is an existing cultural history of Romantic representations of the geographic north in Canadian culture that is still reproduced in present cultural content. However, both levels of crisis involve using technology that depletes natural resources in the name of national economic development. Since there are opposing uses of technology in sustaining the nation, the relationship between the rhetoric of technological nationalism (form) and the North (content) is both fundamental and contingent. It is also partly ambivalent, as it describes a contingent relationship. Indeed, there was no indication of ambivalence in the colonialists' intent and relation to nature, particularly natural resources, as described by Willem-Braun (1997) and Berland (2006). At the same time, there is opposing and, hence, no unique use of technology (rhetorical, political, or economical) when it comes to enabling the nation.

The Problem with Canadian National Identity and the North

The main problem with the popular representation of Canadian landscape and wilderness is that it is not a whole, authentic representation of nature. As Dan Brockington states, wildlife and nature are the "product of careful, calculated manipulations and editing" (2008, p. 565) in cultural practices. From this perspective, popular representations of Canadian cold weather are not a meteorological, but a *cultural* construct of the North that suggests an arbitrary relationship with Canadian national identity (Berland, 1994; Bodroghkozy, 2001). The vast, empty, frozen landscape and symbols of its wilderness represent a Northern frontier that was once colonised by European settlers who used trade and technology (Bodroghkozy, 2001; Hansson & Norberg, 2009).

In a colonialist context, the Canadian North acts as an American 'Other' that can respond to the continentalist threats posed by America. The response is twofold. First, as an 'American Other,' the Canadian North has become a site of imagining strength and endurance against harsh conditions of nature at North America's northern 'frontier.' The conquest of the harsh Northern climate and wilderness creates a condition of "social Darwinism" (Katerberg, 2003, p. 552) and imagines a strong Northern race in Canada. In the Canadian imagination, the Northern location of Canada is not suitable for the 'Southern races' of America. In this respect, Americans cannot adapt to the rigors of the mythic North, so they stay in the south. Canada, by contrast, is considered to be "free, prosperous, and orderly" (Ibid.). Consequently, the Canadian North acts as a site for imagining a strong colonial power defined by conquest and settlement.

Second, the Canadian North acts as an American 'Other' that offers cultural resistance against America's continentalist threats. For Brian Osborne, "the iconography of the North and wilderness has rested upon ideological assumptions that searched for national distinctiveness and rejected [American] continentalist threats" (2006, p. 9). Nonetheless, Canada still imports an extensive amount of American media content. The regular import of content meets the needs of a small audience market that offers limited revenues. It also compensates for the over-expenditure of technology that integrates Canada across vast frontier spaces. But the importing of American media content also fuels the requirement for Canadian content producers to resist American cultural monopoly in North America. In an effort to resist the 'continentalist threats' posed by America, Canadian narratives often imagine Canada as the morally superior nation. Amelia Kalant explains:

> [T]he idea of Canada being almost-American, or drowned out by America but not (yet) American has led to the adoption of a role as interpreter between America and Europe/the world, and as America's moral conscience. Canada does have a soul: if Americanness can be said to be about excelling or success, Canadianness is about being good and moral (2004, p. 34).

The Northern value of morality is expressed in the myth of the Mountie, a "neurotically fastidious, overly polite, and morally pure" (Gittings, 1998) figure in the Canadian North. As William Katerberg (2003) explains, the Mountie is a symbol of peace-keeping and order between the Native inhabitants and white settlers in Canada. In colonising the Northern frontier, these moral overtones are useful in constructing Canadian national identity as the stronger counterpart, or 'Other,' of America's violent, "Wild West" (Katerberg, 2003, p. 545). However, Amelia Kalant states that the depiction of Canada as a vast, empty, snow-covered wasteland ignores "the claims and traces of indigenous peoples [...] along with the industrialisation that was taking place" (2004, p. 55). Canada's (Anglo) national symbols of nature, as Kalant further states, are devoid of the complex political and cultural differences with French-Canadians, the working class, and new immigrants. The images of a hostile and harsh wild North instead represent a need for control through the Anglo-imperialist development of communications technology. The Canadian representation of the North is, therefore, a discursive construct that imagines the Canadian nation as a wild frontier, tamed not by the force and violence that conquered the American West, but by colonisation and civilisation via technological means.

The popular imaginations of the Canadian North lead to another problem: the dismissal of local and regional differences in the geographical north and across Canada. The Canadian North is a metaphor for nature and wilderness. In this view, Canadian nature is usually selected and depicted as part of a vast, frozen, empty, wild, and sublime Northern landscape that needs to be colonised and civilised. These selected representations of nature play a dominant role in legitimising colonialist land claims, the use of communications technology, and the prioritisation of an Anglo-Canadian national identity. In doing so, the land is decoupled from indigenous people, migrants, and their specific cultural practices. Kalant argues that the representations of the North permit the "metaphysical meeting between essential human and nature that modern technology has vanquished" (2004, p. 79). In this respect, the North "erases the telos of human victory that technology promises" (p. 79). In addition, mythic images of Canada-as-the-North are not necessarily the geographical north — that is, sixty degrees and above of latitude.

Studies by Chris Wodskou (2010) and Andrew J. Chapeskie (2001) further show that the problem inherent in cultural representations of the North is an underrepresentation of the complex ecological realities of Canadian nature in the actual geographical north of Canada. Their studies show how these existing representations do not address, for instance, the melting of ice due to global warming and the environmental damage caused by mining and oil exploitation. These exclusions occur because the cultural meaning of the North does not correspond with the geographical north in the Canadian national imagination. Yet, the geographical north is imagined as the *whole* Canadian nation in popular narratives. This underlying tension — reflected in the disconnect between the geographical north and the cultural North — reinforces the ambivalence of Canadian nationhood.

In his radio documentary *Arctic Re-imagined* (2010), Chris Wodskou indicates that popular representations of nature respond to a critical need to restore the north. This restoration is necessary because the frozen landscape that mythically represents the Northern frontier is facing the crisis of global warming. The new conditions arising from global warming are reflective of an ecological and political crisis, and they call for a re-imagination of current issues related to the Northern frontier. One of the current issues is the lack of scientific representations (maps) of the Arctic Ocean floor, which would be used to assess different nations' claims to sovereignty in the north. The government of former Canadian Prime Minister Stephen Harper was engaged in an Arctic agenda geared towards establishing Canada's northern border and sovereignty. This agenda was required to secure natural resources that presumably lie underneath the shrinking polar ice cap. With the help of scientists, the race to map the geomorphology of the ocean could help settle territorial claims in international court. This agenda was represented as the development of a romantic "Far North," but it overlooked climate change and other pressing issues that threaten the northern region (CBC, 2011a).

Critical commentaries, such as those made in *Arctic Re-imagined* (2010), encourage thinking about the implications and consequences of technological nationalism, romanticism, and the North in the present geopolitical order in which technological interventions and the reclaiming of northern territories are overlooked in mythic representations of the North. Wodskou (2010) interprets the inability to represent changing conditions of the geographical north as a failure of imagination on the part of Canadian nationalism. I would rather offer a more pragmatic view (economically and politically) since Canadian identity is developing with an emphasis on a hard reality. On the one hand, most of the Canadian population economically thrives in urban centres of the "South" along the US border. On the other hand, industrialisation, natural resource exploitation, and military defence contribute to the critical condition of the North. The South of Canada is developing at the cost of its North. Instead of acknowledging this crisis, cultural institutions still use romantic images of the North. Indeed, the romantic imagination of the North invites the unsustainable impact of technologies that paradoxically sustain the nation on economic and political levels.

Technological Nationalism and Cultural Productions

Drawing on the paradoxes in sustaining the Canadian nation and the "ambivalence" perspectives of Arthur Kroker, as presented in the previous section, I argue that there is an inherent ambivalence between the form and content of technology when it comes to their use and representation in Canadian popular culture. This ambivalence partly enables the nation. I therefore question determinist approaches towards technology in current literature, and instead observe that the rhetoric of technological nationalism (i.e., form) is both an effect and cause of cultural production (i.e., content) that may use media technologies for their production, distribution, and consumption, mythically uniting the nation of Canada. The rhetoric of technological nationalism is expressed through words, images, texts, and policy documents (content). These cultural productions are literary and visual texts and iconography that act as a source of representations. The "content," representing mythical qualities of technological nationalism, is an effect of the ideological need to develop and sustain the medium or rhetorical form of technologies in constructing the nation. Conversely, the technological production of media content becomes a rhetorical tool, a form that helps to produce and perpetuate mythical qualities of technological nationalism in popular culture. These tools include cultural forms of technology (e.g. filming, broadcasting, Wikipedia) which encompasses the uses of technology. I therefore propose the following bidirectional relationship of cause and effect between form and content:

Technological Nationalism ↔ Cultural Productions
(Form)   (Content)

The relationship between the rhetorical form and cultural content is contingent upon social and political contexts and is therefore subject to changes. From an institutional point of view, the rhetoric of technological nationalism needs to be imposed through federal policies of communications and textual productions. As Norman Hillmer and Adam Chapnick state, "technological nationalism became not just a symbolic strategy but a symbiotic necessity - a rhetoric that they believed they had to use in order to compete for the government contracts that would make their system viable" (2007, p. 48). Robert McPhail illustrates the argument further. He observes that "broadcasting," in particular, "has been charged with the responsibility for promoting the national identity" (1990, p. 144) for economic and political integrity and is increasingly affected by technological innovations in Canada. At the same time, McPhail follows McLuhan and further notes that "technology not only provokes changes within a particular medium, it also forces changes in other media as they attempt to adjust to the altered environment" (pp. 184-185).

One of these altering environments or contexts is the economic and political development of the Canadian nation that requires and prompts technological innovations. As Marco Adria (2010) states, large-scale social movements such as nationalism are only possible with the help of symbols disseminated by technologies. Cultural content produced by media technologies also serves to reinforce national myths for a simpler governance of Canada across regional and cultural diversities. Popular representations of vast and empty lands, for example, also legitimise/call for the implementation of technology to unite the nation. The mythic qualities of technology (content) also cause the need to develop and sustain the infrastructure and its processes (form). In the digital era, hardware and software have further complicated what is form and what is content.

The relationship between the rhetorical form of technological nationalism and cultural content is supported by Marco Adria's understanding of nationalism and technology as existing not in a linear and causal relationship, but in a dialectic one (2010, p. 48). Adria, however, does not situate the relationship between technology and national movements in social, economic, and political contexts. The relationship between technology and nation is contingent upon social and political contexts. These contexts vary. In addition, the relationship between the nation and media technology is an expression of a complex interplay of media producers, texts, and audiences (Bräuchler & Postill, 2010; Corner, Schlesinger, & Silverstone, 1998). There needs to be a clear distinction between technologies and media as technologies as well. Although Adria theoretically explains that Canada is a technologically driven nation, he does not explain how the relationship between technology and nation translates into popular media representations of Canada. The bidirectional relationship between technological nationalism and media technology — and subsequent production of cultural content — can be better understood by considering the social and political roots of technology in Canada. This approach enables the observation of how social and political exploitations of technology, such as technological nationalism, facilitate (in dominant fashion) ideologically driven content production and the use of media technology for dissemination of content.

The cultural productions of media technology reinforce the rhetoric of technological nationalism in popular culture every day. The relationship between technological nationalism and cultural content in media reflects political and economic contexts that dictate the discourses of technology and nation in popular culture. These contexts are not necessarily fixed, and the bidirectional relationship between technological nationalism (form) and cultural productions (content) vary. In addition, the form and content are not always separate entities. The mythical qualities of technological nationalism expressed in content are also technological nationalism as a rhetorical form that feeds on the myth. For example, popular symbols of the Canadian North in cultural content also act as a rhetorical form of technological nationalism. There is no clear distinction between these uses of media technologies and, hence, their relationship is ambivalent. This notion of ambivalence sustains the Canadian nation and creates the basis of its popular representations, as observed in this book.

Conclusion

While existing literature has mostly considered the form and impact of technology on the Canadian nation, this chapter contributed a new view of the mythical relationship between technological nationalism, nation, and nature. This new view helps to understand national symbols in Canadian celebrity texts. The overall relationships explored in this chapter are contingent upon historical settings and intersect in ways that situate and reproduce national ideologies in popular representations. This chapter offered theoretical grounds for the book to explore how Canadian identity is diverse, yet undermined across the nation.

This chapter started with an overview of the literature on Canadian identity and nationalism, which have been captured by technological nationalism. First, this chapter established that cultural productions are both an effect and cause of the rhetoric of technological nationalism in Canada. Media technologies, the production of cultural artefacts, and technological nationalism have a bidirectional and ambivalent relationship. While federal policies and cultural content impose the rhetoric of technological nationalism, cultural content representing mythical qualities of technology creates the conditions for economic, political, and technological intervention that have created and supported the nation. In both cases, the uses of technology enable the nation in ways that are specific to the social contexts in which they are produced. There is, therefore, ambivalence in the fact that technological nationalism can become content, as well as form. Conversely, cultural production (content) can determine the medium of technological nationalism (form). There is no certain identity of form versus content. This ambivalence between form and content is fundamental to the construction of the Canadian nation.

This chapter also presented another important aspect of technological nationalism: scholars' emphasis on the form of the technology rather than its content, and the contexts in which the rhetoric is reproduced. In this respect, there has been significant research on the theory and meaning of the rhetoric of technological nationalism in policies, infrastructure, and impact of its practice. For example, Marshall McLuhan showed that the medium of technology determines content, structures of society, and nationalism. Similarly, George Grant indicated a loss of human experience and regional and cultural differences as an effect of an overdetermined use of technology.

As a second contribution to the study of technological nationalism, this chapter critically examined content in a historical context to show how cultural productions influence technology and, in turn, shape Canadian identity. In other words, if the 'medium is the message,' as Marshall McLuhan suggests, I argue that, in the Canadian context of technological nationalism, the message is also the medium.

Finally, the chapter looked at the use and popular representations of nature —particularly of the North — as national symbols in Canadian popular culture. These popular symbols help to establish a single and coherent Canadian national identity across the nation. Through these symbols, the Canadian North is re-imagined in the form of a united landscape. For the past four hundred years, representations of the North have associated Canada's landscape and way of life with vast, empty, snow-covered wilderness. Texts narrating this wilderness may also demonstrate an economic and political need to be connected by technologies to establish a national community. The mythical 'lack' of Canadian national identity in these images is not just the physical absence of Canadians. Ironically, it is also the presence of an ideology that helps to identify Canada as America's 'Other.' The myth of 'the lack' also negotiates tensions that may exist between regions and between diverse cultural groups. However, national representations of the North may dismiss the complex experiences of regionally and locally diverse people across Canada.

The next chapter looks at how the Canadian state and media attempt to reclaim the North American frontier. In particular, the chapter examines the reclaiming of the frontier through the imagination and construction of 'Hollywood North' as an effect and cause of technological nationalism. The next chapter also explores how the metaphor of Hollywood North figures as a context in Canadian cultural productions of films and celebrities.

4 Hollywood North as the Context of Celebrities

Hollywood North signifies geographical places in Canada. It is also a cultural construct/symbol of the nation. The relationship between the two is overlooked in signifying practices of media, where rhetorical statements overemphasise Hollywood North as the whole of Canada and contest place-based experiences. The economic goals of cities, in association with media, exploit the existing crisis of Canadian national identity that has been extensively explored in academic research. The problem of Canadian national identity forms the contextual framework of the research question explored in the first part of this chapter: What does Hollywood North mean in relation to films and celebrities acting in films? In relation to this question, the second part of the chapter addresses how Canadian media often represent films and movie stars in the cultural space of Hollywood North settings. The reason can be traced back to the economic history of a Canadian film industry that benefits from cultural constructions of Hollywood North. While the growing impact of Hollywood North films on a wide range of celebrity representations is beyond the scope of this chapter, the historical provenance of Hollywood North will be given particular importance in thinking about Canadian celebrity cultures.

In this chapter, I identify these two different, but intersecting, meanings of Hollywood North in Canadian popular culture. I specifically examine how US continental drives and Canadian nationalism underpin the cultural construction of Hollywood North. In light of these two practices, Hollywood North is an expression of the competing dynamics of continentalism and nationalism. In negotiating tensions between these two practices, the Canadian state and cultural institutions produce artefacts that imagine Canada as a Northern frontier that simultaneously adapts and resists the dominance of Hollywood. As an expression of both continentalism and nationalism, the idea of Hollywood North helps to negotiate among the tensions caused by American cultural imperialism and the homogenous representations of the Canadian nation-state.

In order to understand the meaning of Hollywood North as a place, it is important to discuss the development of Canadian popular culture in both historical and contemporary contexts. To date, the origin and use of Hollywood North have been studied by cultural critics such as Serra Ayse Tinic, David Spaner, Michael Spencer, and Mike Gasher. This chapter reviews their work and considers Hollywood North as a material site for the production of US films. However, the colonialist contexts of Hollywood North, and its expressions in cultural productions, such as that of celebrities, have yet to be adequately studied. The second meaning of Hollywood North considers this gap and focuses on Hollywood North as a Canadian cultural construct from a colonialist perspective. It also emphasizes how Hollywood North acts as a context that situates cultural productions of celebrities in Canada. Films and celebrities are often discursively constructed in 'Hollywood North' and identified with the whole of Canada as a frontier region. The systematic way in which America is 'Othered' in the process can be observed in Canadian productions of films and celebrities, and is discussed in the final section of this chapter. In the process, this chapter investigates how social and cultural experiences specific to places both adapt and resist the continental forces of America.

Mapping the location of Hollywood North in both a geographic and cultural context is necessary to understand it as a contextual setting for film and celebrity constructions that need scholarly attention. The Canadian identity of celebrities and other cultural figures, when articulated in locations of Hollywood North, both define and shift understandings of 'who we are' to what Northrop Frye calls 'where we are.' Frye suggests that,

> [T]he Canadian sensibility has been profoundly disturbed, not so much by our famous problem of identity, important as that is, as by a series of paradoxes in what confronts that identity. It is less perplexed...by the question 'Who am I?' than by some ridicule as 'Where is here'" (1980, p. 284).

The analysis presented in this chapter locates two different, but intersecting meanings of Hollywood North that are used to identify complex subjects as 'here.' The chapter also lays the groundwork for interrogating the assumptions inherent in homogenous representations of the Canadian nation-state in other cultural productions of Hollywood North.

Ideas and Origins of Hollywood North

Although the first Canadian films were produced in 1897, Canadian film production picked up with Canadian Pacific Railway (CPR) sponsored films in 1898 and post-World War I developments in 1917-1923. These films encouraged British immigration to Canada and nation-building through technology. During this time, the idea for a northern version of Hollywood can be traced to the popular representation of Canadian film star and cinematic pioneer, Nell Shipman. Her picture personality was strongly associated with the Pacific Northwest in Canada. She wrote several novels and chose acting in films such as *Sons of the Northwoods* (1912) *The Whiskey Runners* (1912), *Pierre of the North* (1913), *Into the North* (1913), *Breed of the North* (1913), *From Out of the Big Snows* (1915), and *God's Country and the Woman* (1916). As opposed to the Wild West in America, the Canadian Northwest was the primary location: an ideological outdoor site of cinematic wilderness, adventure, and heroism. The vision of Photoplays, the Canadian production company for Shipman's film *Back to God's Country* (1919) especially defined its vision in relation to the dominance of Hollywood in the film industry. In its prospectus, Canadian Photoplays Limited expressed that it

> does not expect to compete with the already established studios in the United States in the production of studio-made pictures, but in the great pictures of outdoor life, with their intense dramatic interest, no country in the world can surpass Canada (Morris, 1992, p 104).

The wilderness in Nell Shipman's persona was represented along with the wilderness of the Canadian North. Filmmakers like Nell Shipman, Ernest Ouimet, and George Brownridge could not create a "permanent Hollywood North" (Loiselle, 2003, p. 419) in the 1910s and 1920s. Shipman, however, became an early cinema pioneer and exemplar of stardom set in the Canadian North. She offered a Northern vision as an alternative to Hollywood.

Despite the Northern uniqueness of Canadian cinema, feature-film production faced financial challenges in the 1920s. In 1930, Famous Players, which owned a third of all cinemas in the country, became 100% American-owned — an example of US monopoly in Canada. At that time, the Canadian government hired John Grierson to report on the state of the film industry. Grierson suggested that the

> Canadian government should create a committee that would monitor Canadian film policy [...], that film distribution should be

centralized and further developed and that a more sophisticated and comprehensive sense of propaganda should be developed (Gittings, 2002, p. 79).

In 1939, Grierson's suggestion led to the launch of the National Film Board of Canada (NFB), where he became the Film Commissioner and encouraged the development of patriotic movies. In 1941, however, the government brought a "sad end to one of Canada's earliest and busiest film studios" (Papineau-Couture, 2009) when it shut down the Ontario Motion Picture Bureau and Trenton Studios. Although the government provided legislative support for Canadian film production, film had a limited market, and theatres could not earn a profit on the films produced and distributed in Canada. In 1943, the Federal Communications Commission (FCC) delineated the US border in terms of the "technological network rather than geopolitically" (Braman, 2006, p. 243). The fluid continental boundaries turned the Canadian market into a part of the US market, and spurred the heavy export of American productions, including films, to Canada. US producers handily recouped the expenses of their media products: not only did they reach their profit targets on US domestic sales alone, but they also exported programs to Canada at a fraction of the production costs (Flaherty & Manning, 1993). This process allowed Canadian media to offer cost-effective programming, including content on Hollywood stardom. Canadian theatres and television started to screen mostly American films that generated revenue north of the border, but did not necessarily support the political and economic goals of Canadian nation-building.

In the 1970s, tax shelter legislation was enacted, facilitating the Hollywood North phenomenon and the successful dissemination of American films into the world-wide market (Gasher, 1995; Longfellow, 2001; Wise, 1999). The idea of Hollywood North generally refers to the American film industry in Canada, also known as runaway productions. In Canada, the American film industry thrives in Vancouver, Toronto, and Montreal. The term 'runaway productions' was officially used in the report "Pay Television," by the national newspaper *The Globe and Mail* (Steed, 1981). A particular association between Toronto and Hollywood North can be also traced to 1985. That year, the *Philadelphia Inquirer* published a report called "Toronto has Earned a New Title." This report linked Toronto to Hollywood North:

> Toronto could easily claim the title of Hollywood North, since it now ranks third after Hollywood and New York among North American cities in the production of films for theatres and television and in the making of TV commercials ("Toronto Ranked Hollywood North for Production of Movies", p. 43).

David Spaner notes that the American studio system in Canada practically started in 1986 with a conversation between Toronto-based actor Nick Mancuso and Los Angeles producer Stephen Cannell. On the sets of the NBC TV series *Stingray*, Nick Macunso claimed that, "He [Cannell] is losing his shirt because these shows are costing about $400,000 more than the networks are licensing them for...It was killing me. I said, Steve, let's go to Canada" (Spaner, 2004, p. 73). After Mancuso's suggestion, Cannell checked out the favourable exchange rate in Canada and concluded that any location in Canada would be conducive to American television productions. Macunso started his production work in Calgary but shifted his shooting to warehouses and his newly built North Shore Studios in Vancouver. Vancouver appeared to be the most appropriate because it shared a time zone with Los Angeles. Thanks to better currency exchange rates, cheaper labour, tax incentives, and its Pacific Time Zone, Vancouver became the pre-eminent location of Hollywood North.

Since the 1980s, the film and television industry of Hollywood North has contributed upwards of 262,700 full-time equivalent work positions and generated $20.4 billion in GDP for the Canadian economy (Nordicity, 2013). The high number of Hollywood productions in Vancouver has resulted in Canada acquiring the popular nickname 'Hollywood North' (Dowd, 2010; Leung, 2006; Spaner, 2004). Due to the increasing demands of American runaway productions, and the lack of studio space in Vancouver, additional infrastructures have been developed in Toronto and Montreal. As Canada's principal financial centres, with growing capital and studio space, these cities have facilitated the growth of American runaway productions in Canada. The material practices of generating capital and revenue construct and sustain production sites such as 'Hollywood North.' In light of increasing American film productions, former Toronto Mayor Mel Lastman officially designated Toronto as Hollywood North in 2002. Similarly, the city of Montreal also acquired the nickname of Hollywood North:

> Lights, cameras, and action abound in Montreal, leaving many to wonder whether it is vying for the title of "Hollywood North." For years, the title has belonged to Toronto. But now Montreal is giving the city a run for its money...Seven years ago, there were virtually no American films being shot in Montreal. Now the city is hot, generating almost as much revenue from film making as Vancouver (CBC, 2006b).

The growth of Hollywood North resulted in the development and recruiting of highly skilled Canadian technicians and crews. US television networks are now buying dramas written and produced by and for Canadian TV and set in Canadian locations. These productions include *Flashpoint*, *The Bridge*, and *Corner Gas*, a CTV production. Andy Fixmer states that,

> CTV, Canada's largest private broadcaster, is sharing costs and will air shows at the same time. The results are licensing fees for new dramas that are about half the typical $1.6 million per episode. The pickup of Canadian shows by U.S. networks validates the past 25 years of growth in the countrys [sic] TV industry (2014).

The export of Canadian media productions marks a shift and a contrast to past conditions. In the past, Canadian markers would be removed and locations were often disguised as American cities. Hollywood North was then identified with the Americanisation of Canada. At the same time, the hegemony of American cultural values spurred resistance in the form of an increasing emphasis on the distinct cultural sovereignty of Canada. The North of Hollywood became a critical site for constructing national identity in film and television production and stardom in Canada.

The Meaning of Hollywood North in Popular Culture

Although media reports mark the rise of Hollywood North, the complex ways in which Hollywood North provides meaning, pleasure, and identification received limited scholarly attention. There are two different, but intersecting, meanings of Hollywood North that shape Canadian identity. First, Hollywood North can be understood as a place that is driven by both the material conditions of the American film industry and Canadian state policies. When 'Hollywood' is associated with 'North' in Canada, it carries the idea of a cultural space that is extracted from studio locations and generalised into the nation of Canada. This association leads to the second meaning of Hollywood North: it is a Canadian symbol that acts as a context in which cultural products are generated and place-based experiences are contested.

Hollywood North as a Place

The place of Hollywood North can be understood in terms of the physical/material conditions and state policies engaging with film and other cultural productions. Drawing on Serra Tinic's work (2005), a place can be defined as a geographical area that is known by its physical infrastructure. It is characterised by social and cultural experiences and memories that are specific to material conditions of any given area. As a place, Hollywood North is rooted in the US film industry, also commonly known as Hollywood. It therefore has its origins in the American studio system. The Hollywood studio system can be understood as a structure that represents the consolidation of large studios and corporations (eight in all; five major and three minor) in the USA. The place of Hollywood, however, is a misnomer, because the corporations were not only based in Los Angeles and Southern California, but in other cities such as New York. Hollywood is thus a mystique and fantasy-based concept: it is the greatest corporate invention of the studio system, and it informs the conceptualisation of Hollywood North in Canada.

In Canada, the central locations of Hollywood North are Vancouver and Toronto, where the US film industry is highly reliant on Canadian talent for shooting and editing (Rifkin, 2005). In these cities, Hollywood North is located in settings of film and television production, distribution, and consumption. These locations include studios, casting agencies, on-location sets, and postproduction laboratories. The rise of Hollywood North as a place can be historically traced back to the studio space of the public broadcasting service, the Canadian Broadcasting Corporation (CBC). The unused CBC studios were available as production centres for rent to American films produced in Vancouver in the early 1980s. However, due to severe regional production cutbacks at the CBC, there were no provisions made for growing runaway American productions in Canada. To avoid losing potential productions and their associated revenues, the British Columbia Film Commission and provincial government invested millions of dollars in building new studio spaces. Tinic identifies the new studio complex of Vancouver as a 'Grid.' The Vancouver Grid marks Hollywood's "biggest backlot" (2006, p. 154), thus identifying Vancouver as an extension of the American studio system.

As a physical place, Hollywood North can be defined as a 'locations and service industry' that consists of various Canadian artists' and performers' unions. These unions govern productions and allow their members to work at the basic rate of pay. Furthermore, for American producers, Canadian labourers work at the rate of a lower dollar and tax credits. This supply of low-cost, skilled audio-visual labour is supplemented by tax credits and publicly subsidised infrastructure, which allows for cost-effective outsourcing of American cultural production to Hollywood North (Davis and Kaye, 2009). It is considered part of the Canadian domestic market, but it is dominated by the US Hollywood North, a material effect of US industrial practices in Canada. Furthermore, Hollywood productions in Canada are sanctioned by Canadian governments and institutions and supported by both tax incentives and a favourable exchange rate. From this perspective, Hollywood North is defined as a "locations and service industry" (Gasher, 1995, 2002b; Tinic, 2005) that facilitates American reproduction in Canadian settings.

In the process, Hollywood North generates employment opportunities and revenue for Canadian labour that is often challenged by Canada's greater investment into technology and lack of human resources. In the ideological pursuit of technological nationalism, the Canadian government historically emphasised the development of, and investment into, technological infrastructures rather than media content (Babe, Charland, McPhail & McPhail, Schafer, Vipond). As discussed in the previous chapter, this emphasis forms the core of technological nationalism — a cultural model that contributes to the development of Canadian national identity through technological mediation. To develop Canada as an economic and political unit, and to uniformly administer it across regions, the government has invested in communications infrastructure that includes the 'locations and service industry' of Hollywood North.

As a 'locations and service industry,' Hollywood North is grounded in technological nationalism, as well as a continentalism driven by dominant relations with the US. Continentalism is the integration of the USA, Canada, and Mexico as an economic, cultural, and political unit within North America. The regulations of the Federal Communications Commission (FCC) of 1943, the Free Trade Agreement (FTA) of 1987, and the North American Free Trade Agreement (NAFTA) of 1994 have played roles in developing North America as an integrated unit (Clarkson, 2001; Hoberg, 2000; Brescia & Super, 2009).

The integration of North America has been possible due to the removal of tariffs and investment barriers, a process that converged American and Canadian productions in North America. In Canada, the outsourcing of labour and investments into film and television products and studios have risen since the implementation of the Free Trade agreements. Mike Gasher indicates that, "In light of Hollywood's long established dominance of the continental distribution and exhibition sectors, Hollywood has appropriated British Columbia as part of its continentalization" (2002b, p. 133). In fact, Canada's overall position in continentalism has made it an 'American nation' (Smith, 1994), as reflected in the production of Hollywood North. While free trade regulations attempt to integrate the continent on economic and cultural grounds, these regulations facilitate US cultural monopoly by lowering production costs for Hollywood studios. After filming in Vancouver, Toronto or Montreal, US productions are exported back to Canada for consumption by the Canadian public, with profits going back to the US. Although continentalism constructs a North American unit, it is really an American endeavour that translates into material conditions in Canada. These material conditions give rise to the Canadian notion of Hollywood North, but they are still American in nature.

In the continental production of Hollywood North as a place, governments in Canada play a national role as well. In these practices, the Canadian state intervenes in both public and private institutions at federal, provincial, and municipal levels. Although Hollywood North is a result of American monopolistic capital, it is also supported by Canadian tax credits and promotional material. The economic, cultural, and linguistic practices of continentalism "do not capture the extent to which governmental functions have been redistributed - upward to international institutions, downward to subnational states, and laterally to the private sector" (Clarkson, 2001, p. 501). Indeed, in the material construction of Hollywood North, government institutions play a significant role in the continental drives of the industry. For instance, the British Columbia Film Commission and provincial government of British Columbia play a decisive role in locating and constructing production sites of Vancouver as Hollywood North. In his study, Serra Tinic highlights how the B.C. Film Commission, created by the provincial government of B.C., has played a fundamental role in the material construction of Vancouver as Hollywood North:

> Run by a staff of eight, the commission focuses many of its activities on making the city a production-friendly site. This involves everything from breaking down scripts for locations scouting and maintaining a locations photo library to acting as a community mediator between city residents and business owners when productions take over the city's streets. The commission's primary role, however, is to continually market Vancouver internationally and sustain strong ties to the key market: Los Angeles (2005, p. 34).

The case of the B.C. Film Commission shows how governments and their agencies in Canada offer a multiplicity of services to attract Hollywood productions and mediate between American productions and national businesses. These services redistribute — in ways that are not always explicit — the American commercial activities related to the material construction of Hollywood North. The B.C. Film Commission also illustrates how Canadian institutions serve American interests for the sake of the economic and cultural benefits of nation-building. In light of these practices, Hollywood North is constructed as an interplay of continentalism and national interests.

The construction of Hollywood North as a place can be understood as a rhetorical tool in Canadian nationalism. In effect, governments at all levels in Canada, as well as private corporations, engage in rhetorical practices that discursively construct Hollywood North in popular culture. In the contexts of continentalism and nationalism, language acts as a rhetorical tool in the 'place-naming' of Hollywood North. Place-naming is a linguistic and material practice in which a location is named in such a way that it inscribes politics of histories, habitats, and spatial or environmental perceptions in social and cultural contexts (Jett, 1997). In Canada, the linguistic use of 'Hollywood North' can be understood as a place-name, whereby the rhetorical devices 'Hollywood' and 'North' mobilise discourses of continentalism and nationalism, respectively.

Indeed, the term 'Hollywood' is associated with the economic hegemony of the American entertainment industry, whereas the word 'North' symbolises the frontier region of Canada. These symbols serve the economic and political objectives of both the US and Canada. The use and implementation of the words 'Hollywood' and 'North' thus goes beyond the simple assemblage of letters and syntax — it connotes meanings in real and imagined ways that produce and maintain discourses. These discourses, in turn, frame the systematic production and representation of place-based experiences. For example, in naming Vancouver and Toronto as Hollywood North, it is ideologically assumed that the places are assimilated into North American film production sites. However, the discourses of continentalism and nationalism, in which the place-naming of Hollywood North occurs, tends to neglect the social and cultural experiences that are specific to the actual places.

Drawing on Matthew Rofe and Gertrude Szili, I argue that the place-naming of Hollywood North is neither natural nor neutral. The place-name of Hollywood North is rather an instrument of meaning, and "the ability to control them is directly related to power" (Rofe & Szili, 2009, p. 362). Coining the term 'Hollywood North' — the act of place naming — thus allows Canadian institutions to appropriate and gain power over US practices that normally dominate. The disparate yet overlapping discourses of American cultural imperialism as a continental force, and of Canada's frontier as a national resistance, prompt the usage of the words 'Hollywood' and 'North.' The interplay of these two discursive practices constructs and mediates 'Hollywood North' as a symbol that supports American continentalism and Canadian nationalism, and continues to be widely represented in popular culture.

Hollywood North as a Cultural Construct/Symbol

The continental drives of the US in constructing Hollywood North prompt national resistance by the Canadian nation. This resistance leads to the second meaning of Hollywood North: it is a cultural construct that represents the sovereignty of Canada in relation to the US. This construction is somewhat related to the place naming that I discussed in the previous section, but it is more of symbolic action than a material effect. In the symbolic expression of Hollywood North, the use and representation of the 'North' imagines the whole of Canada as a strong frontier. A frontier is a free land where savagery and civilisation meet, thus marking the strength, self-reliance, adventure, and discovery of nation-building colonisers

(Heald, 2007). Although the frontier is central to the discovery and development of the North American continent, the harsher conditions of the Northern regions create the grounds for imagining Canada as the stronger, more resilient part of the continent. In the term 'Hollywood North,' the word 'Hollywood' is a site of dominant economic and cultural practices of the North American continent. But the Canadian nation-state and cultural institutions use 'North' as a colonialist tool to emphasise a frontier ideology and resist America's cultural dominance via the continental practices of Hollywood North.

When the word 'North' is associated with 'Hollywood,' Canada is imagined in relation to the American Wild West. As William Katerberg points out, the North is "ostensibly a Canadian subject" (2003, p. 545) and defined against the 'Wild West' of America. For Katerberg, "if the West symbolizes something fundamental about the entire American nation, in Canada the imagined West must be understood in relation to the mythic power of the North" (Ibid.). The 'North' of North America, as in 'Hollywood North,' acts as a site of imagining a stronger conquering colonial power. Hollywood North symbolises a stronger frontier than that of the US. From this perspective, Hollywood North acts as a cultural resistance to America's continental practices in film and television in Canada. Hollywood North overlaps with how the wild North "has rested upon ideological assumptions that searched for national distinctiveness and rejected continentalist threats" (Osborne, 2006, p. 9). The cultural emphasis on colonisation is significant in light of an ambivalent identity of the Canadian 'settler' who is imagined as coloniser and colonised at the same time. In our understanding of Hollywood North in a national context,

> it is not difficult to see that [Northrop] Frye's much-discussed 'here' is situated in implicit relation to an imperial centre which determines locations, cultural, global, historical: 'that is where is here?' is a question that makes sense in the context of a process of decolonization understood as the separation of the settler colony from the parent country (Moss, 2003, p. 189).

The colonialist ideology in Hollywood North helps negotiating these tensions in frontier relations with America by locating a stable and coherent meaning of Hollywood North and the whole of Canada as 'here.' Hollywood North is a construct of American continentalism that is also supported by Canadian institutions, but those same institutions coined the term 'Hollywood North' and maintain it as a cultural idea in an effort to appropriate the American cultural industry in Canada and resist the overall US cultural hegemony in technological nationalism.

In essence, cultural productions of Hollywood North are both a cause and effect of the material rhetoric of technological nationalism in Canada. Media technologies, which produce symbols of Hollywood North, combined with economic practices in the runaway film industry, have a bidirectional relationship in technological nationalism. Federal policies and economic practices in trade impose the rhetoric of technological nationalism. Cultural content representing the mythical qualities of Hollywood North creates the conditions for economic, political, and technological intervention that supports the nation. Romantic representations of Hollywood North restore a sense of wholeness and truth that is lost in standardised and mechanised productions of technology. The dominant representations of nature in Hollywood North may represent authenticity and mitigate the tensions created by mechanisation. At the same time, the vast and empty lands in the representations of Hollywood North create the conditions for the national integration of Canada through technology. From this perspective, popular representations of Hollywood North are an effect of technological nationalism and continentalism.

Technological nationalism and continentalism can be expressed through Hollywood North content and form. Again, cultural production of Hollywood North (content) can reinforce the Canadian or American use of the medium (form) in the North. There is therefore no fixed identity of form versus content. This ambivalence between form and content is fundamental to Canadian nation-building. Cultural productions of Hollywood North have a bidirectional relationship with continentalism and technological nationalism, whereby technological nationalism is both the cause and effect of famous representations of Hollywood North. Since there are opposing uses of technology in sustaining the nation, the bidirectional relationship between the rhetoric of technological nationalism and continentalism (form) and Hollywood North as a symbol/cultural construct (content) is both fundamental and contingent. It is also partly ambivalent as it describes a contingent relationship.

In resisting the American drive for continentalism, Hollywood North helps identify Canada as an American 'Other' in popular texts such as film, television ads, and celebrity images. As Christopher Gittings notes, "Canada's cultural representation of its national self is bound up in its construction of a colonising American Other, in this case the Industrial Other of Hollywood" (2002, p. 103). In these productions, Canada is often depicted as morally superior to the USA. These representations will be shown through case studies of celebrity cultures in the last section of this chapter.

Celebrities in Hollywood North

Historically, the construction of stars can be traced to the rise of the Hollywood studio system between the 1920s and 1950s. In the contemporary era — especially within the context of Hollywood North — Canadian media productions have facilitated shifts in, and the restoration of, Hollywood stardom. The dominant role of Hollywood North in Canadian celebrity cultures is observed in two ways.

First, Canadian media often represent an arbitrary relationship between locations of Hollywood North and stardom. This representation occurs despite the fact that stars may never actually be present in the locations. In Yorkville, Toronto International Film Festival (TIFF) supports national discourses especially when Canadian and American stars are represented in the context of Hollywood North. TIFF is engaged in the heavy import of Hollywood films and stars, both American and Canadian, and supports US-based runaway production facilities in Canada. At the same time, media representations of TIFF situate celebrities in the Canadian cultural construct of 'Hollywood North.' As mentioned previously, the continental practice of Hollywood North is a result of American capital but is also supported by government tax credits and promotional material. Symbolically, the 'North' in Hollywood North is a cultural reminder of the Canadian frontier that legitimises further use of media technologies (e.g., runaway film production facilities and broadcast media) to integrate Canada on rhetorical, economical, and political levels. These production facilities also provide material and symbolic grounds to resist Hollywood in the Wild West and retain Canadian sovereignty. Hence, TIFF is a prominent festival that embraces Hollywood films while resisting Hollywood's American Dream in the context of Hollywood North. A section in *Times Out Toronto* guide provides an example of the discursive construction of Hollywood North stars:

> In Yorkville it's not uncommon to see autograph seekers clustering around the exits of the area's five-star hotels...particularly during the Toronto International Film Festival, when the neighbourhood serves as a sort of Hollywood North base ("Yorkville, " 2005).

Here, the gentrified neighbourhood of Yorkville is represented in the national context of Hollywood North. In North America, the gentrification of cities is specific to, and articulated in, a complex interplay of national and continental discourses (Slater, 2002, 2004). From a continental perspective, the annual event of TIFF attracts tourists and bolsters the image of Canada in a way that, in turn, attracts economic investments from the US film industry. Most stars seen in Yorkville perform in American films that are produced in Canadian locations and supported by the runaway film industry in Hollywood North. These productions encourage the employment of Canadian labour and generate revenues through investments by the US film industry in Canada.

At the same time, Hollywood stars at TIFF are culturally resisted by the North in media representations. In this respect, media represent Hollywood stardom in Yorkville in a way that is situated in, and mediated by, Hollywood North. During the ten-day festival, media reports are flooded with claims that Hollywood stars are going 'North' and are better there. Take, for example, the entertainment reports of *eTalk* in Yorkville, which cover "shooting stars in Hollywood North" (CTV, 2009a). In the context of Hollywood North, *eTalk* further states that, "Hollywood is coming to Toronto" and calls Toronto "The New New York" (CTV, 2009b). Here, the 'new' New York represents an American 'Other' conquered in an imagined frontier. Again, a *McLean's* magazine article represents how Hollywood stars at TIFF "just seem to shine brighter north of the border" (Harris, 2007). Another report on TIFF imagines Canadian stars as "North stars" who are "hot in Hollywood" but many of whom "actually hail from the cooler climes of Canada" (Moloshok, 2010). Here, stars in Toronto are imagined as stronger and better American 'Others.' Material and symbolic practices of stardom engage with Northern myths expressed by Hollywood North. These imaginations help to reclaim Canadian stars and, in particular, Canada itself as newer, stronger, and better while still celebrating American stars on a larger scale. In this way, Canadian media representations help to reclaim Canadian stars who have become famous for their work in America or who are underrepresented in their home country. More importantly, the representations reclaim a stronger frontier of the North American continent from which the stars originated and are constructed. The Northern myths help to conjure up images of northern wilderness and imagine Canada as a stronger frontier than its US counterpart. The city of Toronto, and particularly Yorkville, plays a role in articulating national expressions while acting as a site for American stardom.

Stardom at TIFF serves both the US economy and Canadian national discourses. In the context of Hollywood North, TIFF representations of film stars are particularly underpinned by the interplay of America's continentalism and Canada's technological nationalism that provides the conditions to both support and resist the cultural monopoly of American entertainment. In Canada, heavy investments into technological infrastructure and a small market create a lack of economic resources, which, in turn, necessitates the import of American films and stars, as seen at TIFF. The American cultural hegemony involved in this process is simultaneously resisted by the ideological usage of the Northern Canadian frontier, integrated by media technologies. The use and implementation of the words 'Hollywood' and 'North' in media representations of TIFF signify meanings that produce and maintain national discourses in Canada. In this view, Hollywood North stardom at TIFF is a symbolic expression of the competing dynamics of continentalism and technological nationalism. These representations both contradict and overlap in understanding the Canadian nation.

Like TIFF, Canada's Walk of Fame (CWOF) can be read as a complex expression of Canadian nationalism that embraces Hollywood's continental impact. CWOF is a commemorative site that constructs a collective memory of Canada through Northern resistance to Hollywood stardom while emulating its Walk of Fame. CWOF and its media representations focus on Canadians that migrated to Hollywood and reclaims their national identity through the heavy use of Northern symbols. CWOF and media reports routinely use the maple leaf as Canada's national emblem. The CWOF sidewalk particularly embeds names of inductees with marble and granite stars that are 'stylised maple leaves.' The maple leaf symbolises the North through its autumnal change of colour in response to cold climatic conditions that are central to the Northern mythology. In addition, CWOF annual gala uses more Mounties than the stars with whom they pose. Apart from using these official emblems, CWOF routinely uses unofficial symbols of the North in representing celebrities. These symbols include the Canuck and representations of cold weather such as snow and ice. While the Canuck represents heroic strength and endurance in frontier conditions, ice and snow mediate cold weather as a permanent frontier condition — even though Toronto does not have winter most of the year. In light of using these symbols, the CWOF 'sidewalk' reads as a celebrity text that represents an imagined Canadian frontier. Here, the extreme Northern conditions both challenge and empower Canadians to reclaim their North American frontier that the US dominates at cultural and economic levels. We will return to the topic of CWOF media coverage in more details in Chapter 6, but it is worth mentioning here that media often depict CWOF in a way that is representative of Canadian ambivalence in both embracing and resisting Hollywood. The resistance is expressed with a Northern ideology that resonates with the rhetoric of technological nationalism and with colonialist perspectives.

A second approach that follows celebrity cultures in Hollywood North locations often represents them in relation to empty, sublime, and peaceful encounters in Canada's Northern frontier. These cultural constructions of stardom do not necessarily include specific experiences of northern places where fame is imagined. Rather, they help to imagine romantic landscapes that characterise the Canadian Northern frontier. An Air Canada magazine *onAir* illustrates the way in which stardom in Hollywood North shifts celebrations of individual stars to celebration of imagined Northern regions. The opening lines of one its articles state: "They call it Hollywood North for a reason. Here's our guide to getting the star treatment in Toronto – from what to see to where to eat to where to get your beauty rest" (Wilkinson, 2008). The emphasis on Hollywood North as a location of stardom is also observed in the following media statement:

> Vancouver is known as Hollywood North for its many movie shoots and A-list celebrity visitors, and the city boasts several glam places that are ready to buff and beautify. Then, there is B.C.'s laid-back, West Coast vibe. You'll mellow out just experiencing this kind and gentle place; becoming blissed out at a spa is a bonus (Lash, 2010).

A close reading of the media statement reflects a cultural production of stardom in Hollywood North that is accessible to all. But there is an absence of celebrities in the representations of Hollywood North. The cultural representations of Hollywood North emphasise a notion of stardom that anyone can locate and celebrate. In this way, media representations often celebrate locations of Hollywood North rather than celebrating stars.

The media representation of artist Hannah Stone is an illustrative example of Canadian stardom as an expression of the North. According to *Going Coastal Magazine,* Stone is an acrylic ink painter based out of British Columbia who represents popular culture in her art. A report in the magazine, however, imagines her in relation to Canada's Northern mythology. The report emphasises how Stone "glimmers and glitters like a North Star – a Hollywood North star" (Bodmer, Nightingale and Upton, 2010). Here, the 'North Star' is not only astronomical but also a cultural construct that serves as a colonial tool, invoking images of the vast northern lands of wilderness — a 'frontier' that must be controlled and developed. The cultural construction of the 'North' in Hollywood North mediates the art of Hannah Stone as an effect of both her talent and a strong frontier nation.

In general, media celebrate Canadian celebrities along with Northern symbols of the frontier such as Mounties and maple leaves. A *Toronto Life* magazine article illustrates this representation in comparing Canadian celebrity Justin Bieber with comic strip hero Captain Canuck. In Canadian mythology, Captain Canuck often evokes a Mountie with a stylised red and white maple leaf (Dittmer and Larsen, 2007; Edwardson, 2008, 2003). From this mythical perspective, the article refers to Captain Canuck as a "maple leaf-adorned superhero" and asks what "Canadian super-talent has the gravitas, popularity charm and politeness to represent the True North's true hero?" (Vaccaro, 2011a). These representations celebrate Canada's

Northern frontier values and mediate Canadian talent and stardom as an effect of the frontier.

Given these two approaches and the importance of the Canadian North over America, celebrities in Hollywood North are often considered to be distinctive and more powerful than their American counterparts. This is one of the most important aspects of constructing celebrities in the Canadian context of Hollywood North. The moral overtones of being stronger and better are often observed in symbolic representations of Hollywood North celebrities. In most representations, the cultural construction of North is used as a way to imagine the Canadian nation as stronger and more powerful than America. These representations are observed in both Canadian *and* American media. For example, an MSNBC media report represents Canadian stars as "North stars" who are "hot in Hollywood, but many of today's biggest celebrities actually hail from the cooler climes of Canada" (Moloshok, 2010). Canadian celebrity television show *eTalk* illustrates this representation in its reference to 'Hot Hollywood North.' In this respect, *eTalk* further states:

> Hollywood North produces world-class talent that is recognized internationally [...]. As a Canadian entertainment news show, etalk is proud to share homegrown success stories with the rest of Canada. More than just reporting on the big stars in La-La Land, etalk showcases Canada's own shining stars too - from the struggling artists who eventually took Hollywood by storm, to the overnight sensations [...] (CTV, 2009a).

A close reading of the above text shows that the moral superiority of Hollywood North is expressed in relation to Canadian celebrities, as well as American celebrities in Canada. Although Hollywood North symbolically refers to Canada's geographical places, Hollywood North celebrities are not limited to Canadian-bred personalities. In fact, most celebrities mentioned in media reports of Hollywood North are famous for their work in America. They are both Canadians who went to the USA to work and became famous there, and American stars coming to work in Canada in the context of Hollywood North runaway productions. Media representations of these Hollywood North stars draw on classical notions of stardom that originated in the Hollywood studio system.

At the same time, Hollywood North stars serve to reinforce the colonial power of Canada as the better, stronger half of North America. The moral superiority of American stars in Canada is observed in *McLean's* magazine. In reference to Hollywood stars Brad Pitt and Angelina Jolie, the magazine states, "The American stars just seem to shine brighter north of the border" (Harris, 2007). In media representations, both

Canadian and American celebrities are often associated with a stronger value of survival against the odds of a harsh northern nature. The Northern value of moral superiority of Canada over America is claimed on the specific grounds of a wilful survival against the wilderness and cold while also maintaining a socially ordered frontier and preserving an integral culture (Berland, 2006; Hansson & Norberg, 2009; Kalant, 2004; Katerberg, 2003; Mawani, 2007). In this view, Amelia Kalant (2004) argues that "Canada does have a 'soul:' if Americanness can be said to be about excelling or success, Canadianness is about being good and moral" (p. 34). In this context, Hollywood North is morally superior to Hollywood in America. In associating the North with Hollywood, the Canadian nation is constructed as America's better 'Other.' It represents Canada as an 'Other' of America, whereby Canada is imagined as more enduring, integral, and yes, morally better.

From this perspective, Canadian celebrities can be understood in terms of separation from, and opposition to, Hollywood stars in the Unites States (Bodroghkozy 2001; Bow 2008). Canadian celebrities in Hollywood North are framed as a better American 'Other.' In representations of Canadian celebrities, the binary relations with the US are illustrated in a Molson Canadian beer advertisement: "I Am Canadian." The advertisement was part of a series of Canadian television commercials that aired in 2000 and won the advertising industry Gold Quill award in 2001. In the advertisement, Canadian actor Jeff Douglas became an instant celebrity for highlighting binary differences between Canada and America:

> ...I have a Prime Minister, not a President. I speak English and French, not American and I pronounce it 'about', not 'a boot'. I can proudly sew my country's flag on my backpack. I believe in peacekeeping, not policing; diversity, not assimilation; and that the beaver is a truly proud and noble animal. A tuque is a hat, a chesterfield is a couch, and it is pronounced zed: not zee – zed!! Canada is the second largest land mass! The first nation of hockey! And the best part of North America! My name is Joe!! And I am Canadian ("Canadian Commercial by Molson Beer", 2008).

In reviewing the ad "I Am Canadian," Aniko Bodroghkozy notes that Canadian nationalists often set up "a fictive, mythic American Other" (2001, p. 116) against which a sense of self, grounded in difference, is constructed. The representations of Canadian national identity particularly celebrate "the refusal of American values" (Collins, 1990, p. 344). The Canadian identification with an American 'Other' is also seen in representing Hollywood North celebrities as superior to their US counterparts.

Conclusion

Hollywood North acts as a context for understanding representations of Canada in films and celebrity cultures. In this respect, the imagined nature of North is a colonial response to America and identifies the Canadian nation as Hollywood's 'Other.' The term 'Hollywood North' signifies Canada as a geographical place, but it is also a contested cultural construct/symbol that negotiates the tensions inherent in Canadian national identity, especially in relation to America. This chapter interrogated assumptions underlying the relationship between Hollywood North practices and the dominant American cultural industry. In doing so, the intersection of Canadian local and American global emerges as a central factor in the Canadian production of fame. Within this local-global nexus, the contextual setting of Hollywood North is important to popular culture, especially film, as a site of stardom.

Hollywood North is both a material and symbolic construction that identifies Canada as a strong frontier nation in film, television, and celebrity cultures. From this perspective, two meanings of Hollywood North arise: one material, the other symbolic. From a material point of view, Hollywood North is a locations and service industry located in physical places such as studios, post-production labs, and shooting locations in Vancouver, Toronto, or Montreal. From a symbolic point of view, Hollywood North is a cultural construct that helps define the Canadian nation. This chapter asserted that the cultural construction of Hollywood North imagines the Canadian frontier as stronger than that of the USA: it is a better 'Other.'

To this end, the cultural construction of Hollywood North acts as a context in which Canadian and American celebrities act as the 'Other' of America once they are located North of the border. Hollywood North serves to establish the frontier ideology of North America in general and Canada in particular as the superior half of the continent. In Canadian popular culture, the dominant discourses of Hollywood stars need to be both resisted and legitimised for economic reasons. In Canada, heavy investments into technological infrastructure, coupled with a small market, create a lack of economic resources that limits adequate media content. The lack of content is reflected in the small number of media productions and representations of Canadian celebrities in popular culture. For this reason, it is often said that Canada does not have a 'star system.' But this may not be an entirely accurate view because stars are clearly being constructed, supported, and consumed in Canada.

Yet it is necessary for Canadian media to import pre-established content depicting Hollywood stars, both Canadian and American, while depicting Canadian stars in ways that subvert traditional Hollywood fame. The heavy influx of Hollywood stars fosters an American cultural imperialism that spurs Canadian resistance via the affirmation of Canadian nationalism. In Canadian media, one of the ways to resist the effects of American cultural imperialism is to symbolically associate stardom with Hollywood North. The production and reception of American and Canadian Hollywood stars are legitimised in symbolic associations with the North. Here again, the North figures as a colonialist concept that establishes a stronger frontier nation. When juxtaposed against its Southern Other (Hollywood), the North associates its stardom with the better half of North America. This process, in turn, helps identify Canadian stars who have become famous for their work down South and re-imports them (after having been first exported to the US to be constructed as stars) without being subverted. In this way, Canadian cultural producers not only reclaim their stars; they also reclaim a stronger, uniquely Canadian frontier space.

While imaginations of the North help to reclaim Canada as America's superior counterpart, the multiple meanings of the Canadian nation are negotiated in the interplay between American cultural imperialism in continental practices and Canadian nationalism. The interplay of continentalism and nationalism provides the condition to both support and resist the cultural monopoly of American entertainment. From this standpoint, the 'North' in Hollywood North acts as a form of national resistance, while 'Hollywood' supports US continentalist practices. The continental and nationalist efforts are facilitated by the monopolistic control of American corporations and the support of Canadian governments and organisations, thereby complicating the meaning of the Canadian nation in popular culture.

The cultural meaning of Canadian fame unfolds in the existing context of Hollywood North. Canadian celebrities, when situated in Hollywood North, often carry a frontier ideology that is stronger than its southern counterparts. The superiority of the 'North' and the inferiority of the 'lack' function as an American 'Other' in Hollywood North stardom. The notion of Canada as an American 'Other' emerges out of the rhetorical, economic, and political practices of technological nationalism and continentalism. The economic and cultural dependence on America creates a sense of American cultural imperialism that, ironically, is consumed, embraced, supported, and resisted in Canadian popular culture. There is a recurrent representation of how Canada is *not* America, feeding back into the notion of 'lack' that also lays the groundwork for constructing a Northern nation that is 'better' than America. Both myths around the 'North' and 'lack' function in a way that helps to identify Canada as the better version of the North American continent. The 'North' of North America, as in 'Hollywood North,' acts as a site of imagining a conquering colonial power that is stronger than that of the American Wild West. Most Canadian practices and representations in celebrity cultures establish the North as a more robust frontier and, in the process, resist America's Wild West. Similarly, the myth of 'lack' and the national feeling of inferiority, when compared to the hegemony of American culture, are not actually about inferiority. It is a differentiation that is instead expressed as unifying, morally superior, humble, polite, and generally 'better' than the boastful and aggressive promotion of Hollywood celebrities. The strong Northern frontier and Canadian moral superiority thereby intersect with the myth of 'lack' to offer national resistance to American stardom in contradictory ways. In Canada, the identification of celebrities as better 'Others,' a myth unto itself, functions to express this resistance.

The notion of Canada as Hollywood North functions as an American better 'Other' in stardom at TIFF, which is often represented in the context of Hollywood North. At a material level, the representation of Hollywood North encourages investments by the Hollywood film industry, the employment of Canadian labour, and the generation of revenue in Canada. Thus, in representing Hollywood North, TIFF functions as a symbolic extension of America, where Hollywood stars are celebrated and Canadian stars are underrepresented. This unequal representation reinforces the myth of 'lack' by revealing Canada's dependence on American stars, productions, and investments. The Canadian lack mythically acts as a national difference from America. But Hollywood North nonetheless helps to negotiate the 'lack' of Canadian stars by imagining them as superior to their American counterparts because they hail from the superior ('North') part of North America, as represented by Hollywood North. In this context, as case studies show, celebrities are imagined as a better version of their American counterparts that TIFF systematically 'Others' through the North. In the case of CWOF, the superiority of the Northern frontier and inferiority/myth of 'lack' serve to 'Other' America. This resistance is necessary, as CWOF embraces the Hollywood Walk of Fame while recognising the need to reclaim Canadian stars that migrated to America.

Receiving star treatments in Hollywood North or casually walking on stylised maple leaves in the CWOF sidewalk are banal ways of participating in Canadian nationalism. In Canadian discourses of fame, practices and representations often celebrate a constructed notion of Canadianness. Such discourses exemplify these dynamics, as opposed to merely supporting Canadian talent. The case studies show that Canadian representations of Hollywood North stardom (including that of places and audiences) mediate talent as a discursive effect of the national context in which it is produced and received. Here, achievement of Canadian values is popularly recognised and celebrated as a form of stardom. Simultaneously, Canadian media representations of talent resemble and appropriate the Hollywood stardom that dominates cultural practices in North America. Thus, Canadian fame is quintessentially North American: a complex interplay of Hollywood stardom and celebration of Canadian national values. In this celebration, Canadian fame holds varied and multiple meanings. The multiplicity of Canadian fame is exemplified in media representations that engage with national discourses in overlapping or contradictory ways.

The study of celebrities in Hollywood North sets the contextual grounds for critical studies of fame in Canada, and helps to understand Canadian nation-building through notions that support and resist America. In Canadian celebrity cultures, Hollywood North unfolds as an ambivalence that negotiates tensions with American cultural imperialism and the homogenous representations of the nation-state. The ambivalence of Hollywood North is best exemplified in its tendency to simultaneously embrace and resist American celebrity content. This is a rhetorical form of nationalism. In this setting, the celebration of Canadian stars in Hollywood and the reclamation of their Canadian identity through national symbols such as the North also signifies national ambivalence. The paradox in the ambivalence characterises a fame that also marks the progress and success of Canada. The nation, like celebrities, functions on the paradox that exists in its own ambivalence. The question of authenticity in both cases generates and sustains their fame.

5 Celebrities at the Toronto International Film Festival

As I mentioned in the previous chapter, Canadian stars at TIFF are constructed in ways that are aligned with technological nationalism: they are often underrepresented to favour heavy import of Hollywood films and star content. TIFF events largely use Hollywood stardom to support the American runaway film industry in Canada while resisting it with national symbols of the Canadian Northern frontier. The articulation of Canadian national identity in selected film talent is observed when it comes to particular stars promoting their films. The selection of stars is important to consider in national expressions of film festivals. Representation of stars can play a major role in promoting these films. This role is observed especially when media representations strongly support privileged positions of Hollywood stars by promoting blockbuster American films at the festivals.

In Canada, media not only construct stars but also represent them in a way that supports a dominant Canadian national identity. In her work, Liz Czach (2004) observes stardom at TIFF, and, drawing on the thoughts of film director Atom Egoyan, she argues that Canadian organisations do not engage in the "star treatment" (p. 82) of local/domestic talent. TIFF, in her opinion, does not focus on the construction and representation of domestic stars that may offer greater attention to the building of national cinema. Since her publication, there has been some emphasis on stars in Canada. In "Cinephilia, Stars, and Festivals" (2010), Czach illustrates how TIFF shows an "increase in both the participation of stars at film festivals and the ensuing media coverage devoted to fame" (p. 142). In this respect, Czach argues that there is a major shift of attention away from filmmakers towards actors as stars. Czach's interrogation of stardom at TIFF is insightful. Her concern focuses on how stars pose a threat to cinephilia at an international film festival. This chapter further addresses the symbolic constructions of stars in a national context of TIFF, which attempts to subvert the myth that Canada lacks stars. In reality, Canadian stars are significantly less represented than their American counterparts.

Origin and Function of TIFF

TIFF started as the Festival of Festivals in 1976, selecting the best films from other film festivals (TIFF, 2015a). In 1995, it was renamed as the Toronto International Film Festival and has become one of the most pre-eminent international film festivals in the world. It screens more than three hundred national and international films from more than sixty countries. Unlike other film festivals, however, TIFF is open to audiences and distinguishes itself as the world's largest public festival. It attracts around 500,000 people from across the world (Mudhar, 2010a). In response to the success of a large Canadian viewership, the programming of TIFF has now developed events throughout the year. Launched in September 2010, its state-of-the art Bell Light Box building includes 365-days of festival programming that includes lectures, events, and screening of films. In addition, the TIFF Cinematheque is a year-round program that screens classics of world cinema as well as contemporary art house films (TIFF, 2015b).

TIFF's primary mandate is to support filmmaking in both national and international contexts. In order to meet its mandate, Toronto International Film Festival Inc. runs a set of activities that act as "the launching pad for the best of international, Hollywood and Canadian cinema" (TIFF, 2015b). This function is fulfilled via film screenings during the ten-day TIFF annual event. In addition, TIFF offers a monthly subscription called Reel Talk. It is a program for previewing films in relation to the Academy Awards and the best in international cinema, followed by discussions. At the same time, the ten-day festival facilitates business deals for future productions and film screening ("Economic Activity Associated with the 2008-2009 Operations of TIFF," 2010). There are two separate film industry groups promoting films at TIFF: film producers and sales agents selling film rights, and distributors bringing movies to theatres (McDowell, 2009). With these groups, TIFF acts as a 'film market' for Canadian and international films. The need for TIFF to act as a film market resides in the fact that both Canadian and international films receive limited or no distribution in the US. Although the US has a large potential audience, it is saturated by its high domestic production that also dominates the film markets abroad. As Daryl Chin highlights, "American films have broken the dams of all foreign markets and have flooded the fields" (1997, p. 62).

The influx of American films into foreign film markets is so large that it has resulted into collapse of film markets even in cosmopolitan cities like New York (Chin, 1997). Due to a higher demand for American films in both US and foreign film markets, it is important for Canada and foreign countries to distribute their films to a larger market beyond US borders. In response to this need for wider Canadian film distribution, TIFF has grown to become one of the most important film markets that promote national, as well as foreign films looking for international distribution.

Although TIFF's mandate includes international films, Canadian films are its central focus. With the support of the Canadian federal government and the provincial government of Ontario, TIFF functions to support and celebrate the Canadian filmmaking community. As Wayne Clarkson, Telefilm Canada's Executive Director, declares:

> Supporting Canadian talent and creating Canadian content that engages audiences at home and abroad is a unity of purpose we all share...Events such as the Toronto International Film Festival strengthen the industry as a whole by drawing attention to Canadian productions, encouraging a diversity of voices, developing talent and fostering creative collaboration and business deals. Most importantly, these events provide you, the Festival-goer, with an opportunity to discover outstanding works (TIFF, 2009).

In order to fulfil its mandate, TIFF runs a program called Canada's Top Ten that "celebrates and screens the best Canadian features and shorts of the year" (TIFF, 2015b). It also runs a program called the Film Circuit that screens Canadian and foreign films in under-serviced areas of Canada.

Although TIFF's mandate focuses on both Canadian and international films, the ten-day film festival and its media representations have shifted to a celebration of film stars, particularly from Hollywood. To promote films, TIFF events are organised in the form of 'star oriented' or 'star-studded galas.' *Time Canada* magazine illustrates this star orientation in an article titled "How Toronto Attracts the Stars" (Corliss, 2006). This chapter notes that one of the important functions of TIFF is to organise and manage events related to stars. The dominant practice of celebrating stars contrasts with TIFF's central mandate: to focus on promoting films. TIFF, therefore, is not only a festival screening state-of-the art films but also a media event that largely celebrates stars.

TIFF as a Media Event Supporting Stardom

Media constructions of stars are an intrinsic part of TIFF cultural practices. To understand the role TIFF plays in media representation of stars, it is necessary to critically examine the festival as a media event, whereby the festival and media are intrinsically linked. The term 'media event' is derived from the original work of Daniel Dayan and Elihu Katz (1992). Media events have been popularly known as live television broadcasts of historically significant occasions. But an international film festival is now also "seen to constitute another form of media event as it is constructed and articulated across a range of media platforms (trade press, daily newspapers, celebrity magazines, Internet, radio, television, specialist catalogues etc." (Mazdon, 2007, p. 16). In studying film festivals as a media event, 'mediation' is an important process to consider. For Marijke de Valck (2007), the mediation of film festivals refers to a process of value addition that is reworked in relation to specific conditions of a film festival system. The mechanisms involved in creating star spectacle in a spatial setting and organising a timely agenda and press release, are, at a temporal level, some of the key elements in the process of mediating a film festival. These elements not only help to construct TIFF as a media event; they are also central to constructing stars that can add value to the festival's supporting network.

TIFF has shifted from purely a film-based festival to a media event. It is an event where journalism is "both the representation (and interpretation) of festival activities, and in itself a significant mediation and production of the event" (Harbord, 2002b, p. 66). TIFF's reliance on media is evidenced by how the official organisation, Toronto International Film Festival Inc., carefully organises and archives these media representations at its Film Reference Library to promote film research and disseminate a stronger knowledge of TIFF. In establishing relation with the media, the role of press representatives, of stars attending film premieres, and the granting of awards have become fundamental to the festival. As Marijke de Valck writes:

> With the global proliferation of film festivals during the 1980s and 1990s and the consequent increased level of competition between festivals, the formula of premiers, awards, and stars has become an obligatory part of any festival that wants to keep attracting large numbers of media representatives. The greater number of attending press representatives, the greater the chances of success for a festival on the international film festival circuit will be. Some festivals proudly display the number of visiting journalists on their websites (2007, p. 126).

The need for journalists at TIFF is crucial in light of an increasing number of film festivals that compete for press and public attendance. These media representatives and their construction of star-studded events are central to the strategic branding of film festivals.

In covering international film festivals, media endorse their own brand value as well as that of their corporate sponsors. Brand value can be defined as a measurement or perceived quality of a product or service in intangible ways. Wagner Kamakura and Gary Russell specify that brand value is constructed by corporations though "brand name associations and perceptual distortions" (1993, p. 9) that hold similar core values of business and increase equity of a product or service for consumers. Media corporations are among several businesses that associate their brand name with film festivals. They are interested in inscribing the cultural and economic value of their brand in a way that it shares a close fit with their coverage of film festivals and their advertisers. As Lena Mossberg and Donald Getz highlight:

> While the media often prefer to remain independent and objective, they also have a vested interest in securing sponsorship contracts with events to promote their own brand. Only through interaction with the event, tourism organisations, and often cities, will the media be inclined toward, and capable of effectively enhancing the destination or event brand (2014, p. 241).

From this perspective, media representations of TIFF are not independent from the festival's primary activities. Rather, as Marijke de Valck interprets, TIFF and the media are "interdependent and mutually reinforcing," as "both parties benefit from the other and, in this way, the preservation of the larger festival network is supported" (2007, p. 125).

At TIFF, a primary way to support brand value of media is through celebrity endorsements of products and services. TIFF is not only a film festival but also a star-studded event, expressing brand values of corporate sponsors though celebrity endorsements. In general, celebrities play a significant role in enhancing the brand image of media and other corporate sponsors that share business values. First, celebrities are exploited for their 'well knownness' to strengthen media corporations' brands (Boorstin, 1962; Frick, 2004). Second, media corporations cover those very endorsements to highlight their brand quality and the importance of the festival and its corporate sponsors. During the ten-day festival, stars at TIFF add value to the brand image and advertise products or services of both the festival and their sponsors. This 'added value' is achieved at a relatively low cost. Hollie Shaw illustrates the significance of stars in endorsing corporate sponsors on the red carpet at TIFF. In her article titled

"Carpetbragging," Shaw reflects on Alison King, President of public relations firm Media Profile. For King, the "value of festival media coverage aligned with brand would be immeasurable" (Shaw, 2009, p. 12), as the coverage leads to meeting operating costs that can amount to millions of dollars. The endorsements further allow increased visibility of branded products through live coverage of celebrity endorsements of products on red carpet events. At TIFF, many corporate sponsors such as BlackBerry, Royal Bank of Canada, FedEx, Sony, and Cineplex gain added brand value through coverage of celebrity endorsements. The economic exchanges between media and other corporate sponsors through celebrity endorsements show that TIFF is more than a film festival: it is also a star-studded commercial event.

In order to meet branding requirements, national and local media such as the *National Post*, *The Toronto Star*, Global Television, and CTV are saturated with coverage of stars on the red carpet and attending gala parties at TIFF. In the eyes of the public, TIFF is a newsworthy event that the media cover with the purpose of guiding audiences to the best films of the year. A closer look into the news reports, however, illustrates that media coverage has another objective, namely to make visible the celebrity endorsements of sponsoring corporations and, in the process, of TIFF as well. One example of celebrity endorsements is Holt Renfrew's sponsorship of the TIFF red carpet. Holt Renfrew inscribes its logo on TIFF's 150 foot-long red carpet twenty-two times. When high profile stars walk on this red carpet and are photographed and filmed, they indirectly endorse Holt Renfrew by creating a symbolic association between their presence on the red carpet alongside Renfrew's logo. Shaw highlights how celebrity endorsements on the red carpet help the festival and corporations to gain a "free, positive publicity halo of media coverage quantified in terms of advertising spending" (2009, p. 12). She sums up the cost effectiveness of media coverage:

> TIFF packs one of the biggest returns on marketing investment relative to Holt Renfrew's overall marketing budget, which includes traditional and digital media, catalogues, fashion shows, glitzy parties....it is one of our times of year when our media value is the highest...even though the overall spend is less that 1% of the retailer's marketing budget (Ibid.).

In branding the festival, TIFF official sponsors construct it as an 'exclusive' event, and sell it to a large number of markets. These TIFF media events are exclusive because they offer snapshots, interviews, and recordings of celebrity events that are not available to audiences except through the specific media constructing them. In constructing exclusivity, media generate a greater audience to which it can promote its brand alongside that of corporate sponsors and of TIFF venues. Media not only sell an increased value of sponsors' brand image; they also sell an unattainable desire to consume products and access places that are only accessible to stars. These unattainable star-studded events, in turn, attract a large audience curious about the places. These combined practices help to brand both TIFF and sponsoring media as 'exclusive.'

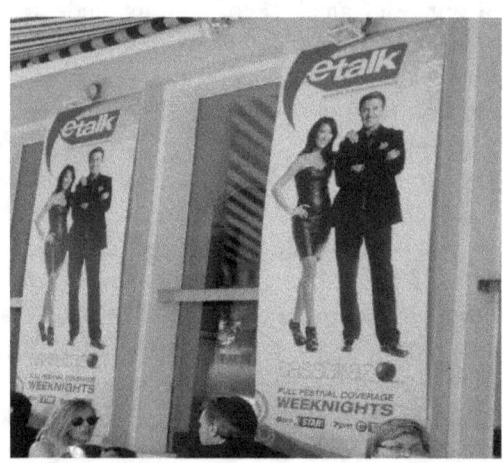

**Figure 1: eTalk Banners Promoting Exclusive Star-studded Media Events
(Source: Samita Nandy)**

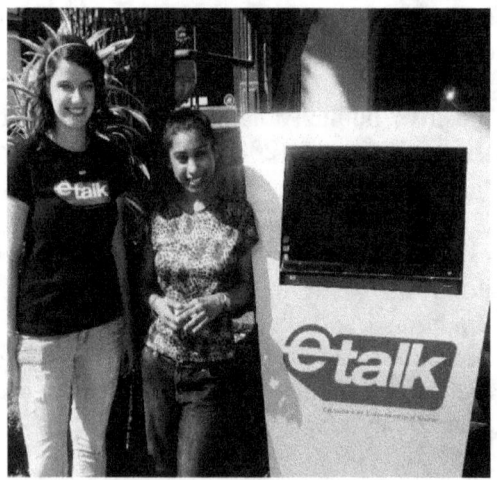

**Figure 2: *eTalk* Interactive Booths Constructing Private Star Experiences
(Source: Samita Nandy)**

The partnership between TIFF and its official sponsor, CTV's *eTalk*, is central to the media branding of the festival as 'exclusive.' Many TIFF media events represent a partnership between CTV, festival sponsors, and venues such as Four Seasons Hotel, Hazelton Hotel, and InterContinental Hotel that accommodate stars attending TIFF. *eTalk* is Canada's most popular entertainment show that claims to offer "exclusive access" to the "most sought-after celebrity interviews" (Garcia, 2008), emphasising that they are taking place at the hotel venues. To build exclusivity for audiences, as seen in my photographs (Figures 1 and 2), *eTalk* invests in promotional banners and interactive booths to share photos and private experiences about stars. In partnership with VISA, *eTalk* also organises a CTV production studio space named the VISA Lounge and conducts celebrity interviews that are not accessible elsewhere. In constructing exclusivity and appeal through celebrities, the studio adds brand value to TIFF, CTV, and VISA. Similarly, *eTalk Festival Party*, *eTalk Tent*, and *eTalk Roots Lounge* are constructed spaces that host celebrity interviews and star-studded events. In situating stars in these media-sponsored events and lodging venues, a symbolic and exclusive partnership between the film festival, corporate sponsors, and stars is imagined. Most constructions of fame are not associated with publicly accessible film screenings at TIFF. However, they serve to brand the festival as an 'exclusive' one. The construction of exclusivity is central to both stardom and to the media branding of TIFF.

In addition to exclusivity, 'live' broadcasts are central to the construction of stars in TIFF media events. Here, the term 'live' refers to first-hand experience of TIFF events that are only accessible through accredited media. This 'live' experience may or may not occur in real time. The 'live' experience is rather a social construction of reality that is not measured by the immediacy of time or place. The construction of 'live' or 'real' experiences at TIFF is often manufactured through the formats and narratives of entertainment magazine shows.

In covering star-oriented events, the format of these television shows creates immediacy of space and time, resulting in first-hand experience of star-studded events that are otherwise excluded from direct public participation. For this purpose, *eTalk* is renamed Live at *eTalk* during the ten-day event of TIFF. It represents TIFF events as 'live' even though they are snapshots of pre-recorded programmes that cover stars at the festival. The show appropriates a tabloid magazine format that utilises narrative devices of both broadcast and print journalism. Research shows that the tabloid magazine format increases sensory arousal, attention, and instantaneous perception on a cognitive level (Caldwell, 1995; Grabe, Zhou, Lang, & Bolls, 2000). In entertainment news, this format uses flashing and enlarged texts. The format also incorporates still and moving images of stars promoting films. A combination of these signs displays a collage of star-studded events and creates a 'live' impression of unedited snippets of stars. On a cognitive level, the rapid clips of texts and images can only be retained in short-term memory and, hence, demand concentration of viewers' direct attention. Spatially, images and texts of stars zoom out and enlarge to create immediacy with viewers. The temporal and spatial mediation of TIFF events, appearing in the form of these snippets of unedited material, manufactures a sense of live coverage of stars that is not accessible to the public. In light of restricted access to stars' actual public appearances, the mediation of TIFF as a 'live' event may resolve audiences' anxiety over not being able to directly access the stars at the festival.

The format of the entertainment shows brings TIFF stars *and* sponsors to the public's attention. Celebrity interviews at the *eTalk* VISA lounge, *eTalk* Tent, and the *eTalk* Roots Lounge, as well as events such as *eTalk* Festival Party are organised by and for a closed network of sponsoring partners. As CTV claims, *eTalk* brings "the Festival experience to fans with a fantastic group of partners" (CTV, 2008e). In order to support the brand image of corporate sponsors, the festival experiences are produced in video segments that are named after the sponsors. In *eTalk*, these segments include LG FilmFest Lounge, VISA Live on the Red Carpet, and RBC Emerging Artist segments. In each incorporated segment, *eTalk* covers star events lasting between thirty seconds and a minute. Each of these short video segments open with a theme and the large, flashing logos of TIFF and corporate sponsors, followed by still and moving images and names of stars. These fast but enlarged texts and images demand the audience's direct attention and give the illusion of immediacy and proximity to the sponsor. As scholar John Caldwell interprets, "the instantaneous perception by the observer of the actual event and by the television view" collapses and "creates a notion of 'liveness'" (1995, p. 367). The 'liveness' replaces the actuality of being 'there' with being 'here.' This mediation of 'live' experiences is central to the construction of both stars and the brand images of TIFF sponsors.

Although TIFF is the largest public international film festival with around 500,000 audience members, the 'exclusive' and 'live' constructions of star-studded media events prevent the equal participation of the public. At TIFF, early sales of festival ticket packages, access to selected films, and star oriented events at TIFF are limited to premium VISA cardholders. Credit card holders receive a unique opportunity to view the best films that are officially sponsored at the VISA Screening Room theatre only (VISA, 2011). The uniqueness and limited accessibility are constructed by offering an emulation of stardom. Indeed, advertisements claim that VISA cardholders can "enjoy celebrity status" (VISA, 2010) and receive refreshments and complimentary snacks at the theatre's VISA Premium Lounge. These advertisements promote VISA in a style that resembles celebrity endorsements of their products and services:

> Want to feel like you're on the a-list? Enjoy the VIP treatment at this year's Toronto International Film Festival! As a VISA cardholder you get priority access to the VISA Screening Room...VISA. The only credit card accepted at the Festival (VISA, 2009).

The premium VISA cards accepted at TIFF are neither affordable nor known to all audiences until they visit the festival or are enticed to subscribe to the high annual fee cards. The inaccessibility to premium services facilitates the unequal access to TIFF film events despite the supposed 'star status' of VISA cardholders. Thus, star-oriented presentations of TIFF, VISA, and other sponsors often exclude equal opportunities to view films in Canada.

TIFF is not just a film festival: it is a media event that constructs and celebrates stardom. Media events at TIFF operate in the following two ways. First, TIFF engages with celebrity endorsements. These celebrity endorsements add brand value to the media constructing stars and to the TIFF corporate sponsors. Second, TIFF organises exclusive opportunities for audiences to attend film-screening events, as advertised in various media channels. Like celebrity endorsements, these TIFF events glamorise stardom by conferring a celebrity status to exclusive audiences. In doing so, the events support corporate sponsors like VISA and their media partners, which fosters 'exclusivity' and a 'live' experience. In both cases, TIFF is a media event that supports and represents stardom and, in the process, mediates the reception of international films and talent.

Representations of Stardom at TIFF

In order to generate audience attention and promote festival branding, media events at TIFF focus on Hollywood films and stars at press conferences. In general, media reports open with statements such as "Hollywood descends on the Toronto International Film Festival" (Johnson, 2006) and "star-driven Hollywood premieres and parties" (Vlessing, 2006) of TIFF. These film stars are promoted because they usually create greater box-office hits and, by extension, add value-impact for the festival. In partnership with media and hotel venues, TIFF devotes careful attention to strategically organising Hollywood films and stars. By focusing dominant media attention towards blockbuster Hollywood films, however, TIFF overlooks Canadian films and homegrown stars. Indeed, quantitative and qualitative studies of media reports reveal the limited representation of Canadian film stars at TIFF.

A quantitative study of media excerpts illustrates how selected Hollywood stars receive stronger coverage than Canadian and international stars do. At TIFF, Hollywood stars such as George Clooney, Brad Pitt, Drew Barrymore, Oprah Winfrey, and Jennifer Connelly have received lengthy front-page coverage. A glimpse into the opening page of Canadian newspaper *National Post* illustrates the major coverage of Hollywood stars on the first day of the 34th annual TIFF. Published on September 11, 2009, the top-third of the front page featured enlarged photographs of American stars Drew Barrymore and Ellen Page promoting their Hollywood film *Whip it* (2009). Notably, the Canadian-born Ellen Page received front coverage because she is now an American star. The rest of the page featured photographs of Amanda Seyfried, Megan Fox, and George Clooney — all American stars.

After the major coverage of these Hollywood stars, there were minor representations of homegrown Canadian celebrities. For example, Canadian-Indian actress Lisa Ray, promoting her Canadian film *Cooking with Stella* (2009), received coverage in a column that occupied only one-sixth of the newspaper's sixth page. The coverage was similar to that of Canadian journalist and celebrity writer Shinan Govani, who received a red-carpet appearance for his novel *Boldfaces Names* (2009). But Govani nonetheless received short coverage on the third page of the *National Post*. On September 16, *eTalk* featured quick snippets of Lisa Ray and Shinan Govani, and both were briefly covered only after long segments dedicated to Hollywood celebrity gossip about Tom Cruise and Jennifer Anniston. These gossips created news on who were part of the "ladies and gents dominating the red carpet" (*eTalk*, 2009) at TIFF. On the same day, Lisa Ray and Canadian director Spencer Maybee received brief coverage that occupied one-sixth of space of the second and third page of the *National Post*. These media reports illustrate that the coverage of Canadian stars is often subordinate to that of Hollywood stars. The coverage of Canadian stars at TIFF usually occupies reduced space or appears in later parts of media content. Even in the TIFF program guide, select Canadian films and talent are relegated to the last pages.

The media representation of these select few stars reflects the Canadian interest in US cultural dominance. Consider America's dominant presence in TIFF industry programs such as the Rising Star Program, launched in September 2011. The program aims to offer professional tools to Canadian film talent and to help launch them into international markets. In a media interview, TIFF co-director Cameron Bailey suggests the urgent need for the program. Bailey "points out that filmmaking in Canada has long resisted a star system" (Vaccaro, 2011b). Karen Bruce, TIFF's

Director of Canadian Initiatives, highlights how TIFF, contrary to its earlier media representations, "is proud of the success some Canadian actors have had in Hollywood, Bollywood, the U.K. and Hong Kong" (Vaccaro, 2011b). This success prompts TIFF to take initiatives to develop and celebrate Canadian film talent through its Rising Star Program. The program, however, emphasises TIFF's strong national links with America's Hollywood. Despite its mandate to promote Canadian talent to the world, the program instead connects "the rising star recipients with Canadian actors who have already established successful careers in the U.S. and elsewhere" (TIFF, 2011c). Here, the 'recipients' are selected to support the Hollywood film industry instead of developing their talent in Canada. A media report illustrates how Katie Boland, one of these rising stars, marks a continuing relation with Hollywood: "Canadian actor Katie Boland [...] was ecstatic Thursday after being short-tracked by the Toronto International Film Festival for a Hollywood career" (Playback, 2011). Although there has been an increasing awareness of Canadian film talent, there is a continued emphasis on Hollywood stardom. TIFF's selective, film-based practices demonstrate how the Canadian nation is imagined and administered in dominant relation to America. This imagination supports American runaway film productions in Canada but contradicts TIFF's mandate to support homegrown film talent.

Canadian celebrities not only receive less media coverage at TIFF, but are also constructed in a way that qualitatively differs from their Hollywood counterparts. In contrast to Hollywood actors who are represented as stars, TIFF promotes Canadian film producers and directors as stars. Even when Canadian actors are celebrated, their representations often carry non-glamorous elements. In representing their stardom at TIFF, media content focuses on issues such as defamation, illness, multiculturalism, and invisibility that counteract the exclusivity and glamour present in Hollywood stardom. In representing Canadian film talent at TIFF, for example, a CBC news report describes "dark shadows" of French-Canadian filmmaker Denys Arcand and highlights that he "has known failure" (Hays, 2007). Similarly, another CBC report describes Kristen Booth, who acted in the two Canadian films *Young People F ---ing* (2007) and *This Beautiful City* (2007), in terms of her invisibility. The report states "Kristin Booth has two films at this year's Toronto International Film Festival, though even if you saw them back to back, you might not recognise her as a star of each" (Onstad, 2007). Arcand's talent is mediated as a form of defamation and Booth is represented in terms of her invisibility. These qualities of Canadian film talents differ from those of Hollywood stars who are mostly represented in terms of their glamour and success.

The talent of Canadian film actor Lisa Ray has been represented in ways that qualitatively differ from Hollywood stars as well. Although Ray's media representations did not carry defamation or invisibility, the media did not focus on her talent either. Rather, her myeloma cancer was the centre of media attention at the 2009 TIFF. Moreover, Ray's Indian-Canadian heritage has been used to demonstrate Canadian multiculturalism. This demonstration is illustrated by a media report, reviewing Lisa Ray's films *All Hat* (2007) and *The World Unseen* (2007), both screened at the 35th annual TIFF. The report claims that Ray had a "Hollywood career" but she was born in "the then-largely white Toronto suburb of Etobicoke," and "this exemplifies Trudeau-era multiculturalism: Her father is Bengali and her mother is Polish" (Giese, 2007). Here, Ray's multiculturalism constructs a "thoroughly Canadian charm" (Ibid.) in an imagined relation to Hollywood. Scholarly literature has taken note of the use of multiculturalism as a means of distinguishing Canada from America. According to scholars, Canadian multiculturalism is discursively constructed on the margins of a core English Canadianness that not only reinforces a dominant Canadian colonialist perspective, but also distinguishes it from America's "melting pot" (Bannerji, 2000; Kalant, 2004; Mackey, 2002). The readings of media reports show that Canadian stars at TIFF are constructed in ways that differ from their American counterparts. Their stardom evokes a constructed notion of Canadianness, rather than talent and success, that is in direct opposition to America.

Another aspect of Canadian stardom associated with TIFF is the conferring of celebrity status to audiences. Audiences, instead of actual film personalities, are referred to as stars in media representations of TIFF. For instance, an article covering TIFF states "the secret of Toronto's success: the audience is the star" (Corliss, 2006). Although the article briefly claims that TIFF is mindful of its homegrown talent, actual names of talented individuals are under-represented. In imagining the 'star-laden power' of audiences, TIFF shifts attention away from individual homegrown Canadian talent in direct violation of its own mandate. The rationale for focussing on audiences as stars can be explained from the scholarly work of Liz Czach, Dipti Gupta, and Janine Marchessault. For Czach, Toronto did not have the "old world charm" (2010, p. 144) associated with Montreal and its Festival des Films. Compared to Montreal, Toronto did not have an interesting image to sell (Ibid.). In addition, TIFF carries a dominant image of Hollywood stardom with which it is difficult to compete. However, the embracing of a large audience demonstrates festival popularity and increases sales. TIFF, then, "turned toward its local audiences, which have been sold ad nauseam as the biggest commodity" (Gupta & Marchessault, 2007, p. 251). In designating audiences as stars, however, the talent of individual Canadians is underrepresented compared to that of Hollywood stars.

Like audiences, Toronto itself is referred to as a star in media representations of TIFF. The attribution of celebrity status to Toronto is reflected in media representations such as the following:

> So before the filmmakers and actors start to strut their stuff at the various gala premieres that are scheduled, it is a good time for all to take a moment to reflect and take pride in this festival, which adds to Toronto's reputation as a rising international star at TIFF (*City in the Spotlight*, 2006).

The festival and media identify specific urban buildings and landmarks of the city as stars as well. For example, the program advertisement of the 39th annual TIFF represents Soho Metropolitan hotel, its residents, and sponsors as Star Power Recharged with bold captions in an advertisement. The advertisement further claims that "This is real red-carpet living in the heart of Toronto's Entertainment District" (*Star Power Recharged*, 2009). Similarly, the TIFF program guide represents a condominium advertisement where Canadian filmmaker Ivan Reitman is visible. Although Reitman is the producer of TIFF's much-hyped, George Clooney-starred *Up in the Air* (2009), he is not celebrated as a star in media events; rather, the condominiums are advertised as the stars in Canada. Here, the stardom of Canadian filmmaker Ivan Reitman appears unrelated to his talent. Instead, his talent is used to ascribe meanings of fame to generic objects (condominiums) in Toronto. Unlike dominant representations of Hollywood stars, these representations do not carry the name and talent of Canadian individuals. Instead, the media emphasise the city and its architecture as stars.

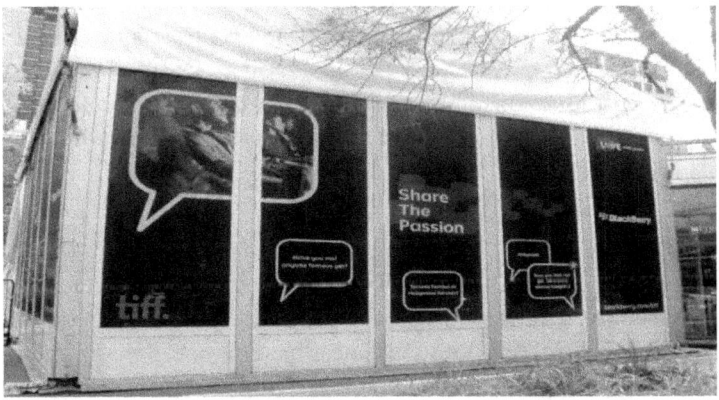

Figure 3: Representation of Toronto Competing for Fame (Source: Samita Nandy)

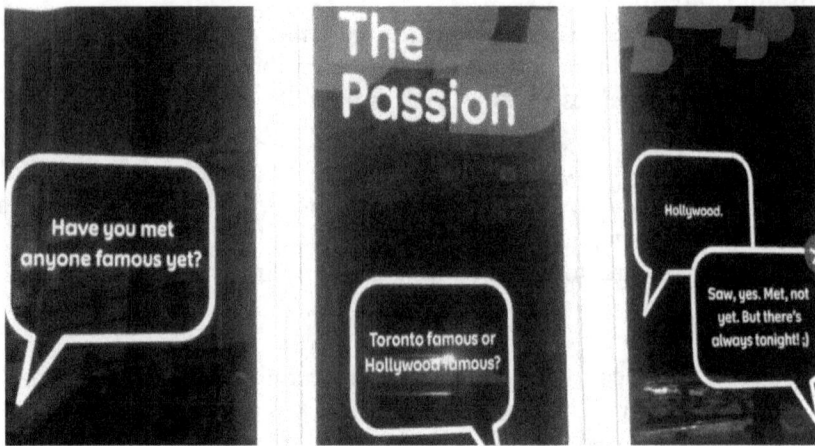

Figure 4: Enlarged Image of Figure 3 (Source: Samita Nandy)

This kind of Canadian stardom at TIFF is limited and mediated as expressions of the audience and the city. The word/sign 'star' particularly becomes an 'absent referent:' its original meaning is transmuted to generic objects. An 'absent referent,' in the words of scholar Carol Adams, "can be anything whose original meaning is undercut as it is absorbed into a different hierarchy of meaning" (2003, p. 209). In the case of TIFF, 'star' does not necessarily refer to an individual personality or talent. Instead, it refers to the city and its audiences that collectively support TIFF's corporate interests in competing relations with Hollywood. Such a discursive construction of the city may offer the illusion of a nationwide fame that symbolically differentiates from and resists Hollywood stardom. This differentiation is illustrated in my photographs (Figures 3 and 4) where TIFF asks if Toronto is more famous than Hollywood. At the same time, the stardom systematically dismisses the specific names of individual film artists while celebrating Hollywood productions of films and stars in Canada. These productions help the economic development and sustenance of the City of Toronto and of its inner neighbourhood, Yorkville.

Stardom in Gentrification of Yorkville

During the annual TIFF event, stars and fans are attracted to specific locations in Toronto. Out of all of these locations, Yorkville is the most important because it attracts and celebrates Hollywood stars and fans. In Canadian media representations, the location of Yorkville is a cultural site that articulates expressions of stardom of Hollywood film actors and of Toronto. In reality, however, Yorkville depicts only a selected area of

Toronto and not the socio-cultural experiences of the whole city. In order to understand the rationale of TIFF and of the media in using Yorkville to imagine Toronto, it is crucial to study the historical relationship between the urban development of Yorkville, the economic development of Toronto, and TIFF stardom. In particular, it is important to understand the gentrification of Yorkville and the ways in which it plays a role in the construction of stardom and Canadian national identity during TIFF.

The rationale for representing Yorkville as TIFF's primary venue of celebrities can be studied through the lens of gentrification in Toronto. Gentrification is the process of economically upgrading inner-city neighbourhoods into upscale areas of commodified culture. From an aesthetic point of view, David Ley (2003) and Vanessa Matthews (2008) define gentrification as a set of practices whereby art districts of high cultural value are appropriated into neighbourhoods with high economic capital. This appropriation is achieved via the market forces of real estate that cater to a new set of residents with greater purchasing power. Yorkville is an example of gentrification in Toronto. Located just north of downtown Toronto, it is an upscale inner-city neighbourhood that has been subjected to the process of gentrification since the 1970s.

In the 1960s, Yorkville was known as an art district with a population of young and low-earning painters, illustrators, novelists, poets, guitarists, singers, and musicians. In the words of Vanessa Matthews, Yorkville was a "bohemian enclave" (2008, p. 2851) with a subversive hippie crowd and artists. This cultural capital of creation, subversion, and innovation, however, was "reduced to economic goods" for capitalist interests and for the development of the nation (p. 2853). Economic investment and redevelopment in Yorkville since the 1970s created what is now an upscale and high-end retail area. During this process, rental costs soared, forcing artists out of their lofts and into to poorer locations. Although there is currently an 'absence' or 'lack' of artists, the cultural capital of art in Yorkville continues to be appropriated by market forces in the name of Toronto's economic development. As a result, Yorkville is now characterised by a high-end retail culture in which boutique shops and lofts have been transformed from a place of art production to a chic, upmarket district catering to tourist consumption. Thus, although the artists and their experimental studios are gone, the aesthetic values of creation, subversion, and innovation still symbolise Yorkville. The cultural and economic capital that turned the neighbourhood into a high-end location, coupled with the area's artistic past, is now exploited to attract festival organisers, stars, and audiences.

TIFF is one of the art festivals that has exploited Yorkville's image for the purpose of selling products and services through celebrity sightings and endorsements (Mathews, 2008). An online media report represents stars at Yorkville in the same fashion:

> Celebrities and cafe society in general love to hang out in this chic shopping and gallery neighbourhood just north of Bloor and west of Yonge. Colin Farrell and Woody Harrelson were spotted there recently for a TIFF-coinciding fundraiser, as were Naomi Watts, Annette Bening and Samuel L. Jackson. Yorkville is home to Toronto's most expensive real estate and finest hotels, including its only five-star: The Hazelton. Who's staying there for this year's Toronto International Film Festival? Their lips are sealed (Peterson, 2009).

Celebrity sightings at TIFF support the development of Toronto as a cultural and economic site. *Toronto Star* reporter Murray White assumes that "Yorkville and TIFF grew together" as a result of a coincidental "thought" in the "shop windows of Yorkville" (2008). However, the strategic positioning of TIFF and the rise of star-studded events in Yorkville are directly related to the consumerist practice associated with the gentrification of Toronto. As Vanessa Matthews observes,

> Celebrity sightings (spurred by the Toronto International Film Festival housing its function annually in the neighbourhood) and high-end shoppers drawn to designer looks and labels project an image of cosmopolitanism to the space" (2008, p. 2860).

In these consumer-based practices, stars and celebrity sightings at TIFF are not necessarily recognised for performative arts; rather, they build the desire to consume stardom and draw audiences and fans to Yorkville (and to the City of Toronto, at large). This observation about stardom is significant because it questions the national myth that Canada does not have stars, as highlighted in Chapter 1. Instead, it shows that stars are indeed represented in Canada and that they support national discourses.

When mobilised by stardom in Yorkville, TIFF audiences and fans perform two national functions. First, at a material level, audiences and fans help to generate economic profits through tourism and consumer practices in Yorkville. Economic development is important to TIFF federal and provincial sponsors such as the Ministry of Tourism of Ontario. Second, TIFF audiences and fans, when represented as stars, help to negotiate tensions that may arise from the underrepresentation of artists in Yorkville and film talent in Canada.

As discussed earlier, audiences and fans are symbolically represented as stars in Canada. In these representations, the stardom of audiences and fans helps to obscure the limited and uneven representation of Canadian film talent at TIFF. As Vanessa Matthews states, "public is defined as a unity to harmonise difference - and works to police and control space and conceal uneven social relations" (2008, p. 2863) with artists. In the case of TIFF, these uneven social relations exist with 'absent artists' of Yorkville and, particularly, Canadian filmmakers and actors who are not equally celebrated. Instead, audiences and fans are rhetorically labelled as stars. It is rhetorical in the sense that it creates a language and discourse that serves economic and political interests. In these contexts, the distinction between signifiers of stardom (e.g., red carpet and paparazzi) and signified or meanings of art (for which Yorkville is historically known) are disrupted (Mathews, 2008). In the case of TIFF, signifiers of stardom may attempt to reproduce the cultural value of Yorkville's art scene from the 1960s. When attributed to audiences and fans, however, these signifiers do not question why Canadian film talent and art are underrepresented compared to that of Hollywood stars. In particular, TIFF's media representations do not examine how the stardom of Canadian audiences and fans and of Hollywood actors support the economic interests of TIFF sponsors at the federal, provincial, and municipal levels.

The City of Toronto and TIFF audiences, when named as stars, offer the illusion of reclaiming Canadian artists and filmmakers that are otherwise scrubbed away by economic interests in gentrifying Yorkville. These signifiers of Canadian stardom are therefore 'absent referents,' whereby the signified (the film talent) is absent. The difference between Canadian stardom and its absent referent is a semiotic one: Canadian stardom is not absent, but its referent is often missing in media representations. This absence of Canadian stardom signifies a national difference from the dominant American stars that are named at TIFF. Moreover, even if Canadian celebrities are named, they are far less represented compared to American Hollywood stars. Both of these cases of TIFF stardom represent Canadian national identity as an American 'Other' while sustaining Hollywood stardom and runaway film productions in Hollywood North.

Conclusion

The case study in this chapter sheds new light on one of the least studied areas in Canadian media practices: how international film festivals play a role in the symbolic construction of stars and of their national identities. The Toronto International Film Festival (TIFF) is an important and representative case in this respect. This chapter showed how TIFF is a cultural site that articulates dominant ideas of fame and nation in media discourses and film festival programming. This articulation is contrary to the myth that there are no stars in Canada. In questioning this myth, the chapter contributed to the broader aim of the book. It demonstrated that there are not only constructions and representations of stars in Canada, but also national expressions in Canadian stardom. By studying the case of TIFF as a media event, the chapter further characterised Canadian stardom as one that is underrepresenting its human subjects — even lacking referents for them. This underrepresentation explains the perpetuation of the idea that Canada has no stars or star system.

The chapter also showed a presence of Canadian stardom at TIFF that both quantitatively and qualitatively differs from that of America. Quantitatively speaking, there is a limited representation of stars in Canada. From a qualitative perspective, Canadian stars are depicted either as supporting Hollywood or as American better 'Others.' In the context of Hollywood North, national expressions at TIFF are a product of two contradictory relations to the US. First, Canadian media offer dominant representation of Hollywood stars in America. In this respect, TIFF privileges Hollywood films and stars over Canadian ones. These privileged practices contradict TIFF's mandate to focus on Canadian talent and 'homegrown' productions, as representation of Canadian stars and promotion of their homegrown films are fairly limited. Second, national discourses in media offer a strong representation of Canada in ways that distinguish it from America. This distinction is exemplified by stars from both nations being represented as newer, stronger, and better in the Canadian context of Hollywood North. The Northern imagination of stardom in Canada can then be perceived as an American better 'Other,' whereby the Canadian North is symbolised as a stronger frontier, as discussed in Chapters 3 and 4.

Apart from symbolising a Northern frontier, Canadian stardom is mediated as an urban and multicultural construct as opposed to a celebration of individual fame. By attributing stardom to audiences and to the city of Toronto, media discourses celebrate a Canadian fame that differs from dominant expressions of America's Hollywood. In working with tourism industries, corporate sponsors, and the government, TIFF not only takes part in reinforcing the urban image of Canada through Toronto but also emphasises the nation's cosmopolitan feel and mobilises economic lures for international tourists and consumers. For this purpose, stars are mostly identified in the gentrified location of Yorkville in Toronto. Canadian celebrities are therefore represented as cosmopolitan and multicultural in contrast to America's 'melting pot' image. These imaginary practices serve national discourses of Canada while sustaining the American film industry in Hollywood North.

The compelling questions of North in Canadian fame will be further explored in the next chapter. Chapter 6 highlights how the City of Toronto uses Canada's Walk of Fame (CWOF) as a commemorative site to construct a collective memory of the Canadian nation through Northern symbols of fame. Like TIFF, CWOF is located in another gentrified location of Toronto that mobilises Canadian touristic, economic, and political interests. While CWOF can be distinguished from TIFF in terms of its focus away from Hollywood, its use of Northern symbols allows for the examination of the Canadian nation and fame in binary yet ambivalent relations with the US.

6 Canada's Walk of Fame

CWOF is a not-for-profit organisation that celebrates Canadian stars with a sidewalk memorial and an annual gala event. Originally inspired by the Hollywood Walk of Fame, the CWOF sidewalk memorial is located along King St. West and Simcoe Street in Toronto's Entertainment District. Stars are inscribed in the sidewalk as stylised granite maple leaves engraved with the printed name and signature of honourees. This site is also supported by an annual gala event that celebrates and pays tribute to its inducted stars. The sidewalk and the annual gala event were established in 1998. Since then, CWOF has been engaged in fame-based practices. CWOF has inducted a large number of celebrities and, to some extent, public personalities that are not necessarily associated with fame. In being inducted into the Walk of Fame, they are celebrated for their national role in Canada.

Josh Stenger and Fan Lin's seminal studies of the Hollywood Walk of Fame can help to shed light on CWOF as an iconographic landmark that constructs public memory of national heritage. Although Stenger and Lin are concerned about the Hollywood Walk of Fame in the city of Los Angeles (LA), their work explores how sidewalk inscriptions of stars serve as iconographic devices that imagine public memory and thereby help to understand collective spaces such as the nation. From this perspective, Stenger and Lin's literature on the Hollywood Walk of Fame is important in the sense that it illuminates the role of CWOF in Toronto. From Stenger and Lin's study, the collective meanings of the Hollywood Walk of Fame can be understood at two different levels: the material and the symbolic.

At the material level, the Walk of Fame is significant because it serves as a centre of attraction for LA tourism even though it is just a selective representation of the city. Under capitalism, cities develop from both the production of manufactured goods and the mass production and consumption of cultural artefacts such as sidewalk inscriptions of stars (Eade & Mele, 2002). Yet, the selective representation generates revenues beyond the municipal level: it also helps to build the nation.

At the symbolic level, the Walk of Fame is a set of signs that invokes cultural meanings of fame, leisure, and lifestyle. As a system of signs, the Hollywood Walk of Fame particularly constitutes an 'urban fantasia,' drawing on icons, stories, and fantasies of the Hollywood film industry (Lin, 2002; Stenger, 2001). Stenger contends that, for tourists visiting the Hollywood Walk of Fame, there is a 'dialogic relationship' between LA's cultural landscape and Hollywood films, whereby the former is mediated by the latter. In mediation of LA's landscape, Hollywood films selectively present parts of the city that can be associated with an urban fantasy. At the same time, public administration and urban planners design commemorative landmarks like the Hollywood Walk of Fame and inscribe cultural mythologies reinforced by films. This inscription leads Stenger to claim that Los Angeles' cultural geography is difficult to distinguish from its "cinematic doppelganger, rendering LA and Hollywood as interchangeable spaces and interchangeable signs" (2001, p. 61). Hollywood then serves to restore a particular kind of public memory of LA.

Given Hollywood's global appeal, the Walk of Fame plays a role in branding LA as a 'world class city.' This branding, in turn, serves national interests. In order to understand how the Walk of Fame supports the nation, it is helpful to consider the work of Stephanie Donald and John G. Gammack (2007). Their work sheds light on how Hollywood's film-based artefacts play a role in branding the city as 'world class,' and how this branding is of national interest. When a city is branded as 'world class,' it is presented as touristic and "as a desirable economic location for investment and as a metonym for the nation" (Donald & Gammack, 2007, p. 8). Donald and Gammack contend that in order to serve these national interests, world class cities are personified with characteristics that also help nation-branding. In the case of LA, the tourism industry helps to market the Hollywood Walk of Fame in a spectacular way. This spectacle shifts attention from problems of urban decline and degeneration that are found in LA, especially the conditions of homeless youths, unemployed minorities, and illegal immigrants (Eade & Mele, 2002). In shifting attention from these problems to spectacle, LA is established as a 'world-class city,' and, in the process, becomes an instrument through which the American government, businesses, and media promote the American Dream on a global scale (Donald & Gammack, 2007).

The Hollywood Walk of Fame functions as a Dream Factory: a mass producing machine that sells the American Dream (Lin, 2002). In selling dreams of fame and fortune, the Hollywood Walk of Fame supports the frontier myth of the American nation and the American Dream. The American Dream is a mythical construct that serves a cultural function by symbolising America as a frontier nation. According to this myth, fame and fortune are achievable via the hard work that supports American civilisation and progress. This achievement can be made irrespective of social class and is central to the American national psyche (Cullen, 2003; Wallmann, 1999). Film scholar Geoff King (2000) explores the relationship between Hollywood films that narrate the American Dream and the frontier myth in America. King points out that Hollywood narratives draw on the frontier myth in which the Wild West functions as the point where untamed wilderness, civilisation, and progress meet in North America. King argues that in order to depict the frontier myth, Hollywood films use narrative devices such as larger-than-life plots and audio-visual special effects. These plots and special effects often support high-speed action and the movement of characters across distances, offering the illusion of conquering time and space. This conquest is often rewarded by fame and fortune: both central components of the American Dream. In the process, civilisation and progress in the frontier myth are affirmed. The Hollywood Walk of Fame is then a film-based artefact that 'sells' the frontier myth depicted in films.

Origin and Differences with Hollywood Walk of Fame

CWOF originated with the mission to "engage Canadians in celebrating those who have excelled in music, sport, film, television, as well as the literary, visual and performing arts, science, and innovation" (*About Us*, 2011). It involves a televised ceremony to honour and immortalise inductees with "their names forever cemented into the sidewalks of Toronto's Entertainment District" (Andres & Kakoullis, 2011).

In 1998, CWOF started small with limited media coverage, and many stars did not show up at the gala, but it has grown over the past years. CWOF inducts Canadian stars known for either international or national work. These stars include homegrown talent such as Anne Murray, Margaret Atwood, and Bobby Orr, but most CWOF stars that receive front-page or opening broadcast coverage are known for their work in the US. These CWOF stars include Jim Carrey, Mike Myers, Michael J. Fox, Pamela Anderson, Celine Dion, Christopher Plummer, James Cameron, and Kim Cattrall. Given its star-studded appeal, CWOF has grown into a major media event and now receives extensive coverage in broadcast, print, and online media, fulfilling the need to recognise Canadian celebrities.

Although the Hollywood Walk of Fame has inspired the creation of CWOF, CWOF organisers claim that there are three marked differences between the two. First, unlike the Hollywood Walk of Fame, CWOF induction is not limited to film stars: it includes individuals from across the arts spectrum. Marissa Soumalias, CWOF Manager of Inductee Relations, states that CWOF is indeed a "knock off of the Hollywood Walk of Fame" (Nandy, 2011a). Soumalias emphasises, however, that Canada has amazing people, not just in film but other areas as well. Second, the selection criteria for inductees to CWOF are different from those of the Hollywood Walk of Fame. The criteria require CWOF inductees to have been born in, or have spent their formative years in Canada. Inductees must also be successful and contribute to Canadian cultural heritage for at least ten years (*Home*, 2011). In addition, inductees are nominated by Canadian citizens and voted by the CWOF Board of Directors. By contrast, stars of the Hollywood Walk of Fame are qualified after five years of achievements. At the Hollywood Walk of Fame, stars also self-nominate and pay for their own sidewalk star. CWOF considers its criteria to be a more legitimate and verifiable way of measuring merit and achievements than those in Hollywood. Third, although inspired by the star-studded Hollywood Walk of Fame, CWOF claims that it does not necessarily honour 'celebrities' or 'fame' as much as it celebrates Canadian excellence and achievements. Soumalias states that, "we no longer wanted to celebrate the fame and celebrity of people" (Nandy, 2011a). In fact, she adds that CWOF aims to "get rid" (Ibid.) of the Hollywood notion of fame in Canada. To subvert Hollywood notions of fame, CWOF renames its Canadian stars as 'inductees' and 'honourees.'

There is, however, a contradiction between the notion of stardom being perceived as un-Canadian and a persistent desire to emulate American fame. Ironically, CWOF induction of artists is a material practice that involves engraving a sidewalk star, which is a symbolic expression of fame. The star is a stylised maple leaf (the official emblem of Canada), but this irony is disguised, emphasising the need to hide the fact that CWOF is actually celebrating the stardom of both inductees and the nation. Furthermore, some CWOF inductees may already have received celebrity status and star-studded appeal for their success in America. Thus, the subversion of fame in Canada is not simply related to talent, achievement, and excellence. It is, rather, a way to establish a national difference with America. Moreover, the subversion is situated within discourses of the Canadian nation in order to emphasise this difference.

In light of this perspective, CWOF discourses do not consider the sidewalk as a celebration of fame. In their discourses, CWOF is constructed as a national heritage site that celebrates individuals famous for their Canadianness. In doing so, the CWOF sidewalk aims to create an iconographic heritage landmark that builds public memory of the Canadian nation. The organisation declares:

> CWOF was created as a permanent place of tribute and recognition for Canadian achievement. What began as a spirited plan to mimic an American idea has grown into a cultural event of its own distinctive character that embraces the glamour of celebrity and the graciousness of our Canadian personality [...] We believe in nation-building (*The Canada Honours*, 2009).

Considering the role of CWOF in building Canadian national heritage, CWOF not only renames Canadian stars as honourees and inductees but also as "heroes" (Nandy, 2011a). CWOF and media reports further represent Canadian heroism with rhetorical expressions such as inductees being a "treasure" that Canadians may "salute" and pay "tribute" with "pride" (*The Canada Honours*, 2009; Hickey, 1999; Muhtadie & Adrangi, 2003; Quill, 1998, 2000). CWOF also expresses the significance of inductees' historical achievements. By highlighting these commemorative acts and by renaming Canadian stars as honourees and heroes, the CWOF constructs inductees' national identity.

The CWOF plays a role in reconstituting Canadian national heritage by addressing the lack of Canadian identity prevailing in the past and by shifting away from the Hollywood notion of fame. Despite the CWOF's commitment to Canadian identity, however, from 1998 to 2010 the CWOF annual gala was organised during the ten-day TIFF festival that largely celebrated Hollywood fame. In light of this association, CWOF has often been perceived as an expression of Hollywood, but Marissa Soumalis and Julianne Taskey refute cultural linkages with Hollywood or Hollywood North. According to them, "the organisation of CWOF during TIFF was a matter of sheer timing, venue availability, and meeting the demands of broadcasters and PR representatives" (Nandy, 2011a). Broadcasters receive better response from CWOF viewers who are also watching the successful, hyped, and Hollywood star-studded TIFF gala. This viewer response to broadcasters' needs was important for two reasons. First, CWOF is supported by its partner Canwest Global Communications Corp, and is a nationally televised event on Canwest television networks, Global TV, and Slice TV. As a result of the same timing, as Soumalias and Taskey assert, some CWOF inductees may attend a film premiere at TIFF (Nandy, 2011a). Alternatively, a film star present at TIFF may attend the annual CWOF gala event. These stars usually receive front page and exclusive coverage when they attend their film premiere at TIFF. The star appearances at both TIFF and CWOF therefore gain cross-coverage in broadcast television and in news publications.

Second, Soumalias and Taskey contend that the international coverage — particularly of Hollywood — around and within TIFF helped to establish the identity of CWOF. As seen in chapters 4 and 5, many

Canadian stars became internationally famous for their work in Hollywood. Thus, CWOF inductees are often world-famous personalities. As CWOF inductee William Shatner states, "All of the [Hollywood] entertainment industry is Canadian" (*2000 The Inductees*, 2008). The global dominance of Canadian stars in Hollywood is illustrated in another media report: "Canada has dominated the entertainment industry for many, many years" and "Canadians played on founding Hollywood and the international film industry" ("Krall, Arcand get stars on Walk of Fame," 2004). The international recognition of Canadian inductees from Hollywood, especially during TIFF, gives a higher status to Canada's Walk of Fame. For this reason, it was initially crucial for CWOF to organise its annual gala alongside TIFF. There is therefore a linkage between CWOF and Hollywood, despite what CWOF staff might claim.

There are two different interpretations of CWOF working in relation to Hollywood in America. In the first interpretation, media identify the notion of fame in the context of Hollywood. In this respect, several media reports interpret CWOF efforts as replicating Hollywood practices. For example, news reporter William Orme considers the CWOF induction as an "Oscar-like punch" (2002). Canadian film critic Geoff Pevere expands on this point:

> [...] Canadians who have made something of a national sport out of celebrity duck-hunting, did not invent the walk of fame. It is true: ideal as the celebrity doormat metaphor might be in this context, it's not our idea [...] the walk of fame is just another idea we borrowed from our neighbours and lamely photocopied (1999).

Other media reports similarly acknowledge that CWOF 'emulates,' 'mimics,' 'rips off,' and has 'copied' an American idea: the Hollywood Walk of Fame (Evans, 2006; Harris, 1998a; Staff, 2001). These media reports situate CWOF within an existing continental framework, as explained in Chapter 4. From a continental perspective, scholars Alan Smith (1994), David Dyment (2010), and Bob Rae (2010) explain that economic factors in continentalism lead America to influence cultural practices in Canada. This economic influence leads to what is discursively constructed as an emulation and mimicry of American ideas in Canada. As a result, both nations share central features and values in many of their cultural practices. This sharing of cultural values is reflected in the construction and representations of CWOF.

In the second interpretation, CWOF can be read as a complex expression of Canadian nationalism that embraces the continental impact of Hollywood. A number of media reports interpret CWOF as a symbol of Hollywood North that represents Canadian contradiction and complexity by both embracing and resisting Hollywood. This complexity underpins the following *Reuters* report on CWOF:

> Step aside Tinsletown. Toronto, dubbed 'Hollywood North' for its active film industry, has its own star-studded 'Walk of Fame,' and its biggest red carpet yet was rolled out on Saturday for this year's Canadian inductees. Actor Michael J. Fox and director James Cameron were among those honoured in front of hundreds of reporters and fans in the city already flooded with celebrities for the Toronto International Film Festival (Sibonney, 2008).

Similarly, *The Los Angeles Times* comments on the CWOF: "It's a chance to see ourselves as others see us and, in this case, observe a certain smugness in the way Los Angelenos regard the self-promotion efforts of Hollywood North" (Orme, 2002, p. 14). However, an article in the *The Watcher* responds to this promotional effort by stating that, "Although savagely mocked in a recent *Los Angeles Times* story as yet another attempt by Toronto to lay claim to being Hollywood North, Canada's Walk of Fame is actually an appropriate pat on the back" (*Star Struck*, 2002). These media statements can be read as expressions of a complex sense of Canadian nationality that embraces Hollywood while resisting it with a Northern ideology. These statements are discursive practices that support the rhetoric of technological nationalism, as explained in Chapter 3. From this perspective, CWOF imports American content and the idea of Hollywood Walk of Fame, but resists America in order to maintain a national identity that resonates with colonialist perspectives. The following sections will illustrate how national identity is constructed through a set of three interrelated national myths in CWOF discourses.

The Myth of Inferiority in CWOF Discourses

While CWOF reproduces Hollywood fame as a superior symbol of success, media discourses treat CWOF practices from the view of an 'inferiority complex.' The myth of 'inferiority' in Canada historically emerged in response to economic and cultural threats of Americanisation and the perception of US superiority. The myth negotiates tensions of how Canadian cultural, military, economic, and technological practices cannot compete with those of the more dominant America. The Canadian 'inferiority complex' has been widely studied as a 'national crisis' (Astakhov, 1960; Capel, 2007; Charlesworth, 1935; Craig, 1997; Jackson, 2001; Kim, 1993). The national 'inferiority complex' myth is historically reflected and reinforced by the lack of heroes in Canada, and it prevents giving adequate recognition to Canadian talent (Reynell, 1949; Saul, 1997).

Scholar Hugh MacLennan (1977) explains the 'lack' of heroes by pointing out how the founding groups in Canada were defeated peoples: the English by the Americans and the French by the English. Similarly, the Natives share a history of conflicts and struggles in Canada. These founding people (French, English, and Natives) have been divided into different regions without celebrating their individual heroes. This lack of celebration emerged in favour of celebrating a monolithic English Canadian identity and conforming to the status quo of a core, English Canadian heroism (Francis, 1997). Yet, "English Canada has not produced many heroes" due to the "overwhelming influence of American culture on our lives" (p. 112). From these perspectives, public discourses imagine Canada as a nation of losers paralysed by fear, failure, and a dearth of heroes. This imagination is then reproduced as a myth of inferiority in cultural productions (Kim, 1993; MacLennan, 1977; McGregor, 1985; Saul, 1997). CWOF practices are situated within these existing national discourses, and they support the myth of inferiority in Canada. This myth of inferiority is reproduced in low-key representations of CWOF inductees compared to Hollywood stars.

The dominant representation of Hollywood often results in embracing American stars while representing Canadian heroes and celebrities in subordinate and inferior positions, as shown in Chapter 5. Instead of recognising national heroes and celebrating meritocratic fame, most CWOF productions celebrate Hollywood icons and reclaim Canadians who have become famous for their work in America. The act of reclaiming famous Canadians in Hollywood is a discursive effect of a Canadian identity crisis, wherein Canadian cultural institutions fail to produce their own talent.

This reclamation is crucial in the context of an existing problem of Canadian national identity crisis. A commemorative audio-visual presentation of the 11th anniversary of the CWOF recognises this form of reclaiming. The presentation opens with an archived news report that announces a "national crisis – one which may have effects on the Canadian way of life" ("Canada's Walk of Fame 10 Years," 2008). The report sets CWOF practices as a need to grapple with the existing identity crisis. For some media reporters, the replication of Hollywood practices in CWOF further illustrates a national identity crisis. In the words of journalist Christopher Harris (1998a), the CWOF sidewalk itself can be understood as a "tired emulation of what Hollywood did decades ago" (*Opinion*, 2008, p. 84). He continues by stating that the act of emulating is a "kitschy manifestation of Toronto's continuing identity crisis" and Canadians "grappling with identity" (Ibid.). The Canadian media treatment of the reproduction of the Hollywood Walk of Fame can be understood from the view of Canadian philosopher John Ralston Saul (1997). For Saul, Canada prefers to be like other nations rather than recognise its own differences. Consequently, Canada reclaims its personalities who immigrated to the US and became famous for their work there, rather than recognising homegrown talent. In the case of CWOF, the simultaneous emulation of, and resistance to, Hollywood's Walk of Fame reflects an 'inferiority' complex" and a sense of Canadian failure.

At the same time, the induction of Canadian stars paradoxically helps to establish a Canadian identity (Staff, 1999a). CWOF is a cultural site where Canada's 'inferiority complex' and national identity crisis are expressed in the discourses related to the induction of stars. In these discourses, I identify various ways in which the 'inferiority complex' around CWOF inductees is expressed. These CWOF expressions largely suppress or subordinate stardom in Canada. In the process, CWOF often constructs 'anti-fame' that subverts American stardom while strengthening Canadian national discourses.

By suppressing stardom, CWOF aims to resist the American star system and expressions of Hollywood fame that the CWOF sidewalk emulates. A *Globe and Mail* report on the first CWOF induction is an example of this suppression. The second page of the report opens with bold headlines: "Fame is not a very Canadian word" (Harris, 1998a). The report then describes celebrating Canadian stars as an "act of shameless self-promotion" (Harris, 1998a). The report ends with the following question:

> Will, in the end, Canada's starry Walk of Fame turn out to be a thousand points of light or just one particularly pedestrian stretch of sidewalk? The answer to that may depend on whether Canadians really are in a mood to embrace their stars – or are happier just to keep walking all over them (Ibid.).

The expression 'walking all over' evokes an 'anti-fame' view of Canadians who choose to ignore and suppress their stars. The suppression of stars overlaps with existing discourses expressing 'lack' of Canadian heroes. Studies by scholars Adam Carter (2003) and Fiona Tolan (2005) explain the recurrence of these discursive practices in cultural productions. Carter sheds light on various literary practices in which Canadians neither name nor celebrate culturally different citizens. This absence is constructed in favour of sustaining a collective sense of English Canadianness. It also serves to create a national difference from America that celebrates Canadian national heroes. In Canada, this practice of 'namelessness,' as Carter calls it, may establish a nationwide 'lack' of heroes that, ironically, offers a "unifying function of a national character" for Canada (2003, p. 5). In the case of CWOF and media productions, inductees are often unnamed when they are represented. This practice of 'namelessness,' in turn, supports the suppression of fame and the Canadian myth of inferiority.

Film critic Geoff Pevere uses literary devices that contribute to existing 'namelessness' and the suppression of CWOF stardom in media and national discourses. In one of his *Toronto Star* columns, Pevere uses the expression 'celebrity doormat metaphor' to imagine the suppression of CWOF inductees. He particularly describes the CWOF sidewalk as "a place where everybody can go to wipe their shoes on people they normally wouldn't allow in the same room with and we can all go to scuff our heels and spit out our gum" (1999, p. A34). From this perspective, he defines the CWOF as "a mechanism for preventing social breakdown, as a place where all Canadian citizens can harmlessly ventilate their desire to stomp on their betters," which "can be seen as necessary agents in the prevention of complete social collapse" (Ibid.). Here, CWOF stars are not only constructed as 'faceless,' as Pevere suggests in his column, but also as 'nameless' (Carter, 2003) and collectively suppressed in favour of celebrating an existing 'inferiority complex.' The suppression of CWOF inductees, then, marks an irony in the celebration of Canadian nationalism.

At the same time, Geoff Pevere and Greig Dymond (1996) indicate the irony inherent in such national practices in their book *Mondo Canuck: A Canadian Pop Culture Odyssey.* In this book, Pevere and Dymond explain the irony of Canadian nationalism and how it helps us to understand the function of the 'inferiority complex' that is embodied in the 'anti-fame' suppression of CWOF stars. They argue that, "[t]he cultural conditions of Canada, a country where everybody watches TV that comes from somewhere else...[renders] Canada [as] as nation of chronic, ironic, detached observers" (1996, p. 196). For Pevere and Dymond, cultural productions consumed in Canada often originate from other countries, mostly America, indicating the irony of being Canadian. In media discourses, the suppression of Canadian icons due to US cultural imperialism is therefore an authentic way of being Canadian. As seen in the case of CWOF, the suppression of Canadian icons also supports national discourses that Canadian cultural practices cannot compete with the more dominant practices of fame in the US. The media statement made by CWOF inductee Geddy Lee supports these discourses: "We're always happy to have more people walk all over us. It's part of our great Canadian identity" ("What it Means to Them," 1999). The irony of this statement lies in way Canadians celebrate their national identity while they simultaneously support a deep inferiority complex (as observed in their suppression of CWOF inductees). The particular expressions of 'anti-fame' in the myth of inferiority subvert US celebrity culture, which, ironically, creates the ideological conditions that sustain CWOF. This irony forms the basis for Canadian nationalism and intersects with the CWOF's initiatives.

A similar way in which the 'inferiority complex' around CWOF inductees is played out is via the subordination of Canadian talents and personas. This subordination overlaps with the suppression involved in Canadian 'anti-fame' but differs in the way that it adds an inferior quality of talent and presents public personalities in a negative way. The subordination of Canadian personalities is an expression of a national 'inferiority complex' and is supported in CWOF media discourses. The following examples exemplify this subordination.

In a supplement of *The Toronto Star,* Christopher Hutsel writes about Canadian folksinger and CWOF inductee Gordon Lightfoot. The opening page of the report starts with the headlines, "It's everyday theatre having the stars underfoot: Mother Nature, little boys, collies can be impolite to our greats" (Hutsel, 2002, p. R1). Here, Hustel plays on the word 'foot' and uses it as a pun to suggest, literally and figuratively, meanings related to the subordination and desecration of CWOF stars. Using his last name, Underfoot, the media report represents stars as being stepped on, and ways in which people, weather, and dogs may ignore and even soil the Walk of Fame stars. Although the opening line of the report acknowledges Gordon Lightfoot's talent, Hutsel describes him as a 'sole' that has the strength to endure people stepping all over him: "Some shoes walk around him, some hop over him – others step right on our folk icon" (Ibid.). Hutsel continues writing about people who "gleefully tromp on their finest" (Ibid.). From this imaginary perspective, he cites inductee Joni Mitchell in making a request to Toronto pedestrians: "If you're crossing over my star, I prefer you don't spit there – and curb your dog elsewhere" (Ibid.).

In these commentaries, the metaphorical treatment of 'stepping over' is a way to diminish Canadian personalities. This subordination is comparable with descriptions of CWOF in Claire Bickley's report. Her *Toronto Sun* article "Legends Get Star Treatment" cites CWOF inductee Donald Sutherland: "I am thrilled and honoured. I want to warn you that it's real bad luck if you step on [the star]" (Bickley, 2000). Although the 'warning' in the second sentence can be seen as a light-hearted comment, it demonstrates a lack of confidence in its expectation of behaviour that subordinates. This leads Sutherland to pre-emptively call for respect. Bickley restates the second sentence in a bold and enlarged text box and emphasises the 'bad luck' that comes from treading on stars. By using this literary device, Bickley supports existing national discourses through which Canadian personalities are subordinated.

The subordination of Canadian talent within national discourses of an inferiority complex is further reflected in the acceptance speech of inductee Kim Cattrall. Cattrall is well known for her role in the American television and film production *Sex and the City*, but she was raised in Canada. At the 11th annual gala of CWOF, Cattrall stated that, "I would also like to thank Samantha Jones, honouring not so much for the Walk of Fame but the Walk of Shame" (*2009 Tribute Show*, 2009). The reference to CWOF as a

Walk of Shame is an expression of embarrassment for the inferior quality of Canadian talent. In *The National Post*, art critic Robert Fulford writes about CWOF inductee Kenny Gardner using words like 'shameful,' 'embarrassing,' and 'infamous stars' (2002). This embarrassment also characterises his negative representations of Canadians who are inducted into CWOF. For example, Fulford writes that, "Canada needs a Walk of Shame to recognise our infamous stars" (2002). For him, Canadian stars with an international reputation have "seriously contributed to the degradation of an art or craft" (Ibid.). These representations suppress fame and collectively support national discourses of an 'inferiority complex' in Canada.

Other media representations subordinate Canadian fame through regional discrimination within the nation. In a *Toronto Sun* newspaper report, journalist Kieran Grant does not focus on talent in CWOF but instead indicates how a CWOF star was subordinated on grounds of being French-Canadian. He illustrates this region-based national identity in relation to French-Canadian inductee Maurice Richard. In his acceptance speech for the CWOF award, Grant writes, Richard "pointed out jokingly that, in his early days as a top-scoring Montreal Canadiens great, Toronto crowds used to boo his appearances" (1999, p. 77). Grant selectively focuses on the regional expression of Richard's speech. In doing so, Grant emphasises the bilingual makeup of the Canadian nation and the presence of French Canada that is otherwise, as Michelle Byers points out, not present in the English-dominant productions (2008, p. 71). In this way, readers in the French province of Quebec are able to identify with the regional character of the national meta-discourse of Canada in CWOF practices of fame. At the same time, Richard articulates his expression within existing Canadian discourses that support an 'inferiority complex' exemplified by the domination of French-Canadians by English Canadians in Toronto. Through regional subordination, the report contributes to a cultural understanding of how Canadians are not adequate in terms of dominant practices of fame. It thus creates a national difference in contrast to America while supporting an English Canadian conception of the nation.

In some media reports, the myth of inferiority is expressed through the interrogation of CWOF inductees' achieved status. The interrogation reinforces an absence of recognition that actually limits inductees' achievements. CWOF organisers and media often raise rhetorical questions like 'Who?' 'What?' and 'Why?' that support the limitation in media reports. For example, in describing the progress and success of CWOF, founding director Peter Soumalias ironically emphasises that, "We got a lot of, 'Who? What? Why?'" (Harris, 2008). Soumalias' questions relate to the past but they abruptly suspend narratives celebrating CWOF inductees in the present. A *Marquee* magazine article contains this interrogation of achieved success, wherein CWOF inductees are associated with the rhetorical questions "Who?" "What?" and "Why?" (Gardner, 2000). The interrogation also surfaces in the following *Toronto Star* news report on CWOF:

> The Canadian Walk of Fame is an object of quite genuine pride. Most days it's Toronto's citizens and Canadian out-of-towners who step their way respectfully around the names of people they know and admire, even as the tourists, more often than they should, ponder too loudly, "Who's that?" (Quill, 2000, p. A30).

In this report, arts writer Greg Quill establishes CWOF as a cultural site of pride. But at the same time, he undermines its recognition by assuming that tourists would question 'Who's that?' This uncertainty reflects an 'inferiority complex' in which Canadians believe that their stars will not be recognised by visitors; that their stars have not achieved international recognition.

In order to understand how these rhetorical questions figure in CWOF and media discourses, it is useful to draw on what scholar Charles Taylor (1997) calls the 'politics of recognition' in Canadian history and literature. For Taylor, an urgent need for identity, often designated by questions of 'who we are,' is usually linked to recognition of self or its absence in others. Taylor contends that if recognition comes out of urgency or need, as in the Canadian myth of identity crisis, it does not assure equal dignity and respect. Thus, collective questions like 'who are we?' dismiss rather than affirm identity. Although Taylor's work mostly focuses on minority groups in Canada, his proposition can be applied to collective practices of CWOF and media reports that interrogate, rather than celebrate the achieved status of individual stars by questioning 'Who?' 'What?' and 'Why?' These rhetorical questions presuppose a lack of recognition and acceptance of CWOF inductees as an effect of the myth of inferiority, and they mediate Canadian talent as a political expression of Canada. Media discourses then conflate national identity with star recognition, undermining both.

The 'inferiority complex' around CWOF inductees is also expressed by imagining their unconventional practices. These practices are unconventional in the sense that they do not meet dominant standards of fame in America. In some media reports, the personality traits of CWOF inductees are described in ways that are unusual and do not meet conventional star behaviours. This unconventional description is another way of expressing the 'anti-fame' that resists dominant practices of American celebrity culture and instead celebrates the Canadian nation. In a *Toronto Star* (2000) report, television critic Rob Salem subverts dominant expressions of fame in his interview with actor Martin Short. Salem asks

Short about growing up in Hamilton. Short replies, "Canada is just a very nurturing place and accepting of great diversity, and it inspires you to feel less like a freak within your own skin. Eccentricity is allowed" (Salem, 2000, p. C4). While Salem expresses Short's eccentricity, arts writer Greg Quill speaks of the awkwardness of CWOF stars: "Most people feared the worst, that the Walk of Fame would celebrate fleeting celebrities [...] And though the stars did, for the most part, show up – albeit humbly and awkwardly [...]" (Quill, 2000). *Toronto Star* reporter William Orme points out the awkwardness in a patronising headline as well: "Aww, your own Walk of Fame. How Quaint" (2002, p. J4). These expressions support a national myth of inferiority whereby celebrating Canadian talent is not an expected behaviour that can meet American standards of fame. Thus, CWOF practices of fame establish a national difference from the US.

CWOF as National Pride and Heritage

While CWOF is associated with a myth of inferiority, it is, ironically, also imagined as a site of national pride and heritage. CWOF inducts and celebrates stars that are already famous — mostly in Hollywood — as opposed to celebrating Canadian achievements (Doyle, 2011). There are various ways of expressing national pride through celebrating CWOF stars. For example, as a commemorative site, the CWOF organisation works in partnership with the Federal Government of Canada, the Provincial Government of Ontario, and the City of Toronto. The Federal Heritage Department supports CWOF practices in a way that constructs and celebrates Canadian cultural tradition. In establishing CWOF as a national heritage site, official statements at the federal and municipal level often imagine inductees as national heroes, as well as agents of legendary pride. Former Canadian Heritage Minister Sheila Copps and former Toronto City Mayor Mel Lastman, for example, rhetorically express the heroism of CWOF inductees. Minister Copps believes that CWOF offers a "new chance to share Canadian heroes" (Grant, 1999, p. 77). Similarly, Lastman refers to CWOF inductees Donald Sutherland and Neil Young as Canada's "two great ambassadors" (Bickley, 2000). These statements form official expressions of CWOF as a site of heroism and pride for the Canadian nation.

Another way of expressing national pride in CWOF inductees is through the selective representation of their acceptance speeches and official declarations. In receiving the CWOF star, the following inductee acceptance speeches show how their understanding of achievement and excellence is specific to their national pride:

I just want to say this about Canada. You can take the girl out of Canada, but you can't take Canada out of the girl (Francis Bay cited in Zacharias, 2010).

You can describe me as an actor, as a comedian, but you cannot describe me completely without saying that I am Canadian (Mike Myers cited in "What does it mean to be Canadian," 2010).

Canada is a peaceful, progressive country that has set the stage for the rest of the world and continues to do so. We are a young nation, full of openness and peacefulness and I am so proud to be a part of this country. I will always represent Canada to the best of my ability in a peaceful, compassionate way (Lang, 2011).

In the case of international stars inducted into CWOF, expressions of Canadianness can be perceived as loyalty to Canada or a sense of national belonging. There is a deep sense of repatriation in bringing overseas successes back home. Although the inductees did not receive opportunities to achieve success in Canada (they had to move to Hollywood or other places abroad), they maintain a fierce loyalty to Canada as the origin of their talent. CWOF selects and appropriates the parts of their statements that express Canadianness and routinely reproduces them in their official publications, such as their commemorative magazines, audio-visual presentations, and Internet homepage. The appropriation of original CWOF gala speeches is a rhetorical practice that mediates inductees' public addresses as a live performance that bears witness and testifies to Canadianness. This rhetorical practice is subject to public scrutiny that helps imagine an authentic Canadian national community. CWOF then uses this information to increase public awareness about expatriate Canadians in Hollywood, as well as to authenticate them as Canadians. Otherwise, the Canadian provenance of CWOF inductees goes unnoticed. As a final consequence, this constructed authenticity reclaims those emigrated stars and imagines a stronger Canadian national community in which those Canadians who are more successful abroad than in Canada become a matter of national pride.

Another way in which media express national pride is by frequently labelling CWOF inductees as Canucks. The word 'Canuck' refers to English Canadians and acts as an informal marker of Canadian origin. Research on comic books such as *Captain Canuck* and *Johnny Canuck* shows how the image of the 'Canuck' has been established as a national superhero. Canuck, as a reference to a Canadian hero, articulates a "national identity against that of USA" (Dittmer & Larsen, 2007, p. 741) and displays qualities of tremendous strength, endurance, moral integrity, and restraint. These are mythical traits of Canadianness that cultural institutions discursively use to interpolate Canadian identity and reproduce it via the cultural production of Captain Canuck (Dittmer & Larsen, 2007). Media reports on CWOF engage with these national discourses so that audiences can resonate and identify with the inductees. In these reports, CWOF inductees often figure as Canucks and articulate a sense of national heroism that is morally stronger than that of the US. For example, in news headlines and commentaries, CWOF is labelled as the "Canuck Walk of Fame" (Grant, 1999). Again, inductees are described as having "Canuck roots" (Salem, 2000), are "Stellar Canucks" (Harris, 1998b), and act the role of "Canucks Who Walk the Walk" (Bickley, 2001). Another media report describes CWOF inductees as "Canucks [who] can't seriously expect the bogyman of fame to pass their country by" (Harris, 1998a). These CWOF statements not only imagine inductees as Canadian national heroes but also as holders of meritocratic fame that is morally stronger than that of America.

In other CWOF and media productions, expatriate Canadian stars are represented in association with Canada as their 'home' and 'family' (Lypchuck, 2002; *Star Struck*, 2002). For example, in the CWOF 11th anniversary audio-visual presentation, inductee Shania Twain states that, "Canada is my home – I am a Canadian through and through" ("The Canada Honours," 2009). Similarly, *The Toronto Sun* interprets the CWOF induction of Donald Sutherland and Neil Young as "legends" in the Canadian "homeland" (Harris, 2008). Both Canadian stars immigrated to the USA and have been famous for their work there since the 1960s. The rhetorical expression of Canada as their 'homeland' helps to reclaim their national identity. The rhetorical function of 'home' and 'family' in CWOF media events can be understood using the theoretical perspectives of scholars Rudolf De Cillia (1999), Martin Reisigl, (1999), Ruth Wodak, (1999), and Erin Manning (2003). In general, words such as 'home' and 'family' are linguistic devices that draw on notions of familiarity and intimacy. In doing so, these devices play a role in the discursive construction of the 'sameness' of national identities (Cillia, et al., 1999). The function of the word 'home,' for example, is an expression of the nation that Erin Manning studies in her work. Manning sheds light on how the Canadian nation is imagined as 'home.' In this respect, the word 'home' often functions at a connotative level of meaning that signifies belonging to a domestic and private space. The homogenous notion of what it means 'to be at home' naturalises and normalises a cohesive discourse of national identity and, in the process, stabilises national territories that are otherwise unstable (Manning, 2003). In these national discourses, CWOF figures as a site that produces rhetorical expressions of 'home' to reclaim the Canadian identity of Hollywood stars.

In expressing Canadian national heritage and pride, CWOF practices and media representations also intersect with official and iconic representations that symbolise the Canadian nation, especially the strength of the Northern frontier. In media reports, CWOF stars are invariably represented along with national symbols such as the federal mounted police force, or 'Mounties,' the maple leaf, and the Canadian national flag. The iconography of these selected symbols represents the Canadian nation and evokes images of the strong Northern frontier (Edwardson, 2008; Osborne, 2006). In both its annual gala and in cultural artefacts such as vignette presentations and commemorative audio-visual presentations, the CWOF appropriates the image of Mounties in the Great White North. In CWOF representations, inductees are escorted by, and photographed with, one or more Mounties. The significance of posing with Mounties is so high that, at times, there are more Mounties than stars.

Media representations of Mounties at CWOF restore an imagined Northern frontier experience by invoking a mythical sense of social order and control that historically emerged from the Northern frontier. This myth harkens back to the beginning of Canadian Confederation, when Mounties kept peace and order in the North-West Territories. Today, this myth is reproduced in CWOF media reports such as "Mounties [are] armed with nothing but smiles" (Farquharson, 2005). Here, the word 'armed' signals the ability to keep peace and control while negotiating tensions with 'smiles' that signify Canadian attributes of friendliness and politeness. The Mounties are often positioned alongside motorcycle police officers, symbolising the maintenance of a social order (Quill, 2000). This symbolism is emphasised in another media report on CWOF: "Four Mounties, two in full-dress uniform, guarded the celebrities' podium while troubadour John McDermott sang the national anthem" (Quill, 1998). In the Canadian national anthem, the epigraph "we stand on guard for thee" follows the line "The True North strong and free." Here, the act of 'guarding,' as mentioned in Chapter 3, invokes Canadian images of the Northern frontier that Mounties historically guarded and controlled. Scholar Renisa Mawani argues that this epigraph from the anthem suggests that, in Canada, "nature, alongside law and liberty, are key cultural signifiers of a national distinctiveness [...]" (2007, p. 716). Positioning Mounties to guard the podium during CWOF ceremonies invokes the symbolic guarding of a strong, free, and sovereign northern frontier.

The symbolic representation of Mounties and of the 'True White North' is also illustrated at the 11th CWOF annual gala. As seen in their audio-visual presentation, CWOF celebrates the induction of fashion duo Dean and Dan Caten, who created the international clothing label DSquared2. Before presenting the induction award to the Caten brothers, the CWOF gala displays a vignette highlighting their fashion shows and designs. In the fashion shows, Mounties and models wear fur, symbolising 'fur trade colonialism' (Cavanagh, 2009) in an imagined frontier whereby selected animals have been cruelly exploited for nation-building. These fur-wearing models, guarded by the Mounties, are presented with a recurring background song: "Take out to the Great White North. Take out: it's a beauty way to go!" (*2009 Tribute Show*, 2009). CWOF understands the celebrity status and success of the Caten brothers in relation to the exploitative power of Canada's Northern frontier. Here, success does not necessarily mean the achievement of their talent so much as the conquest, achievement, and maintenance of the nation through the frontier experiences of Mounties in the Great White North. The presence of the Mounties is important for Canada and its Walk of Fame as a symbol of 'authority' in celebration of talent. Here, the talent and success of individuals are culturally projected onto, and appropriated by, the Canadian nation as a whole. This appropriation is required to repatriate a national feeling diminished by individual stars who often immigrate to the US and abroad to achieve success.

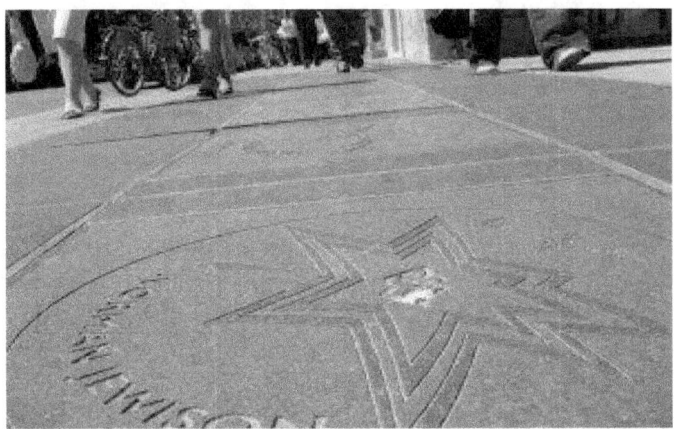

Figure 5: Stylised Maple Leaf Star for Inductee Norman Jewison
(Source: Samita Nandy)

In addition to using Mounties in induction ceremonies and vignette presentations, CWOF and media reports also employ the national emblem of the maple leaf. The use of this emblem symbolises the Canadian nation and the Northern nature of its frontier. Since its inauguration, the CWOF sidewalk embeds the names of inductees with marble and granite stars that are 'stylised maple leaves.' As seen in my photographs (Figures 5 and 6), these stylised maple leaves in the CWOF sidewalk are rendered as stars. These maple leaves/stars reinforce a collective memory that authenticates a relationship between the Canadian nation and nature on the one hand, and a

Hollywood-inspired notion of stardom on the other. This constructed authenticity of the Canadian nation, juxtaposed with a symbol of American cultural hegemony, signifies the complex and often contradictory relation between Canada and the US. Yet these symbolic representations are important to the process of re-appropriating Canadian stars who have become famous for their work in the US and who may not be recognised as Canadians.

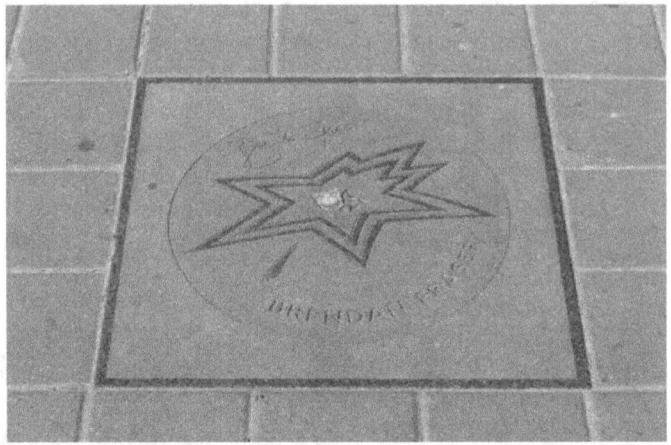

Figure 6: Stylised Maple Leaf Star for Inductee Brendan Fraser
(Source: Samita Nandy)

In other instances, the maple leaf is represented in the extensive use of the Canadian flag during CWOF induction ceremonies. In light of these representations, a *Globe and Mail* news article once raised and addressed the question: "the best symbol for Canadian-born talent? A maple leaf, of course" ("Maple Leaf: A touch of home," 1999). Similarly, a *Toronto Star* report opens with the line, "Canadian stars keep track of the Leafs as names are unveiled" (Gordon, 2002). These media statements on the maple leaf, along with CWOF practices, play a role in mediating Canadian talent as a construction of the nation. In popular references, the maple leaf authenticates the Canadian nation, its vast frontier, and harsh climate upon which it was founded. As discussed in Chapter 3, the official symbol of the red maple leaf conjures up images of changing maple tree colours in seasonal cycles that are specific to the arrival of winter. The symbol of the maple leaf particularly signifies the cold, Northern climate that historically challenged and stimulated the socio-economic prosperity of Canada. In this collective act of remembrance, the use of the maple leaf, as an embedded star in the CWOF sidewalk, shifts from its state of nature to an 'invented tradition' of Canadian nationalism. As an invented tradition, the maple leaf becomes an element of nature that plays a role in the cultural maintenance of the Northern frontier on which the Canadian nation was built.

For the CWOF, cold weather also plays a national role in imagining Canadian stars and representing Canadian fame. In general, news headlines about CWOF emphasise the importance of winter weather with the appropriate expressions: 'True North,' 'northern climate,' 'mountain,' 'wind,' and 'Mother Nature' (Crossingham, 2009; Farquharson, 2004; Hutsel, 2002; Staff, 1999a). These expressions help to imagine Canadian stars in the context of rugged and harsh Northern frontier conditions. In the context of an imagined frontier, the opening line of a CWOF chapter is significant. The chapter connects inductee Howie Mandel to winter: "You can take the boy out of Toronto but you can't take the Toronto winter out of the boy" (Rumack, 2009, p. 61). Mandel then wonders if he is responsible for "shovelling the snow" (Ibid.) off of his or somebody else's star. Only after establishing Mandel's relationship with snow does CWOF describe his induction and talent in the entertainment industry.

As seen in the above examples, both CWOF productions and media reports routinely use meteorological elements such as snow, ice, and cold to represent inducted stars. In this context, weather is a cultural expression of an imagined frontier. Although winter in Toronto lasts for approximately four months, CWOF inductees are often imagined in Northern conditions of cold climate throughout the year even when it is not winter. For Peter Soumalias, one of the pragmatic issues of Canadian winter is that when it snows, the CWOF sidewalk and embedded stars cannot be seen (Evans, 2006). This occultation of stars by snow on the sidewalk is reminiscent of the subordinate representations discussed in the previous section. Symbolically, by emphasising and normalising the cold weather and snow as Canadian attributes, the seasonal disappearance of stars is re-claimed by CWOF as a standard aspect of Canadianness, as represented in those stars. The physical reality of snow is further transferred to the symbolism of what it means to be year-round Canadian. In CWOF reports celebrating stars, there are statements that elaborate elements of Canadian winter but are unrelated to expressions of talent. Drawing on the work of scholar Jody Berland (1994), ethnometeorological studies on Canadian weather shed light on how representations of Canadian climatic conditions are not natural. The media representations of cold weather are, in fact, cultural constructs that mediate national identity in a way that mythically represents the endurance and strength of an imagined frontier. The CWOF sidewalk represents the Canadian frontiers, Northern or Southern, where extreme weather conditions both challenge and empower Canadians to claim the territorial space of their nation. In the CWOF sidewalk, it is the 'human will' and the tolerance for harsh Northern seasonal changes that inducted stars endure in a heroic manner.

CWOF inductees do not simply symbolise talent and achievement: they also symbolise national heroism in Canadian frontier conditions. The heroic strength of CWOF stars is often imagined in relation to America's Hollywood through Canadian weather. The following media representation compares 'Hollywood-Canadian' inductee Michael J. Fox with other CWOF inductees through cultural constructs of weather:

> Unlike its Hollywood counterpart, Canada's Walk of Fame is subjected to everything that our northern climate has to offer. Michael J. Fox – inducted in 2000 – probably thought he'd seen the last of our winters but, if anything, it seems to have snowed a little harder on his plaque. Today there's some dirty slush on Neil Young, and perhaps metaphorically, a patch of ice on snowbird Anne Murray (Hutsel, 2002).

In the above anecdote, expatriate Canadian star Michael J. Fox is imagined as receiving 'harder' snow than resident Canadian celebrities such as Neil Young and Anne Murray (Hutsel, 2002). Michael J. Fox is not only a Hollywood icon, but also a Canadian who is imagined to have overcome the harsh Northern winter. In contrast, resident celebrities receive "some dirty slush" or a "patch of ice" (Ibid.). In this representation, the Canadian fame of Michael J. Fox can be read in two complementary ways. First, his stardom is evidence of his talent and achievements not only in Canada but also in globally known Hollywood. Second, his Canadian origins imbue him with the strength of an imagined frontier experience that his Hollywood counterparts lack. CWOF inductees that have 'made it' in Hollywood can then be awarded both the status of true international stars and the qualities of a stronger frontier. This attribution is useful to amplify the impact of Canada's perceptions of itself and in constructing a strong national identity.

In expressing conditions of an imagined frontier, CWOF articulates a 'moral soul' that is better and stronger than that of American stars. With CWOF, Marissa Soumalias asserts, there is a strong emphasis on Canadian stars being kind, humble, down-to-earth, and friendly (Nandy, 2011a). Along with politeness, these are traditional symbolic characteristics attributed to Canadians. The imagination of these personal traits is an expression of moral consciousness in Canadian identity. This Canadian strength of a moral 'soul' is understood in a binary relationship with America, as discussed in Chapters 3 and 4. As Amelia Kalant observes, "Canada does have a soul: if Americanness can be said to be about excelling or success, Canadianness is about being good and moral" (2004, p. 34). Arts writer Greg Quill shares this belief in his newspaper report and imagines CWOF stars having a 'down-to-earth charm,' 'politeness,' and 'humility' (2000). In contrast to strengths in Canadians, the "gasping celebrity worship" in America is a cultural practice that Canadians "seem to abhor" and "fear the worst" (Ibid.). In undermining the Hollywood Walk of Fame, CWOF displays moral superiority.

In his media report, film critic Geoff Pevere also imagines CWOF within existing national discourses of Canadian moral superiority:

> The walk of fame [CWOF] is that rare example of a successful American pop cultural concept that did not instantly blow northward. Perhaps this is due to the northern puritanical temperament, which mistrusts any form of fame that is not earned in winter on skates, but the fact is the walk of fame had to take the same route into Canada as that taken by draft-dodgers and fugitives [...] (Pevere, 1999).

Pevere situates CWOF in Northern discourses of Canada and imagines that its deferred achievement in fame is a particular result of the superior Canadian puritanical or moral standards of the North (1999). In this discursive framework, the CWOF values of endurance do not trust practices of instant fame in America. Instead, CWOF calls for an authentic kind of fame that can endure and tolerate challenges to achievements. The value of authenticity is particularly grounded in the ability to overcome the harshness of the Northern frontier. From this point of view, CWOF stars are stronger, more heroic, and more resilient than Hollywood stars.

CWOF's treatment of inductees also shows an emphasis on Canadian values such as a sense of humour in addition to a tolerance for cold weather. A 2009 CWOF commemorative magazine article illustrates how Canadian stars are celebrated for their strength and humour. The magazine opens with the headline, "True North, Strong, and Funny: Canada's Legacy as the World's Preeminent Nation of Comedy" (Crossingham, 2009). This article imagines the strength of CWOF inductees on two levels. First, as the headline suggests, the true and strong characters of CWOF inductees resonate with the imagined frontier experience of the North, which is recouped into the struggles of Canadians that find success in Hollywood's Wild West frontier. In the article, a half-page photograph of a polar bear with a microphone symbolises Canadian stars in an imagined Northern frontier. The headline and the photograph help to imagine harsh Arctic conditions where CWOF inductees — like polar bears — must survive. These Northern conditions are further associated with inductee Howie Mandel, as mentioned earlier. Although Mandel is now based in the US, the article helps to reclaim Mandel's Canadian identity by arguing that he can be taken out of Toronto, but that the Toronto winter cannot be taken out of him (Rumack, 2009). Scholar William Katerberg elaborates on these representations of CWOF inductees in cold conditions. As discussed in Chapter 3, the harsh Northern winter conditions make the Canadian frontier experience stronger than that of the America's Wild West (Katerberg, 2003). The North plays a mythical role in building a physically and morally better race in Canada when compared to its southern counterpart, thus imagining a positive Canadian national identity.

Second, CWOF stars are imagined as 'funny' in that humour is a comic relief and survival strategy to resist American dominance. The CWOF website emphasises the number of comedians inducted and asks, "What makes Canadians so funny?" (CWOF, 2011). For CWOF, being funny is a national attribute of Canadians. Given the myth of the 'Great White North,' CWOF inductees are imagined to bear endurance against harsh conditions, including the American dominance that they resist with humour and comic relief:

> We're still making the Americans laugh. But what are they actually laughing at? There is something bothersome about being a nation of comedy – it sort of puts us in our place. After all, what victim of childhood bullying has forgotten that the secret of survival usually revolves around being able to make the bullies laugh? [...] It's our demure and considerate exterior that gives us such prized access – we're only allowed passage into the guarded inner sanctum of Americanism because no one actually considers us a threat of any kind (Crossingham, 2009).

Here, the word 'bullying' refers to America's dominant cultural and economic practices. In light of these practices, the induction of Canadian comedians such as Mike Myers, Jim Carrey, Seth Rogen, Will Arnett, and Russell Peters can be understood as more than just a recognition of their achievements and talents: it is also a recognition of their Canadian attributes. For example, Russell Peters is known for a number of stand-up comedies where he uses irony to point out what it means to be Canadian and what the Canadian accent sounds like. Peters was not inducted for his comedic talent alone, but also for ability to perform Canadianness via his ironic, ambivalent, and funny observations.

The CWOF celebrates inductees for their talent and for their Canadian values. These values are central to the construction of national pride and heritage because they represent moral superiority and operate within an existing discourse that supports the superiority of the Canadian Northern frontier over that of the American Wild West. The CWOF therefore imagines inductees as better, stronger, and morally above their Hollywood counterparts.

Strong Frontier / Inferiority Complex

The CWOF invokes competing discourses of a strong Northern frontier and of an inferiority complex. Both discourses act as a national resistance to Hollywood and the American Wild West in a contradictory way. Canada's frontier experiences created the conditions for what scholar Amelia Kalant calls 'moral superiority' over America. This 'moral superiority' contradicts the supposed 'inferiority complex' in Canadian representations of CWOF stars. Claire Bickley expresses this complexity in her *Toronto Sun* news article, "Legends Get Star Treatment." Bickley observes that the 3rd CWOF annual event had a stage that was "flanked by Canadian flags and Mounties" and onlookers singing the *South Park* song "Blame Canada" (2000, p. 55). Although the invocation of 'Blame Canada' might be a mere imaginary construction, it conjures up the inferiority complex associated with CWOF inductees. At the same time, the maple leaf in the Canadian flag and the Mounties symbolise a strong Northern frontier. The strong Northern frontier/moral superiority thus collide with the inferiority complex to resist Hollywood stardom from which, ironically, the CWOF emerged.

Classical notions of stardom in the US are rooted in the American Dream, an expression of the Wild West frontier (Guilbert, 2002; Rothman, 2004). CWOF inductees, represented by symbols of the Canadian North, challenge Hollywood stars that emerge out of the ideology of the American Wild West. This challenge is metaphorically illustrated when CWOF inductees not only receive a star on the Hollywood Walk of Fame, but also a stylised maple leaf on the CWOF sidewalk. The stylised maple leaf symbolises the strength of the Northern frontier that challenges that of the Wild West. In light of this symbolic strength, media represent CWOF stars as receiving a recognition that "means a lot more" (Staff, 1999b) and facilitates "twice the traffic," (Quill, 1998) since they have received a walk of fame star in both Canada and in America.

The mythical representation of an inferiority complex in CWOF inductees contradicts and resists the American Dream and Hollywood stardom in two ways. First, the CWOF invokes national discourses that draw on the Canadian ideology of an inferiority complex. In this mythical perspective, Canadians are humble and reserved compared to the bellicosity of Americans who proudly celebrate their star status. Second, CWOF inductees are presented in a low-key manner that resists the glamorous notion of American fame. As discussed earlier, low-key representations of the CWOF as 'humble' and 'awkward' contrast with American 'fleeting celebrities' that Canadians downright fear (Quill, 2000). The low-key personality traits of Canadian stars constitute 'fear' and 'abhorrence,' and they are direct responses to American cultural practices. The contrasting of low-key Canadian personality traits against America's embracing of fame, in turn, imagines resistance to, and a distinction from, American nationalism. These inferior personality traits negate American cultural monopolies by forging a distinctly Canadian identity. Thus, the 'inferiority complex' is not about actual inferiority; rather, it is a tool through which Canadians position themselves as superior to Americans.

Although the CWOF and Canadian media construct fame in a negative manner, this construction is not necessarily defamatory because they consider 'anti-fame' to be a distinct form of popularity that contrasts with the American celebratory approach to fame. The notions of anti-fame and inferior personality traits are a mechanism through which the CWOF displays its greatness in resistance to its origin in the Hollywood Walk of Fame. This kind of resistance to the American notion of fame, in turn, undermines the American Dream and limits US domination of Canadian popular culture.

The irony in CWOF stardom is threefold: First, despite engaging in the Canadian 'inferiority complex,' the CWOF celebrates a multitude of stars that demonstrate superior Canadian talent. Second, although the CWOF attempts to subvert the American notion of fame, it largely celebrates the talent and fame achieved by Canadians who immigrated to the US. This celebration leads to the third irony: although the CWOF claims to celebrate Canadian achievements, as opposed to fame, it nonetheless inducts and celebrates famous stars. The celebration of stars, therefore, contradicts the Canadian 'inferiority complex' and embraces the very notion of American fame that the CWOF claims to reject. Scholars Imogen Tyler and Bruce Bennett (2010) argue that paradoxical relations of superiority/inferiority, normality/abnormality, and judgment/shame are central to celebrity cultures. The ordinary weakness brought forward by an 'inferiority complex' is one of the major myths that work as a paradox with extraordinary achievements in Canada. It thereby creates appeal in relation to sometimes subordinated, or even occulted, Canadian stars that the CWOF otherwise celebrates. What Tyler and Bennett identify as a complex set of contrasts also reflects ambivalent ideas about the Canadian nation. Moreover, the use of words such as 'inductees,' 'honourees,' and 'talent' instead of stars helps to negotiate the tensions inherent in Canadian national ambivalence.

Conclusion

The chapter started with an overview of how a nation's walk of fame can act as a commemorative site that celebrates national public memory. Drawing on existing literature and practices of the Hollywood Walk of Fame, this chapter showed how the CWOF situates itself in multiple, intersecting discourses of the Canadian nation that simultaneously overlap, conflict, and contradict. In representations of CWOF celebrities, there is no singular true or authentic notion of Canadian national identity. Instead, CWOF practices present a layered and ambivalent construction of Canadian nationhood in which legendary pride paradoxically affirms a threatened national identity. The ambivalence of Canadian national identity is expressed through ironies of fame in the CWOF. These ironies subvert Hollywood Walk of Fame notions of stardom and interrogate CWOF inductees' fame in relation to a Canadian inferiority complex. Nevertheless, CWOF inductees demonstrate superior talent that is emphasised via rhetorical expressions of a stronger Northern frontier, even though this talent is cultivated in the US. These practices reflect the existing ideology of an ambivalence in Canadian identity. The CWOF manages the ideology by constructing stars in a context that reclaims a Canadian national pride that is otherwise hidden in mythical representations of the inferiority complex. This chapter demonstrated the irony of Canadian national identity in relation to fame through a set of three interrelated national myths: an inferiority complex, the superiority of the Northern frontier, and the 'Othering' of the US through Canadian national myths that subvert or undermine America's dominating power.

In doing so, the CWOF embraces traditional practices of fame but also questions those practices with frequent usage of words like inductees, honour, success, and achievement instead of the classical terms 'stars' or 'celebrities.' The simultaneous destabilisation and strengthening of the Canadian meaning of fame reflect the national context in which it is produced and mediated. These challenges to traditional understandings of fame employ contradictory myths with regard to Canadian national achievements. These myths both reject and embrace stars, and, by extension, they contribute to a discourse that simultaneously postulates an ambivalent national identity regarding Canadian fame and mitigates the tensions inherent in Canada's national identity crisis.

This chapter also contributed to popular understandings of contemporary notions of Canadian heroes and stars. While existing literature mostly speaks of the absence of stars in light of the Canadian inferiority complex, this absence nonetheless resonates with popular representations of CWOF. These representations indicate how Canada cannot match the global appeal of a Hollywood entertainment industry that sells the frontier ideology of the American Dream. This is not to say that Canadians do not embrace American stars and entertainment productions: on the contrary, they do. When it comes to the 'fame and fortune' of their own stars, however, Canadians display a mythical inferiority complex and a humility that reflects their country's subservience to American cultural practices. These myths often prevent Canadians from honouring their own heroes. At the same time, Canadian stars who have achieved fame in the US are represented as better than their American and other Canadian counterparts. The CWOF and media illustrate Canada as a strong Northern frontier, thereby contributing to a representation of Canadian stars as superior to American celebrities. Indeed, Canadian stars are more than stars: they are legendary national heroes. These complex practices interact to construct a multi-faceted and ambivalent Canadian nationality.

The next chapter continues to explore Canadian national identity by studying how reality TV shows construct and represent celebrities. It sheds light on how these shows engage in national discourses through practices of fame. In particular, the next chapter will explain how Canadian national identity is expressed through cultural understandings of fame by employing questions of authenticity in regionalism and American/local production of celebrities. The ordinary and authentic character of celebrities demonstrates the unique ways in which national identity is constructed in Canada.

7 Celebrities in Canadian Reality TV Shows

Canadian reality TV programs are often associated with symbolic expressions of different kinds of fame. These expressions are variably found in settings, format, and narrations in relation to celebrity hosts and contestants in the TV shows and their media representations. In Canada, reality TV programs offer different opportunities to construct national identity through fame. Often, these shows help to construct Canadian celebrities through narratives associated with national myths such as those around ice and technology in an imagined Northern frontier. Other shows appropriate various Canadian markers that articulate national identity in regionalised/localised ways. In both cases, the aim is to resist American cultural domination.

In the next section, I introduce Canadian homegrown and franchised television shows. In the following sections, I examine the ways in which each reality TV show constructs and represents the fame of hosts and contestants. In exploring their fame, I focus on Canadian expressions that celebrate both talent and the nation. Although these contrasts are central to any kind of fame, reality TV shows emphasise them to a greater degree. These contrasts, in turn, help to authenticate the Canadian national context in which fame is constructed.

Canadian Reality TV Programs

There are two kinds of reality TV programs in Canada: homegrown and franchised. *Battle of the Blades* and *The Greatest Canadian* are examples of homegrown programs, in the sense that they are an original concept produced and distributed by Canadian public or private media companies.

Other reality TV shows, such as *Canadian Idol* and *So You Can Dance Canada*, are franchises of foreign shows. *Battle of the Blades* will be studied here as representative of Canadian homegrown reality TV programs. The program features ice hockey, Canada's national game and most popular sport overall. It features eight National Hockey League (NHL) male hockey players paired with eight female figure skaters. The pairs perform figure skating routines and viewers vote to select the best. The bottom two pairs return the following night, and a panel of four judges eliminates one pair. The final cash prize of $100,000 is donated to a charity of the winners' choice.

The format of *Battle of the Blades* resembles that of international reality TV shows such as *Dancing with the Stars* and the UK-based *Dancing on Ice* (Strachan, 2010). However, the content of *Battle of the Blades* is specific to Canadian production and cultural contexts. The CBC, Canada's public television service, created and produced the program. Since its premiere in 2009, the show was hosted by Toronto's historic Maple Leaf Gardens, a famous ice hockey arena. The show featured ice hockey players that are national stars in Canada. With an initial viewership of two million, *Battle of the Blades* was one of the CBC's most successful shows. The show became so popular that its executive producer Kevin Albrecht, received calls from US, Russia, and Czech Republic producers who wanted to 'copy' the idea of the show (Elash, 2009). In fact, John Brunton, another executive producer of *Battle of the Blades*, confirmed that the show was accepted in "Sweden after inking its first deal to bring the Canadian format overseas" (Szklarski, 2010). This deal marks a significant shift from the past, when Canadian producers had to import American and other foreign shows.

Compared to homegrown reality TV shows, franchised shows construct Canadian identity in a way that explicitly highlights national differences with America and other counties. Programs such as *Canadian Idol* and *So You Think You Can Dance Canada* are international co-productions and global franchises that grew out of the UK original show *Pop Idol*. The latter was created in 2001 by Simon Fuller, producer of 19 Entertainment and Fremantle Media (Holmes, 2004). Soon after its creation, the production companies started to offer international licenses to purchase the *Pop Idol* format. Similar formats of reality TV programs such as *Fame Academy* and *Popstars* failed to secure popular viewership. However, when *Pop Idol* judge Simon Cowell pitched the format to US network executives in association with the idea of the 'American Dream,' the franchise was successfully adopted and implemented in the US (Moran, 2010). In 2002, *American Idol: The Search for a Superstar* reached twenty five million viewers (Holmes, 2004). In light of this popularity south of the border, Canada's first reality TV show, *Canadian Idol*, was launched by

CTV in 2003 as an international co-production between Fremantle Media and Toronto's Insight Production. Similarly, *So You Think You Can Dance Canada* is a licensed franchise of the US-based *So You Think You Can Dance,* created by Simon Fuller as a spinoff of *Pop Idol.* Premiering in 2006, *So You Think You Can Dance Canada* was a popular reality TV show that was produced by CTV in association with Danse TV Productions Inc. in Toronto.

Both *Canadian Idol* and *So You Think You Can Dance Canada* were based on global television formats but used local Canadian markers to establish national differences from America. The shows held nation-wide auditions for vocal artists and dance performers, respectively. After the top twenty contestants were selected, weekly shows were held, during which contestants demonstrated different generic styles of performances in front of a panel of judges, hosts, and a studio audience. Viewers across Canada then voted for their favourite contestants by calling or sending SMS messages. Every week, voters and judges eliminated two contestants until the top ten contestants remained, their fate to be decided by the public. The final contestant was voted as Canada's favourite performer and often earned celebrity status. As the following sections will demonstrate, the process by which hosts and contestants of reality TV shows have been constructed as celebrities supports Canadian national discourses.

Battle of the Blades

The setting of *Battle of the Blades* used the ice rink to celebrate talent. In this setting, ice hockey serves a national function by stabilising and normalising the whole of Canada as a frontier. As mentioned in Chapter 3, ice represents Canada as the North in popular culture (Chapeskie, 2001; Grace, 2001; Hulan, 2003; Kalant, 2004; Katerberg, 2003). *Battle of the Blades* celebrated talent in ice hockey whereby the ice rink is a metaphor for the Canadian North, especially its geography and meteorology (Grace, 2001; Howell, 2001; Uher, 2008). It is a symbol of an imagined Northern frontier. In this imagined frontier, frozen conditions, as discussed in Chapter 3, inspire the use of technology to unite the nation. The popular imagination of ice figured in national representations of *Battle of the Blades.* In her media article, Anita Elash describes that *Battle of the Blades* became popular by "putting reality TV on ice" (2009). In the Canadian imagination, *Battle of the Blades'* "popularity may be no surprise, given the amount of ice that forms during long, Canadian winters" (Elash, 2009). Yet, in reality, the winter in southern industrial cities such as Toronto does not last as long as it does in the northern regions. Even when winter does hit Canada's southern industrial cities, it does guarantee snow, and slush is as likely as ice. The mediation of ice in Toronto as a permanent Northern construct stabilises and normalises Canada as a frontier nation.

The ice hockey rink at Maple Leaf Gardens, where *Battle of the Blades* was set, enables these national functions. Conn Smythe built the Maple Leaf Gardens for Toronto's National Hockey League (NHL) Team in 1931. Since the Great Depression, the Maple Leaf Gardens successfully supported ice hockey as a 'national pastime' where 'Leaf' players became icons of the Canadian national consciousness (Cox & Stellick, 2006; Riendeau, 2007). In this historic setting, *Battle of the Blades* evoked cultural memories of Canada — especially that of the North — through the stardom of iconic hosts Rob McLean and Kurt Browning as well as ex-NHL players.

The narratives in *Battle of the Blades* articulated an imagined Northern frontier through the fame of its hosts. Both hosts of *Battle of the Blades* gained success and fame on ice. While Rob McLean is popular for hosting Saturday night ice hockey games on CBC, co-host Kurt Browning is well known as an inductee to Canada's Sports Hall of Fame and Figure Skating Hall of Fame. As the *Battle of the Blades* website promoted, Browning won many national and world championships in figure skating. He is also famous for entertaining audiences in the Canadian tour for *Stars on Ice*, a program dedicated to constructing Canadian ice skaters as stars. In the case of *Battle of the Blades,* promotional material and scripted narratives symbolised ice as an imagined frontier that fosters success and fame.

An opening segment of a *Battle of the Blades* episode illustrated the importance of ice as symbolism. The episode opened with a theme called Country Night. To illustrate this theme, the ice-skating rink was illuminated with shades of orange and green colours, signifying the harvest season in the Prairie region of Canada. Host Rob McLean appeared in the spotlight and started skating in this setting while narrating lyrics of a song: "I am rooted in the Prairie world [...] it is a land I do my dreaming in" (CBC, 2010e). He then focused on an imagined Northern frontier and narrated that its landscapes are a 'mirror of home' whereby the 'open,' 'vast,' 'beautiful,' and 'limitless' land enabled him to 'dream' and achieve success in Canada (CBC, 2010d). McLean's lyrics overlap with dominant Canadian narratives that represent the Northern frontier as an enabler of conquest and success. As discussed in Chapter 3, the Canadian North is a cultural site for imagining strength and endurance against harsh frontier conditions. In *Battle of the Blades*, the ice skating rink (ice being a symbol for nature) was a metaphor for Canada as an authentic, Northern frontier nation.

In romanticising the North, McLean used the expressions 'open' and 'mirror of home' (CBC, 2010d) to signify the Canadian nation, where 'open' and 'home' refer to the Prairies and the North — but not necessarily all places in Canada. This selective accommodation prioritises Canada's frontier regions as opposed to situated experiences in specific locations of the country. As scholar Erin Manning (2003) explains, the use of the word 'home' is a linguistic and spatial device that naturalises exclusionary practices towards various racial, linguistic, and cultural groups in Canada. Manning adds that the word 'open' is a mythical construct that legitimises Canada as a harmless and generous nation that enables success. In this view, McLean stated that the lyrics "could have been written for Kurt Browning," as Browning achieved success and fame on ice as well. *Battle of the Blades* reinforced Northern narratives through the success stories of its hosts, both of whom became famous on ice — the symbol of the Great White North. These narratives not only help to celebrate the fame of hosts and contestants; they also celebrate the Northern frontier as a source of Canadian strength and identity.

Battle of the Blades expressed the fame of its contestants and, in the process, imagined a frontier nation as well. The show reconstructed the fame of ex-NHL stars on ice to reclaim and enable an imaginary Canadian frontier. The narratives and format of *Battle of the Blades* contrasted the ordinary with the extraordinary on ice to help construct this frontier mythology. The title of the show, *Battle of the Blades*, referred to the ordinary struggles of ex-NHL hockey stars who battle the ice armed with metallic skates. The 'behind-the-scenes' format further highlighted this process by exposing the mundane and banal incidents — the trials and hardships — that occurred while the ex-NHL stars practiced their performance on the ice-skating rink. These incidents specifically took place when the hockey players were learning to figure skate. The trials of learning to figure skate stood in opposition to the extraordinariness of their past hockey performances.

The ex-NHL players are already famous for their performance in Canada's national game. Yet, the show attempted to transform hockey players into figure skaters; a process that involves relearning old skills and reclaiming control over the ice. This reclamation is significant in light of the fact that hockey games in urban centres have replaced wilderness conquest as a nation-building process. Thus, the ice-skating rink played a dual function. First, using ex-NHL hockey players on the ice-skating rink celebrated the North as a popular national pastime. Second, the transformation from hockey player to figure skater acted as a new 'skill frontier,' where ex-NHL stars unlearned their existing meritocratic fame and gained technological control over ice using sharp 'battle blades.' Their new fame relies on the paradox of ordinary struggles in figure skating and extraordinary merits in ice hockey. This paradox enables the hockey players' new fame, on which the progress and success of the frontier nation rests.

The stardom of *Battle of the Blades* hosts helps to further undermine and reconstruct the existing fame of ex-NHL stars. For example, before contestants Isabelle Brasseur and Todd Warriner performed in the third week of the second season, host Kurt Browning walked from the backstage to the ice-skating rink and described himself to the audience/fans:

> I am used to this backstage stuff. I am walking towards the ice...maybe there is a camera in my face, doesn't matter – I have been there before. Can you imagine how foreign this must be for all our hockey players?...With their jerseys and helmet you're like the guy beside you, replaced with a weird pair of skates that don't work right...once they pass the curtain – poof – now they are on stage...Spotlight right in your face. That's new. Thousands of eyes staring just at you instead of the team...let's check in with Isabelle and Todd (CBC, 2010d).

Here, Browning highlights ordinariness on two levels. First, he refers to 'backstage stuff' to signify ordinary activities of figure-skater training in the behind-the-scenes portion of the show. Second, he refers to ex-NHL stars as being like the 'guy beside you' and contrasts this ordinariness to being extraordinary in 'spotlight' (CBC, 2010d). Browning's commentary, coming as it does from a famous figure skater, suggests that the paradox between the ordinary and the extraordinary is something with which he is intimately familiar. He is "used to this backstage stuff" with a "camera in [his] face" (CBC, 2010d). However, Browning imagines that this paradox is new for hockey stars, for whom walking from the backstage to the spotlight, a moment that symbolises fame, is "foreign" (CBC, 2010d).

Indeed, fame becomes new for ex-NHL stars who are retrained as figure skaters, and in the process of re-earning this fame, these former hockey stars reconquer an imagined frontier. Otherwise, ex-NHL stars are familiar with the spotlight and camera in the context of their past hockey glories. The image of Browning 'walking towards the ice' is a cultural reminder of an imagined frontier that must be reconquered by hockey players as Canada's national heroes. The imagined frontier can only be reconquered if ex-NHL stars retrain as figure skaters and reconstruct their fame in the process. The ice is thus an imagined frontier to be reclaimed by ex-NHL stars who transform from famous hockey stars into figure skaters, a process through which they discursively construct the progress of the nation and its national pastime all over again.

Media representations of *Battle of the Blades* reconstructed ex-NHL stars' fame within national discourses. The media represented the hockey players experiencing 'blood, sweat, and tears' on ice. For example, a CBC press release claimed that, "The hit series Battle of the Blades is back on CBC Television for another season that promises more drama, blood, sweat, tears" (CBC, 2010b). In a CBC blog, Sandra Bezic, judge and producer of the first season, similarly emphasised that, "[v]iewers will get a glimpse into the blood, sweat and tears that go into the training, beginning with a behind-the-scenes special [...] It's not always pretty tempers flare, injuries occur - and it can get very intense as the competitive juices start to flow" (CBC, 2010a). In the blog, ordinary figure-skater training struggles contrast with the extraordinary merits of hockey players on ice. John Brunton, *Battle of the Blades* executive producer, illustrated this paradox further:

> We didn't show a lot of the blood, sweat and tears last year. We didn't show the injuries that some people were going through or some of the bad accidents. Part of it is that we were really interested in focusing on what was on the ice. But afterward, we thought, what they all went through was unbelievable. I mean, they'd take their skates off and their feet are bleeding. So we are going to see more of that preparation (Mudhar, 2010b).

In media representations, the rhetorical use of the words 'blood, sweat, and tears' can be read in light of scholar Colin Howell's work in *Blood, Sweat and Cheers: Sport and the Making of Modern Canada* (2001). For Howell, the history of 'blood and sweat' constitutes narratives of building the nation through sport. During the industrial development of Canada, Howell contends, urban sports such as hockey became a social technology that gradually replaced rural blood sports involving cruelty to animals. The urban sports unfolded "lines of demarcation" between the "civilised" and the "savage" (Howell, 2001, p. 12) that fascinated Canadians. This demarcation prompted Canadians to strengthen the regularity and efficiency that marked the progress of the nation. This progress involved blood and sweat in struggles to civilise wilderness as it replaced blood sports during the urban development of Canada. Media representations of *Battle of the Blades* used narratives of 'blood, sweat, and tears' that overlap with that of Canadian nation-building history. Blood symbolises the ordinary struggles that built the Canadian nation. In general, the paradox between the ordinariness and extraordinariness of hockey players is central to constructing their fame. As explained in Chapter 1, stars are sustained by 'contrasts' between the ordinary and the extraordinary, epitomised by the performance of 'presence' and 'absence,' e.g., what happens on and off stage (Ellis, 2007; Geraghty, 2007). This paradox enables hockey players' fame, on which the progress and success of the nation rest. The reconstruction of fame through national discourses of 'blood, sweat, and tears' once again subdues an imagined frontier that was lost through industrial practices such as urban sports.

Like the rhetorical use of the words 'blood, sweat, and tears,' media representations of *Battle of the Blades* often used the term 'rookie.' Media representations and narratives of the show referred to ex-NHL hockey stars as 'rookies' who need to achieve meritocratic figure skating skills and "survive Boot Camp" (CBC, 2010a) in figure skating. In these media representations, ex-NHL hockey stars are described as 'rookies' because they are not equipped with skills to cope with the challenges of figure skating. Yet, the Northern image the ice-skating rink acts as a rhetorical tool that transforms them into reality TV stars. Thus, while standard notions of fame are undermined through the use of the word 'rookie,' both harshness and triumph on ice underpin their fame. In media, the rhetorical use of 'rookie' begets ex-NHL stars' reclamation of an imagined 'skill frontier,' thereby strengthening the nation that they represent.

Apart from using ice-laden frontier myths, *Battle of the Blades* constructed national differences between Canadian and international contestants. It localised ex-NHL stars to Canadianise the show's otherwise global format and content. These contrasts locate the stars in a national context with which Canadian audiences can identify. Media representations highlighted this nationalisation of stardom. For example, John Brunton, *Battle of the Blades* executive producer, noted hockey stars' Canadian identity in relation to international stardom:

> We've been approached by some international superstars that really like the project and so we're looking at: Should we consider a star that emerged out of the Olympics on the figure skating surface or a famous international Russian hockey player paired up with a Canadian figure skater? (Szklarski, 2010).

Here, Brunton suggests an international appeal in casting Olympics "superstars" (Szklarski, 2010), but he also emphasises the Canadian identity of homegrown figure skaters by pairing and contrasting them with a Russian hockey star named Valerie Bure. These contrasts in stardom create local differences out of global formats and content and reinforce Canadian national pride.

The creation of national pride through fame is heightened in CBC blogs. For example, a CBC blog stated that, "Bure is no stranger to representing his nation against a strong Canadian team" (CBC, 2010c). Here, Valerie Bure is presented as a foreign obstacle with which ex-NHL, as symbols of Canadian nationalism, must contend. The blog further imagines national tensions between Canadian and Russian hockey stars:

> Battle of the Blades competitors have already been warned: the Russians are coming. And leading the charge is former right-

winger Valerie Bure [...] Valerie is a spy. He's a Russian spy [...] Nobody loves Russians (CBC, 2010c).

Here, Canadian national pride is imagined in relation to a confrontation between Canadian and Russian stars, the latter characterised as hated 'spies.' The Canadian media representation of Russian hockey stars as 'spies' can be interpreted from the perspective of scholar John Soares (2008). In his study, Soares explains how the historical and political context of the Cold War in 1972 served to construct the national identity of Canadian ice hockey players. During the Cold War, Canadian ex-Prime Minister Pierre Trudeau took initiatives to create the 1972 Hockey Summit, whereby hockey players played a role in strengthening international relations between Canada and the Soviet Union (Buckel, 2008).

During this Summit, Canadian identity was articulated through two contrasting practices in relation to national sovereignty. First, Canadian hockey players played a diplomatic role as cultural and educational exchange agents with the Soviet Union. These exchanges were meant to be independent of American foreign policies. From this view, Canadian hockey players distinguished themselves from Americans, thereby helping Canada resist becoming "too Americanised as a nation" (Buckel, 2008, p. 69). Second, Canadian hockey players in the Summit were differentiated from their Russian counterparts on grounds of national ideologies. The style of Russian hockey reflected its communist ideology. While Russian hockey players embraced collective teamwork, the Canadian style of hockey demonstrated individualism. From these ideological perspectives, Russian hockey players lacked the individual talent that is central to a player's stardom ("Sports in the Cold War," 2007). In contrast, Canadian hockey reflected a sense of individualism that is key to both Canadian democratic political ideology and stardom in general. This ideological perspective was so strong that sometimes Canadian hockey players engaged in violence against opponents instead of working together as a team ("Sports in the Cold War," 2007). In this historical and political context, *Battle of the Blades* imagined ideological tensions with famous Russian hockey player Valerie Bure as if he was a 'hated' opponent and 'spy' from the Cold War-period. In doing so, *Battle of the Blades* not only celebrated the individual talent and stardom of hockey players, but also Canadian national ideologies constructed out of global tensions with foreign nations.

Canadian Idol

The program and media treatment of host Ben Mulroney in *Canadian Idol*, the first Canadian franchised reality TV show, helps to understand Canadian stardom in a national context. In *Canadian Idol*, Ben Mulroney's fame was reconstructed despite the fact that he was already well known as the son of ex-Prime Minister Brian Mulroney. Ben Mulroney's stardom not only advocated the celebration of talent but also of the Canadian nation. This occurred on two levels. First, the popularity of Ben Mulroney was reconstructed in association with popular locations in Canada. An opening segment of *Canadian Idol* is significant in this regard. One of the segments of the *Canadian Idol* auditions opened by foregrounding Ben Mulroney in popular locations such as Niagara Falls and the CN Tower, two symbols of the Canadian nation. The Canadian symbols helped to distinguish and privilege Ben Mulroney as a popular figure in relation to auditioning contestants. More importantly, they helped to authenticate Canada by negotiating tensions between nature and technology, as discussed in Chapter 3. While the CN Tower symbolises Canada as a technological nation (Kroker, 1984), Niagara Falls symbolises authenticity in nature, which Canada exploits for technological pursuits. Representations of Niagara Falls mediate nature in a way that legitimises and authenticates technological practices in Canada. These representations privilege both Canadian nationalism as well as Ben Mulroney's role in celebrating Canadian talent.

In this national context, the camera took multiple close-up shots of Ben Mulroney while he ran mundane errands for the preparation of the contestants' auditions. Here, *Canadian Idol* highlighted Mulroney's ordinariness in pre-production stages of the show, as close-up camera shots mediated the exclusivity and intimacy that were central to the extraordinariness of Mulroney's public persona. As Richard Dyer explains, "close-up reveals the unmediated personality of the individual, and this belief in the 'capturing' and the 'unique' 'person' of a performer is probably central to the star phenomenon" (1998, p. 15). In this setting, Mulroney raised a question regarding his authenticity. While running his mundane errands, he faced the camera and directly asked, "OK so do you want to get to know the real me?"(CTV, 2008a). At this moment, a song started to play in the background with the lyrics "you can be the hero" (CTV, 2008a). In a national context, the narrative of the song authenticated Mulroney's fame as a performance of Canadian heroism.

An intertextual reading of a media interview further addresses Ben Mulroney's question with regards to authenticity and legitimises his fame as a Canadian hero. In the interview, Mulroney claims:

> The perfect host for *Idol* should be slightly more interesting than vanilla . . . Fashionable, but not like he's trying to upstage anyone. Funny, but not necessarily a comedian. Confident, but not necessarily cocky. He should be like a good child: speak when spoken to and recognise his place in the family. This show is first

and foremost about the singers, and then about the judges, and maybe if we're lucky after that, and we have time, it should be about the host (Baltruschat, 2009, p. 43).

Here, Mulroney indicates paradoxes that are central to his fame and national status. First, Mulroney claims that *Canadian Idol* is primarily about singers while the host is secondary. The irony is that Ben Mulroney is a host who is already extraordinary as a national icon. As a host, he starts both the auditions and the semi-final shows where his unique personality sets him apart from the ordinary contestants. At the same time, Mulroney is represented in ordinary ways such as being a "good child" and part of a "family" (Baltruschat, 2009, p. 49). The paradox between the extraordinary and the ordinary in linguistic and visual expressions allows him to interrogate the meaning of his authentic self. The interrogation is demonstrated in his self-directed question "do you want to get to know the real me?" (CTV, 2008a) The question remains unresolved via the continued curiosity of Ben Mulroney's authenticity. Moreover, in addition to addressing his question, the background song "you can be the hero" (CTV, 2008a) inscribes a 'heroic fame' whereby his fame is associated not with musical talent, but with a demonstration of national values.

Indeed, as the son of an ex-Prime Minister, Ben Mulroney inherited national fame from his father's political career. This fame is further highlighted in media representations of his stardom. An opening paragraph of a *Toronto Star* news article described Ben Mulroney's stardom in a way that celebrated his national status:

> The children of former prime ministers, especially those who spent a good part of their childhood at 24 Sussex Dr., as Mulroney did, tend to hold the public's attention. But in the last few years, Mulroney, 32, the eldest son of Brian and Mila Mulroney and now the co-anchor of CTV's *eTalk Daily* and host of *Canadian Idol*, has become a celebrity in his own right (Chung, 2008).

Similarly, in a *McLean's* magazine article, journalist Jonathan Gatehouse described Ben Mulroney's national status as a "star" (2003, p. 20). For Gatehouse, Ben Mulroney's national status represents the "access to the famous and powerful," and is "beyond the reach of even the most successful television personalities" (p. 23). As an ex-Prime Minister's son, Ben Mulroney had access to pre-established fame, having spent time with other celebrity politicians such as former US president George Bush Sr, Jean Chretien, and other notables (Gatehouse, 2003). In light of his father's national acclaim, Gatehouse claimed that Ben Mulroney "is the only person who has any idea what it's actually like to be famous" (p. 23) on *Canadian*

Idol. The media representation of Ben Mulroney's national stardom is crucial to *Canadian Idol* because, as Gatehouse states, "one of the things that makes [Canadian] Idol compelling is the untainted, unabashed vision of celebrity that it sells" (Ibid.). More importantly, the authenticity addressed in his fame helps to negotiate tensions arising from an existing identity crisis in Canada.

The construction of Ben Mulroney's stardom in a national context can be read from the scholarly perspective of Chris Rojek (2001). For the media, Mulroney's stardom is what Rojek calls 'renown.' Mulroney gained initial popularity through an exclusive access to his father's network of celebrity politicians and other public personalities. Indeed, the image projected by celebrity meetings constitutes symbolic/political capital that raises one's public profile (Hart & Tindall, 2009). Ben Mulroney's celebrity status, however, extended beyond the network of celebrity politicians. Media capitalised on his existing fame by offering him work at *TalkTV* and, later, a job at *eTalk*, Canada's most popular entertainment magazine. Mulroney topped these gigs off with his job as host of *Canadian Idol*. Mulroney did not land these jobs based on his merit or talent alone: his performance of Canadianness at a national political convention ensured his future public status. When his father Brian Mulroney was not able to attend a national convention of the federal Conservative Party, Ben Mulroney was asked to drop by and wave the 'family flag.' He also gave interviews in both English and French at that time (Gatehouse, 2003, p. 21). In this way, Mulroney created national appeal through bilingualism. He carried this national appeal to *Canadian Idol* and its media representations.

Ben Mulroney's fame through his father's political connections was reconstructed through his role as a TV host, a gig that helped him reinforce national ideals in ways that eluded his father. As the Prime Minister of Canada, Brian Mulroney signed the Free Trade Agreement (FTA) with the US, a move that facilitated greater Americanisation and spurred yet another Canadian identity crisis that just cried out for an "all-Canadian hero" (Jackson & Ponic, 2001, p. 50). Ben Mulroney appears to have fulfilled this heroic role via his nationwide fame in *Canadian Idol*. He became famous by transforming a political windfall inherited from his father into a patriotic defence against the effects of Americanisation. As Jonathan Gatehouse explains, "Part of the younger Mulroney's appeal seems to be inextricably linked to his father's controversial legacy" (2003, p. 22). This political link undermines the classical definition of Hollywood fame and establishes a Canadian fame that is free from American domination. In undermining Brian Mulroney's "controversial legacy," Gatehouse refers to Ben Mulroney as a "winner" and a "Canadian Idol" (p. 20). These media representations are heroic expressions that subvert the FTA and the effects of Americanisation on Canada.

Although fame-based practices in *Canadian Idol* overlap with *American Idol* in the US, Ben Mulroney's fame may have helped to negotiate tensions originating from the FTA (introduced by his father) in Canada's favour. In the process, his fame helped to resolve the Canadian national identity crisis. From this perspective, Mulroney's fame is a political act that differentiates Canada from the US. Clearly, Mulroney did not earn his 'Canadian Idol' status on musical talent. Instead, his fame refers to his winning ability to perform Canadianness and spur a renewed national identity. Thus, *Canadian Idol* winners can be associated with Canadian notions of fame, in which the host plays a role in representing what it means to be a Canadian celebrity by questioning past Canadian myths of inferiority and promoting the admiration of fame as a new Canadian value.

Ben Mulroney's national role as a celebrity host in *Canadian Idol* is comparable to that of *Battle of the Blades* hosts Rob McLean and Kurt Browning. This role can be further understood from the scholarly perspectives of Julie Rak (2008). Rak refers to famous hosts like Ben Mulroney as 'celebrity advocates' because they are famous in the present time and confer meaning of fame to contestants they represent. In Canadian reality TV shows, the relationship between the individual and his/her Canadian contexts is central to the construction of celebrities (Rak, 2008). She analyses the first homegrown reality TV show, *The Greatest Canadian*, to demonstrate this construction. In this show, the biographical narrative of 'top ten' Canadians acted as "the nexus between the individual and his or her social context," whereby ordinary people get a "lucky break" (p. 60) that is more contingent on their Canadianness than on their merit. Rak's perspectives demonstrate how celebrity hosts like Ben Mulroney, Rob McLean, and Kurt Browning perform different national functions in Canadian reality TV shows.

The celebrity hosts popularise and glamorise past Canadian ideals and target them to a younger audience. In doing so, the idea of a celebrity turns into performance. In *The Greatest Canadian*, the celebrity status and 'rhetorical flair' of already famous host George Stroumboulopoulos was so pronounced that it contributed to the win by otherwise little-known politician Tommy Douglas (Rak, 2008). At the same time, however, *The Greatest Canadian* undermined the fame of the top Canadians in a manner similar to that of *Battle of the Blades*. In his role as a celebrity host, George Stroumboulopoulos both undermined and rejected the celebrity status of Tommy Douglas, comparing the politician to legendary American actor James Dean in the film *Rebel without a Cause* (Stern, 1955). Stroumboulopoulos stated that, unlike Hollywood rebels, who are traditionally associated with fame, "we" (Canadians) have political "rebels" (p. 61). In shifting focus from Hollywood to politics, Stroumboulopoulos denied fame to Douglas while maintaining his own identity as a 'celebrity guest.'

This act of undermining talented Canadians is yet another function of Canadian media. In this respect, the "lives and personalities of the advocates seemed to have even greater importance than the life of the person for whom the celebrity was advocating" (p. 58). Indeed, politicians' fame does not carry the same weight as those of film, television, and sports personalities. By comparing Tommy Douglas to James Dean and labelling Douglas as a 'rebel', Stroumboulopoulos actually established stronger fame for Douglas, transforming a mere political symbol into a vehicle for opposing the American Dream and Hollywood fame. Furthermore, Tommy Douglas was not a garden-variety politician: he was the man who envisioned and established Canada's single-payer universal health care program, which remains a major mark of distinction between Canada and the US. Thus, the symbol of Tommy Douglas undermines the classical definition of Hollywood fame and domination by America. As the first homegrown reality TV show, *The Greatest Canadian* set a framework for both questioning past Canadian myths of humility in the face of stardom and activating new Canadian values, including an interest in fame. The appeal of Canadian celebrity cultures through reality TV hosts is a new Canadian value that was not present in the past.

In conferring fame to contestants, reality TV show hosts use scripted anecdotes to narrate Canadian authenticity. This kind of authenticity is central to the long-term fame of contestants and to the nation in which they become stars. The response by *Canadian Idol* host Ben Mulroney to Season Six contestant Earl Stevenson is worthy of note. In appreciation of Stevenson's performance, Mulroney claimed: "I hope that Canada gets this cause you are the real deal, my brother – you are the real fame!" (CTV, 2008c). Here, Mulroney constructed Stevenson's fame within the paradoxes of the extraordinary and the ordinary in Canada. First, Mulroney created a notion of exclusivity/extraordinariness by singling Stevenson out from the rest of Canada. He then exclusively referred to Stevenson's talent and stated that, "I hope that Canada gets this" (CTV, 2008c). On another level, Mulroney also created a sense of ordinariness that can be contrasted to the extraordinariness of Stevenson's talent. In this respect, Mulroney related to Stevenson on ordinary grounds by calling Stevenson his "brother" (CTV, 2008c). The contrast between extraordinariness and ordinariness questions authenticity; in other words, who Stevenson really is. However, Ben Mulroney also performs and mediates authenticity by idealising how "real" a Canadian Stevenson is: "you are the real deal, my brother – you are the real fame!" (CTV, 2008c). Mulroney maintains the paradox between extraordinariness and ordinariness by articulating Stevenson's singularity in relation to the whole of Canada while also observing Stevenson's singular talent. Through this paradox, Mulroney conferred stardom on Stevenson and claimed that he was the real fame, i.e., fame as a performance and mediation of Stevenson's authentic talent in relation to the whole of Canada.

In addition to using a celebrity host and expressions of national pride, *Canadian Idol* emphasises particular regions in order to popularise contestants. Canada is a mosaic of different cultures that exist in five regions: North, Pacific Coast, Prairies, Central Canada, and Atlantic Canada. For Canadian cultural productions, multiculturalism, a mosaic of different cultural identities, distinguishes Canada from America's 'melting pot' (Flaherty & Manning, 1993). In *Canadian Idol*, representations of regional identities act as stand-ins for multiculturalism (B'béri & Middlebrook, 2009). This representation supports a core Canadian identity around which visible minorities are marked and maintained on the margins of multiculturalism (Mackey, 2002).

Like regions of the North, West, and East, *Canadian Idol* identifies French Canada in ways that help to signify a French-Canadian region for Quebecois contestants. This identification distinguishes them from the rest of English Canada and supports a core English Canadian identity. Yet, at the same time, the distinction reinforces the idea that the Canadian nation was built by joining these two identities. The identification of a French region reinforces the bilingual make-up of Canada. To reflect this bilingualism, host Ben Mulroney sporadically tosses French words into English evaluations. For example, Mulroney said 'Merci' three times to emphasise his gratitude in French to the 2006 Quebec contestant Eva Avila (CTV, 2008f). Such French expressions within predominantly English monologues serve to underline the presence of the French region of Quebec, which, as Michelle Byers (2008) points out, is otherwise not present in English language TV shows. The low frequency of French expressions shows how the evaluation of talent is marked around a dominant English Canadian identity in Canadian reality TV programs.

In *Canadian Idol* and other franchised shows, the articulation of a region-based identity serves to popularise contestants on national grounds. This identification is crucial in regions where there is a relatively low voting audience. The regional identification is familiar enough for viewers/fans to develop an affinity with contestants. During weekly performances, judges and hosts make continued references to their regions in order to familiarise voting audiences with contestants. In Season Two of *Canadian Idol*, the music evaluation of contestant Kalan Porter was significant. In his evaluation, Porter was associated with Southern Alberta, a sub-region of the Prairies. At that time, judges made mythic associations to "the West, whiteness, family values, religiosity, innocence, youth and so on" (Byers, 2008, p. 31) that are not specific to his talent. Similarly, hosts and judges often referred to the regional identity of contestants from Newfoundland, Labrador, and Quebec in the evaluation of contestants. In an episode of Season Six, for example, host Ben Mulroney described contestant Mitch Macdonald in terms of being from a 'small town' of Port Hood in Nova Scotia (CTV, 2008b). At the same time, Mulroney claimed that there was an "East coast thing going on" (CTV, 2008b) for MacDonald. In both comments, Mulroney perceived Macdonald's musical talent in relation to his town as a marker of his region.

Season One *Canadian Idol* contestants Jenny Gear and Jonathan King were also evaluated based on their respective regional characters. In the evaluation, Gear and King were associated with their 'rustic' home of Newfoundland (Byers, 2008). They were also associated with an equally 'rustic' character that emphasised a regional identity in Atlantic Canada. These associations, of course, had little to do with their musical talent. *Canadian Idol* judge Jake Gold reflected on and reinforced this region-based recognition. In his comment on the performance of contestant Craig Sharpe, Gold stated that, "You're from Newfoundland so there is a good chance you're going on... the people in Newfoundland know how to support their people" (p. 32). Such evaluations support national meta-discourses of Canada having a regional character.

On regional identification, audiences/fans are able to vote for their region's contestant. The shared recognition of a region-based national identity reflects in online fan interaction as well. Scholars Boulou B'béri and Ruth Middlebrook observe that online users frequently label contestants with the help of stereotypical regional expressions such as 'Newfies,' 'Newfiegurl,' and 'French Frogs' (2009, pp. 33-35). Similarly, in the case of Season Six contestant Earl Stevenson, an online fan stated that, "You have the "it" factor and we're all voting for you here in southern Saskatchewan!" (Kat, 2008). These linguistic practices show how audiences are familiar with region-based identities and how those identities play a selective role in popularising contestants irrespective of their musical talents. The nation, like the contestant, is imagined as a 'competition' between its regions.

In conferring region-based recognitions, *Canadian Idol* contestants are popularised in association with urban centres rather than rural areas. This popularity further helps to symbolise Canada as an industrial and technological nation that developed against a wilderness frontier, as discussed in Chapter 3. In franchised reality TV programs like *Canadian Idol*, auditions taking place in cities play a major role in establishing an urban-based regional identity. These cities include Vancouver on the Pacific Coast; Edmonton, Regina, and Winnipeg in the Prairies; Kitchener-

Waterloo, Toronto, Ottawa, and Montréal in Central Canada; Halifax and St. John's in Atlantic Canada, and Yellowknife in Northern Canada. The "pre-selection of audition locations is a frame that divides Canada into a set of regional identities with dominant urban centres" (B'béri & Middlebrook, 2009, p.30). Limiting auditions to cities also prevents qualified candidates from rural areas from participating on those auditions. After the auditions, contestants perform and become popular in Toronto, Canada's largest urban centre. Toronto's reputation as the 'centre' of Canada was echoed in a *Canadian Idol* song during the show's first season. The lyrics of the song state, "Choose Me, Choose Me and the one you are looking for [...] Canada can you see me as your Canadian Idol [...] Tell me, Tell me, Tell me - are you going to Toronto – I wanna be a Canadian Idol" (CTV, 2003). The song shows the importance of the city of Toronto in popularising contestants as national idols.

Celebrity hosts and judges popularise contestants on grounds of their urban-Canadian identity and, in the process, establish a national difference from America. This national difference plays a role in the awakening of Canadian talent. Often, Canadian judges evaluate contestants in a way that is morally superior to that of their American counterparts. Reflecting on the moral disposition of *Canadian Idol*, Susanne Boyce, CTV president of programming, claims that shows such as *Canadian Idol* are 'good-natured' and "fit our Canadian sensibilities. There's competition, but nobody wants anybody to die" (Gill, 2004). Here, the imagination of *Canadian Idol*'s 'good nature' intersects with Canadians constructing a 'better' nation than America. Boyce further asserts that, "You have to be better than the American version because Canadians can compare the two [...] The expectations are huge" (Ibid.). Indeed, the proximity with America actually enables Canada to assert itself as a nation. In *Canadian Idol*, the representation of Canadian talent not only occurs in moral relation to America but also in response to the threat posed by American shows and Americanisation. These threats inspire a national drive to create Canadian talent and stardom in a national context. The national difference from America, coupled with regional differences within Canada, allows national audiences/fans to identify with both the contestants and the nation.

In addition to using national expressions, *Canadian Idol* contrasts the ordinary with the extraordinary to popularise contestants and construct their celebrity status. This contrast occurs via the interplay of selection criterion, staging, settings, and narratives of the show and media. *Canadian Idol* carefully selects ordinary semi-professional and non-unionised performers based on their audition and show performances. This selection criterion sets ordinary performers apart as extraordinary contestants who are then advertised in nationwide media events. In these staged events, contestants are selected on the basis of their vocal merit as well as for their on-air presence (extraordinariness) and their ability to be ridiculed (ordinariness) for humorous effect on the show (Baltruschat, 2009). These criteria allow the program and the media to popularise contestants within a standard format of 'admirable behaviour.' Once selected, contestants must perform exclusively on the show's television stage, called the Idol House. Contestants are also offered luxurious accommodations and "star treatment," which are publicised in promotional material and "behind-the-scene clips" (CTV, 2006). The construction of a luxurious lifestyle and the appeal of stardom popularises the contestant as extraordinary:

> While the Idols were surely enjoying living it up in a swank downtown hotel during the Top 22 phase of the show, it doesn't compare to the star treatment of the Top 10 and a spot in the exclusive Idol Mansion (CTV, 2006).

While the 'behind-the-scenes' format highlights contestants' ordinariness, the luxurious production settings emphasise how extraordinary these contestants actually are. Ordinary contestants are paradoxically extraordinary because they are "incredible yet inaccessible" (Dubied, Dubbey, & Gorin, 2009). Reality TV contestants' fame relies on this paradox. More importantly, the inconsistency between the show's extraordinary accommodations and the contestants' ordinary backgrounds raises questions of authenticity. Media reports articulate the 'star treatment' of contestants in relation to this authenticity.

Canadian Idol also mobilises its audience to help popularise ordinary contestants as extraordinary celebrities. Their interactions reflect and reinforce reality TV contestants' stardom. The production company provides the interactive digital means for audiences to familiarise themselves with contestants and popularise them. Producers use techniques such as text-message voting systems, downloadable cell phone ring-tones and music clips, online chat rooms, and blogs to facilitate online audience interaction with contestants even after the show is over. In Season Six of *Canadian Idol*, for example, contestant Earl Stevenson interacted with audiences in a way that extended the shelf life of his fame even after his elimination from the show:

> Don't change who you are - your voice, your persona, your presence, your charm [...] Rock on! You're a winner & a star! (Kat, 2008).

> You are an incredible star already, you need to get busy recording right away. I'm waiting, just like all the others, to hear more of you (Catt, 2008).

You are famous already; know you have an army of fans!
(Helen, 2008).

I would pay to see you sing and perform - your [sic] a unique
talent with major star power (Sandra, 2008).

These blogs show that audiences/fans used symbolic expressions of fame to
assert that Earl Stevenson is a winner, famous, and a star — even though he
lost on the show. The blogs not only reflect contestants' popularity, but
they also help to maintain audience loyalty, which generates revenue
during and after the program.

The media and fans play a shared role in how some *Canadian Idol*
contestants make the transition from the temporary, constructed fame of
reality TV to a status of more permanent and widespread Canadian
celebrity. More importantly, the media representations support the shift
from limited notions of fame to ironic, yet valued, celebrity cultures in
Canada. The media representation of 2004 *Canadian Idol* winner Jacob
Hoggard in September 2010 is an example of this new, ironic fame. In his
performance, Jacob Hoggard sang the first single "Cha-Ching" off of his
band's third album, *The Show Must Go On*. Throughout the song, Hoggard
reflects on his experiences during the *Canadian Idol*'s second season:

Who's the biggest loser?
I'll bust the biggest boozer
Bigger ratings for MTV

All the soul survivors
Still stranded on the island
Lyin' through their teeth for money

In the *Vancouver Sun* newspaper, journalist Graeme McRanor expands on
the "fame-seeking characters" and "greedy executives exploiting fame-
obsessed contestants" (2010) that Hoggard targets in his lyrics. Ranor
responds to these lyrics and notes how the band "pokes fun at fame-
seekers, including themselves" (Ibid.). The irony in questioning fame while
constructing ordinary talent as famous is perhaps what characterises
Canada's rising celebrity cultures.

Indeed, the construction and maintenance of homegrown versions of
fame is relatively new and strangely ironic for both TV show contestants
and cultural industries in Canada. The new rise of fame is depicted in
CTV's report "Idols still getting used to newfound celebrity status" (Block,
2008). The report quotes a fan named Shirley Brule and represents her

"sense that [Canadian Idols are] famous, maybe not [sic] to the extent of Britney Spears, but they're still really known to people in Canada" (Ibid.). Here, the irony is that *Canadian Idol* contestants do not meet American standards of fame, epitomised by Britney Spears, but are still famous to fans in Canada. This irony characterises the rise of celebrity cultures and the media constructions of Canadian celebrities. For example, journalist Graeme McRanor reflects on Hoggard's fame-criticising lyrics: "It's ironic, of course, given frontman Jacob Hoggard's history as a Canadian Idol contestant [...]" (2010). In describing the performance of fame as 'ironic,' McRanor helps to reconstruct and reclaim the fame that Jacob Hoggard once received as a *Canadian Idol* in 2004. At the same time, the media mark a noticeable shift towards a rising fame that was previously absent in Canada.

So You Think You Can Dance Canada

A glimpse into *So You Think You Can Dance Canada* demonstrates how media and the show played a role in constructing the fame of its host and contestants as well. Media representation of host Leah Miller shows how she was constructed as a celebrity through authenticity that emerged out of the paradox of her ordinariness and extraordinariness. Consider a *Flare* magazine article written by Hannah Sung, which uses three different narrative devices to demonstrate Miller's ordinary and extraordinary qualities.

First, the article opens with a rhetorical question, "So you think you know who Leah Miller is? Think again. Hannah Sung speaks to the rising star behind the tears and the triumphs" (Sung, 2009). Here, 'tears' and 'triumph' refer to the ordinary struggles and hard work that were involved in Miller's achievement of extraordinary success (Ibid.). The rhetorical use of 'tears' is a signifier of ordinary emotional revelations that mediate authenticity through the legitimisation of real-life experiences (Biressi & Nunn, 2005). The article also uses 'triumph,' however, to signify the extraordinary stages of her competitive and glamorous life in the public realm. These extraordinary achievements include Miller's nomination for the Best Performance or Host in a Variety Program or Series in the 2009 Gemini awards, as well her winning the Viewers' Choice Gemini Award for Hottest Canadian Female in 2008. The paradox of Miller's simultaneous ordinariness and extraordinariness raises questions of authenticity that are addressed through ordinary emotional revelations.

Second, Miller's authenticity is mediated by boldface words. In boldface and uppercase fonts, the headline of the article opens with the words, "DANCING QUEEN LEAH MILLER" (Sung, 2009). These boldface fonts emphasise Leah Miller's innate talent and merit as a dancer. The boldface particularly mediates her talent as a 'royal fame' in dancing.

Readers can also draw on their knowledge of the show that rates dancing talent and merit across Canada. The headline, "So you think you know who Leah Miller is?" is a rhetorical question that resembles the title of the reality TV show *So You Think You Can Dance Canada*. This headline allows readers to reflect on and reinforce knowledge of actual contestants' innate dancing qualities. This knowledge, in turn, helps to authenticate Miller on the basis of her real efforts and success in dance, rather than on mere personal accounts from her life. The knowledge of innate talent restores a primordial source of nature in self that is central to authenticity.

Third, Miller's authenticity is expressed through a black-and-white photograph. Positioned against the bold font headline, the photograph shows Leah Miller screaming ecstatically with her eyes closed. Traditionally, photojournalism has used black-and-white images to draw on past methods of recording the "real" and to "appear more truthful, serious, and artistic" (Thompson, 2010). The photograph mediates Miller's authenticity as a constructed notion of 'serious truth' within a paradox of ordinariness and extraordinariness. This paradox persuades readers to seek the truth behind the host. It is in the resulting paradox of Miller's ordinariness and extraordinariness that journalist Hannah Sung imagines her as 'the rising star' in Canada. This stardom, in turn, confers meanings of authenticity and increases audience rating and voting.

In *So You Think You Can Dance Canada*, media representations and judges' evaluations help to both authenticate and popularise contestants. In the Waterloo-based magazine *The Record*, an article focuses on judge Jean Marc Genereux, who evaluated contestant Jonathan Arsenault in Season Three. According to the article, Arsenault suffered from a malformed blood vessel that gave him migraines and occasional seizures. However, his health improved and he reached the Top 5. This personal story involving ordinary struggles signified authenticity and led Genereux to claim that Arsenault was "a real guy" and "the real deal" (Staff, 2010a). Here, 'real' is a performance and mediation of authenticity that emerges within the contrast of ordinary struggles and extraordinary merit, and it supports the construction of fame. Thus, Genereux mediated Arsenault's dancing talent as a performance of authenticity.

In addition to media representations, local stories and descriptions of community events act as narrative devices that popularise contestants on grounds of their authenticity and Canadianness. These activities help to set Canadianness apart from global forms of standardised identification that are used in franchised formats. Like *Battle of the Blades* and *Canadian Idol*, *So You Think You Can Dance Canada* presented contestants' individual profiles before they performed. Although the practice of profiling contestants is an internationally recognised reality TV format, local stories popularise contestants in a way that is already familiar to audiences in the country where the show is franchised. For example, *So You Think You Can Dance Canada* employed local settings, such as region, hometown, and schools when profiling contestants. This helps to familiarise audiences with contestants who might share contestants' local and regional backgrounds. Regional markers also help to construct a region-based national identity and, in the process, localise Canadian contestants within a globally franchised program. For example, host Leah Miller often greeted people with the French 'Salut' to distinguish Quebec-based Canadian dancers in the shows. Similarly, French-Canadian judge Jean Marc Genereux once evoked images of delicious French dishes when evaluating the dance talent of a Quebecois contestant (CTV, 2010b). As explained in the case of *Canadian Idol*, these infrequently used French expressions underline the presence of the French region in Canada that is otherwise absent from English Canadian reality TV. These linguistic markers also help to localise contestants in a global programming format and to establish a national difference from America's 'melting pot.' In his media report, television critic Rob Salem suggested that *So You Think You Can Dance Canada* contestants were "far more regionally representative than their American counterparts, which also speaks to their overall excellence" (2008).

There are many other instances where *So You Think You Can Dance Canada* and media used local, hometown stories to popularise contestants. For example, a headline in a Surrey, British Columbia newspaper focused on the elimination of contestant/Surrey resident Kirsten Wicklund (Staff, 2010b). News stories preferred to highlight local information — such as the high school Wicklund attended — rather than focusing on her dancing talent and the talent of other contestants. An article in the Waterloo-based magazine *The Record* took a similar approach to a show contestant. The article reviewed the rising popularity of Season Three contestant Jonathan Arsenault because he lived in the adjacent city of Kitchener. In fact, the magazine emphasised Arsenault's Kitchener roots several times. *The Record* used Arsenault's hometown as a rhetorical device in order to familiarise local audiences — particularly fans in the Waterloo-Kitchener urban area — with a hometown contestant. For example, the article described how Arsenault was a "2002 grad of Kitchener's Eastwood Collegiate", and cited the *Toronto Star*'s Debra Yeo, who noted that, "Jonathan Arsenault, 25, of Kitchener, was my hands-down favourite" (Staff, 2010a). In constructing Jonathan Arsenault as Canada's favourite performer, familiarity with his hometown took a dominant position. Local stories are specific to the nation in which the original format is franchised. In Canada, urban markers such as Surrey, Waterloo, and Kitchener set contestants apart from other international stars — especially American ones.

In popularising *So You Think You Can Dance Canada* talent, media and the show often differentiated judges and contestants from their American counterparts. Often, media represented Canadian talent judges as morally superior to American ones. For example, an article in the *Hollywood Report* states, "In the Great White North, talent competition series like *Canadian Idol, Battle of the Blades* and *So You Think You Can Dance Canada* tend to prefer nurturing over nastiness when it comes to judging contestants" (Vlessing, 2011). *So You Think You Can Dance Canada* judges were so polite, positive, and nice to even 'flawed couples' that they lacked critical balance in showing areas of improvement and reasons for elimination, while the American version of the show covers them — often in abrupt ways (McNutt, 2009). For example, judge Jean-Marc Genereux once claimed that, "America has amazing dancers…but we have nothing to be ashamed of. I realise now how much depth we have" (Quail, 2008). Genereux's expression 'nothing to be ashamed' implies a sense of disbelief, in which Canadians felt ashamed of their supposed dearth of talent when compared to the wealth of talent in the culturally dominant US. This discovery led Genereux to claim that Canadians have greater *depth* than Americans do.

The ways in which national differences are created against America suggest both a national inferiority complex and an awakening of talent that marks the rise of Canadian fame. On one hand, Genereux's realisation of 'depth' marks a sense of inferiority and a crisis point for Canada's national identity born out of the need to overcome American dominance. Here, 'depth' refers to a Canadian character that was forged in the Northern frontier; a character that is morally superior to that of America (Kalant, 2004; Quail, 2008; Salem, 2008). The articulation of 'depth' marks a nationwide awakening and a discovery of talent that was previously denied to Canadians.

A similar response occurs in a comment made by America's *So You Think You Can Dance* judge Marry Murphy: "The talent you have in [Canada]…I just can't believe it!…Even at the auditions, the level was so incredibly high. I'm amazed at what they've been able to do here, and it's only the first year" (Quail, 2008). This observation of how Canadian contestants are actually talented indicates a 'disbelief' as well as an 'awakening' and a 'discovery' of innate talent that can be celebrated through fame. These narratives lay the foundation for celebrating Canadian fame, a foundation that did not previously exist. They challenge both past cultural constructions of talent and the Canadian inferiority complex. Although the inferiority complex functioned culturally to establish national differences with America, it was also a real perception on the part of Canadians who thought that they were less capable than, and less talented than, Americans. In the end, Canadian reality TV fame is largely based on a celebration of national values, not innate talent. But there is also a growing recognition of Canadian talent and a conscious awareness that Canadian fame should be celebrated as a national value.

Like the judges, host Leah Miller described dance contestants as cute, sweet, and polite. In describing their personality Miller further stated that, "They're better looking than the American dancers....Wait until you see them – they're all super cute and sweet" (Quail, 2008). The underlying premise can be read in the context of Miller's other commentary, wherein she explicitly stated that Canadian contestants are extremely polite and gracious — even when criticised. Unlike American contestants, Miller claimed that, "Canadians are so polite compared to the Americans. They're just like, 'OK, thanks for the opportunity" (Quail, 2008). For Miller, Canadianness is performed through expressions of being 'cute,' 'sweet,' and 'polite' that morally differentiate it from American bellicosity. At the same time, these positive qualities are central to fostering newly recognised Canadian talent. There is a sense of transition in how Canadians celebrate talent that marks the unleashing of a previously suppressed Canadian style of fame. While hosts express Canadian talent in moral relation to America, they also acknowledge how its qualities are central to the construction of fame as a rising Canadian value.

Conclusion

This chapter set out to examine its central question: how do Canadian reality TV shows play a role in constructing Canadian celebrities and supporting national discourses? The chapter looked at popular TV shows such as *Battle of the Blades*, *Canadian Idol*, and *So You Think You Can Dance Canada* in order to explore some of the discursive constructions of celebrities in Canada. The chapter considered celebrities in both homegrown and franchised reality TV programs. Case studies of these programs showed that reality TV celebrities support national discourses and represent Canadian values on two levels.

First, both homegrown and franchised shows construct particular kinds of national identities through notions of fame. Homegrown reality TV shows such as *Battle of the Blades* reproduced Canadian myths around ice, symbolising an imagined Northern frontier. At other times, both homegrown and franchised shows represent an urban-based regional and local identity in discourses of fame. In most of these cases, national identities in fame serve to differentiate Canada from America, where most of the shows originated and became popular. Celebrities in franchised reality TV shows particularly appropriate Canadian markers that articulate national identity in regionalised/localised ways and resist American cultural domination. The popular recognition of Canadians having a superior 'moral soul' is another cultural practice that differentiates them from dominant, fame-based American practices. These practices counteract the perceived inferiority of Canadian talent.

Celebrity hosts in reality TV programs such as *Battle of the Blades*, *Canadian Idol* and *So You Think You Can Dance Canada* have expressed fame in a way that affirms the presence of emerging Canadian talent and the rise of Canadian celebrity cultures. This popular recognition of emerging talent in Canada is a way to affirm Canadian values that were not present in the past. Some narratives and media representations express disbelief that talent is actually present in Canada. The disbelief functions in a way that marks a shift away from past practices when Canadian fame was intimately connected to the Hollywood star system. This chapter observed celebrity hosts that advocate reality show contestants while also supporting the performance of Canadian national identity. In particular, they play a role in questioning both the classical definition of Hollywood fame and past myths of inferiority that subordinated Canadian talent. These case studies showed that reality TV hosts' stardom often helps to undermine and reconstruct contestants' fame in a way that reclaims Canadian values. For example, the stardom of *Battle of the Blades* hosts is used as a cultural reminder of ice as an imagined frontier that forged Canadian national fame — a frontier reconquered by talented former NHL stars. Central to this mediation of talent is authenticity whereby a performed Canadian reality, fame, has become a new Canadian value.

In most cases, fame in reality TV distinguishes talent as a performance, as well as a mediation of the achievement of Canadian values. In a Canadian context, reality TV programs highlight the winning contestant as the nation's 'favourite,' as opposed to its 'best' performer. While winning contestants are recognised for their merit, their talent is mediated in a way that is favourable to maintaining Canadian national discourses. Thus, the fame of Canada's 'favourite' contestants does not necessarily refer to merit or talent, at least in the classical meaning of fame. Instead, 'favourite' in the Canadian context refers to an authentic personality with innate national qualities. In the context of a past identity crisis, establishing the 'favourite' Canadian personality is important for reality TV shows. It also secures votes and revenues from a relatively smaller, yet fiercely loyal, domestic audience who can identify with reality TV participants on both national and local grounds. The popularity of 'favourite' thus refers to how 'best' performances are mediated through national discourses and presented as performances of Canadian values. Central to this mediation of talent is authenticity, whereby a performed Canadian reality of fame has become a new Canadian value.

The next chapter will continue to examine how this authenticity not only legitimises celebrities but also the Canadian nation, this time in an Internet setting. The chapter will examine whether or not traditional media representations of online celebrities engage with Canadian national ideologies. In examining these ideologies, the next chapter will allow us to verify whether offline constructions of national identity are maintained or subverted in online productions and representations of fame.

8 Online Celebrities in Canada

An important aspect of Canadian fame has been the advent of decentralised, participatory Internet/Web 2.0 technologies. Although the infrastructure, policies, and content are to some extent subjected to corporate and governmental support and influences, the Internet is an affordable and accessible media technology that audiences and fans use to construct and circulate celebrity texts. In the Canadian context, user-generated content on talent is important to fame given Canada's limited production capitals and the dominance of the Hollywood studio system (as seen in Chapters 4 and 5). With these contexts in mind, this chapter will explore two questions: First, have Internet practices shifted the ways in which Canadian stars are constructed and maintained in national discourses? Second, how are online celebrities' national identities expressed in Canada? Studying media representations of online celebrities helps to illuminate the cultural processes and practices that are involved in constructing their online fame in Canada. At the same time, a study of their online celebrity texts shows how they intersect with offline representations of Canada and articulate national identity.[3]

Online Fame – General Concepts

Before I delve into the question of how online celebrities are constructed in relation to the nation, it is important to define who and what an online celebrity is. I define an online celebrity as a public personality who is popularly recognised on the Internet. There are two distinct types of online

---

[3] Soon, there may be no difference between online and traditional media stars but, in this book, I am studying a period where this distinction is still important.

celebrities. First, there are online only (or fame due to online presence) celebrities. This type of online celebrity refers to Internet users, bloggers, or fans who are constructed as celebrities and who may or may not cross over to achieve celebrity status in traditional media. In this chapter, case studies of Justin Bieber and Maria Aragon will illustrate how online fans become celebrities. Second, there are traditional celebrities, who now have an online presence. This type of online celebrity refers to those who are already famous in print and broadcast media industries but are also present on the Internet. Canadian star Lisa Ray's media representations will be presented as examples of reinforcing offline fame by establishing an online presence.

Online celebrities are both similar to and different from what Matt Hills calls "sub-cultural celebrities" (2006, p. 6). Hills refers to sub-cultural celebrities as well-known individuals within fandom who interact with other fans through niche media. These celebrities include Internet fans who share media texts in closed networks of fandom. As is the case with online celebrities, sub-cultural celebrities offer an alternative insight into talent. Traditional media industries usually do not offer these insights. However, online celebrities differ from sub-cultural celebrities in the sense that their fame is not limited to fans in a closed network. Online celebrities are able to reach out to a mass audience in the same manner (or increased) as industrially produced offline stars. Nevertheless, Internet fame is a distinct sort of celebrity: it is often temporary, fragile, and understood to be fleeting unless it connects to sociological conditions in the offline 'star system' and is maintained within existing social discourses.

The construction and maintenance of online fame share similarities with the fame constructed by traditional media industries, but there are also key differences. The similarities include binary oppositions between 'extraordinary' and 'ordinary' conditions and its 'presence' and 'absence,' e.g., onscreen/off-screen, public/private, and distant/close (Ellis, 2007; Geraghty, 2007). Star images are thus incoherent: they are sustained by 'contrasts' between the performing 'presence' and 'absence,' i.e., what happens 'off-stage' (Ellis, 2007; Geraghty, 2007).

In the case of online celebrities, the incoherence that characterises the ways that they differ from the conditions of offline stars — part of the reinvention of star image — generates an appeal for curious fans. The central difference between online and offline constructions of fame lies in how Internet users can control the variability of these 'contrasts' through active participation. This variability heightens the incoherence and, consequently, results in a reinvention of the star image. This heightened reinvention marks a significant breaking point from earlier practices of fan gaze towards traditional celebrity texts such as posters and autographs. In the past, fans would engage with celebrity texts in ways that were fixed in time and space. The lack of two-way communication and active participation with celebrities led early researchers to conceptualise fans as 'passive consumers and cultural dupes' (Jenkins, 2006). The impact of Internet technologies, however, has turned the production, distribution, and reception of celebrity texts into a participatory process. In this respect, fans have greater control and can reproduce texts in various ways to construct popularity. These changes also shift the traditional meaning of fame into one that is immediately accessible to active Internet users, and it can generate 'overnight sensations' in the right conditions.

To understand the sociological conditions of online fame, it is important to address two major questions: In an offline setting, who can become an online celebrity? Moreover, what are the sociological conditions of an online celebrity's production? Here, with inspiration from Francesco Alberoni's work (1972), I introduce three different micro and macro sociological conditions that are necessary for attaining the status and textual representation of an online celebrity. These conditions will be applied to the case studies of Canadian online celebrities presented later in this chapter. There are microsociological conditions for the construction and maintenance of an online celebrity in everyday life. These conditions are 1.) Social mobility (i.e., anyone can change his or her social status based on achievement or visibility); 2.) the social role of a hero who may or may not have served a community but is nonetheless a role model for self-achievement, and 3.) emotional affinity in para-social interaction with fans. By contrast, there are macrosociological conditions required for online celebrities. These conditions are 1.) a large audience or large number of fans (e.g., at least over a million online users); 2.) the development, use, and convergence of technologies in mass communication (i.e., the Internet, telecommunications, print, broadcast media or film), and 3.) broader media discourses in which online celebrity texts are produced. Once these criteria are met, traditional media often represent online celebrities within existing social discourses. These offline representations, in turn, help celebrities' Internet fame, which is otherwise fleeting in nature.

The sociological conditions for the construction of online celebrities are parallel to what Francesco Alberoni (1972), Richard Dyer (1998), and Barry King (1991) identify as the classical conditions for the industrial production of stardom in traditional settings. These conditions have long existed in the Hollywood studio system (Strinati, 2000). Francesco Alberoni (1972) identified that these factors operate and determine the nature of production, distribution, and consumption of a heavily controlled star. In this context, Alberoni uses the phrase 'powerless elite' to describe traditional celebrities in Hollywood. He suggests that the institutional power of celebrities is very limited or even non-existent. For him, the celebrities' lack of power contrasts with their actions that "arouse a considerable [...] degree of interest" (1972, p. 75). Unlike the Hollywood studio system, however, the cultural processes of online celebrity constructions do not necessarily require the industrial control that involves the ownership of production, distribution, and reception. For online celebrities, the conditions shift from benefitting lawyers and bureaucrats in favour of decentralised expressions of individual talent. In contrast to the control of the studio system and other media corporations, centralised media networks generally do not regulate internet sites. In this social setting, the semiotic construction and maintenance of an online celebrity text vary in ways that make the text immediate and accessible to Internet users and fans, thus making the text subject to reinvention.

Celebrities who have become famous in traditional media can also advance their fame on the Internet. In these cases, media often contrast extraordinary performances in offline settings with ordinary expressions on the Internet. The media construction of celebrities often relies on these contrasts. On the Internet, celebrities can share individual expressions through their own media texts on websites. Celebrities frequently use blogs as extra-textual devices to construct and maintain their self-images beyond their primary texts in popular media. Through blogs, celebrities can post entries about their ordinary selves, and any viewer or fan can read and respond to them. Based on origin of production, there are three types of celebrity blogs that are produced by three different entities. These include: 1.) cultural industries, 2.) celebrities, and 3.) fans. Some cultural industries, such as television stations and tabloid press create and maintain celebrity blogs where fans can interact with celebrities. These blogs can be considered part of a coherent system of celebrity promotion that carefully attracts targeted audiences (Marshall, 2006). In many other cases, celebrities maintain their own websites or blogs.

In producing and maintaining personal websites and blogs, celebrities have opportunities to post professional and personal information about themselves. Sometimes, celebrities respond to comments on fan sites as well. Such practices indicate that, as David Marshall (2006) argues, the traditional 'representational gap' between the celebrity and fan is narrowing. For Marshall, the narrowing of the 'representational gap' between the celebrity and the fan is driven by the emphasis on the 'presentation' of self. He states that the ideology of individualism has always been a central element of consumer culture. Celebrity cultures have been part of "discourses of self" that make "individuality concrete and real" (2006, p. 635). This discourse is what drives the construction and maintenance of the rhetoric of authenticity in the construction of fame. In order to establish authenticity, celebrities are usually constructed through the extra-textual dimensions of private, ordinary self on the Internet (Marshall, 2006).

The contrast of ordinariness on the Internet with the extraordinariness of offline talent, coupled with accessibility and immediacy, is central to the construction of celebrities online. The rise of Internet celebrities has become ubiquitous. As scholar Rachel Derkits argues, the "decreased barrier to access online provides an opening for new formations of celebrity" (2004 p. 27). In fact, journalist Rob Williams adds that, "A person getting famous after being discovered online is becoming more and more common" (2011). One of the online celebrities that illustrate William's report is Susan Boyle, who became famous after performing on *Britain's Got Talent*, after which 32 million viewers saw her singing on YouTube. Also, US-based Tila Tequila became famous for having over 1.3 million friends on MySpace (Grossman, 2006). Traditional media such as *Stuff*, *Maxim*, *Time* and *Penthouse* then featured Tequila, further enhancing her popularity. This offline fame, in turn, led to her selection as a host for Fuse TV's *Pants-Off Dance-Off* and MTV's popular reality show *A Shot at Love with Tila Tequila*. Similarly, Canadian blogger Lara Doucette became one of the Internet's most popular online celebrities. Doucette became popular as a videoblogger on *Tiki Bar TV*, one of the Internet's earliest and most popular video podcasts. Thousands of Internet fans celebrated her online performance. She became so famous that the CBC hired her to host its late night program *Exposure*.

The above examples show how talented individuals can gain popular attention on the Internet. Mainstream media, including prime-time broadcast news, then proclaim the artistes to be celebrities and often represent them within existing social discourses. Online celebrities sustain their fame by subjecting themselves to the larger, on-demand gaze of millions of fans through both online and traditional media. In this way, online celebrities are associated with offline fame. To illustrate the creation of an online celebrity in the Canadian context, I first look at Justin Bieber's fame and examine how he has been represented in national discourses. I then follow with two other cases: Lisa Ray and Maria Aragon.

Justin Bieber

Justin Bieber is a Canadian teenage pop star who has become globally famous for his musical talent. Born in the Canadian town of Stratford, Ontario, Bieber was a fan who received initial recognition for his online performance of songs from artists like Usher, Ne-Yo, and Stevie Wonder. He attracted a worldwide audience of around ten million online viewers when his mother, Pattie Mallette, posted his performances on YouTube (MTV, 2009; Stevenson, 2009). In 2008, Bieber's online popularity caught the attention of Atlanta-based Scooter Braun, who became his manager. Soon afterward, Bieber obtained a recording contract with Island Records and released his first single, "One Time" and his debut album, *My World*, in 2009. It topped worldwide music charts. Since then, producers, media, and fans have constructed and represented Justin Bieber as a star in Canada and abroad. Bieber's fame mostly relies on his meritocratic talent. It also relies on questions of authenticity within the paradox of the 'extraordinary' and 'ordinary' that are specific to global and national/personal contexts.

In general, media reports describe Bieber's extraordinary talent with expressions such as 'teenage sensation,' 'superstar,' and 'megastar.' At the same time, the reports indicate his ordinariness in two different ways. Media recognise how ordinariness complements his extraordinariness — it offers a familiarity with which millions of young fans can identify Justin Bieber as an extraordinary case of merit-based talent. CTV news expressed the extraordinary role of Bieber's ordinariness when reporting on the promotion of his film *Never Say Never* (2011) at Toronto's Royal York Hotel. "Bieber, indeed, is a star of another era - the social networking, era, to be precise" (Droganes, 2011), CTV stated. The specific reference to 'social networking era' indicates an ordinary, everyday life situation in which Bieber's mother simply wanted to share her son's videos with relatives by posting them on YouTube. Nonetheless, viewers worldwide saw these online videos and recognised Justin Bieber's extraordinary talent. Bieber's ordinariness thus complements his extraordinary achievements.

Justin Bieber is known for overcoming ordinary struggles in the private space of his home, which contrasts with his extraordinary achievements in the public realm. In this respect, media emphasise Bieber's ordinariness in terms of his struggles growing up in a poor home where his mother held two jobs and raised him as a single parent (Hertz, 2010; Stevenson, 2009). In light of this background, CTV showed how Justin Bieber was ordinary and, hence, 'not perfect' when he arrived at Toronto's Royal York Hotel to promote his film *Never Say Never* (2011). The report then cited Bieber as saying that, "I'm a regular teenage boy [...] Lots of people think I'm made by some factory machine. But I worked hard to get here [...] I'm going through different struggles and different things in my life" (Droganes, 2011). These expressions of ordinariness contrast with Justin Bieber's extraordinariness as a singer. Although Bieber's authenticity is often questioned, it is simultaneously addressed through his ordinariness, which is central to the construction of his stardom.

After a series of media events, Justin Bieber tweeted "The media talk a lot about me. They make up a lot of lies and want me to fail" (Everett-Green, 2014). His claim appeared on Twitter right after his tweet announcing his wish to officially retire. The radical expression in his tweet was a response to how media representations distorted his image. These representations included him spitting on fans and urinating in a restaurant as a form of public spectacle. For example, the opening headlines of *The Toronto Star* newspaper stated that, "Justin Bieber Pees in Restaurant Mop

Bucket: Video" (Arpe, 2013). The report included a video that appears to show his emotional excitement while urinating in public and laughing about the public act with friends. Several media reports also showed how Justin Bieber was excited about spitting over a hotel balcony in Toronto. The photograph of him spitting received wide circulation and created a stir among readers. While media representations of Bieber's emotional state helped create a public spectacle and sell newspapers, the reality of his emotions and the display of his authentic self are questionable. For example, the alleged public urination video does not show Bieber's face or anyone else's for that matter. It is entirely likely that group of teenagers recorded the video and sold it as an example of Justin Bieber's emotional excitement. The authenticity of the spitting video is also disputed. Several media reporters, including a representative of Bieber himself, claimed that the photograph of the pop star's spit was superimposed. In addition, absurd headlines such as "Justin Bieber Fans Plan to Clone Him from His Spit" (Josh, 2013) indicated the social construction of his spitting. In any case, none of these heavily circulated representations were related to Bieber's musical talent. These images reconstructed his emotional state of pleasure in order to sell him as a public spectacle. The commodification of these imagined expressions created the conditions for further (profitable) scandals and gossip.

The commodification of Justin Bieber's emotional state and the creation of scandals were also exemplified in representations of his arrest for two charges in one week, one for assaulting the driver of VIP Limousines Toronto on December 30, 2013, and the other for driving under the influence of alcohol in Miami on January 23, 2014. On January 29, 2014 a live telecast of Justin Bieber's arrest at Toronto Police Service's 52 Division headquarters became a media spectacle. At that time, 52 Division transformed into a cultural site that articulated the legal and moral territories of the Canadian nation in relation to the controversial stardom that Justin Bieber acquired in America. The television crewmembers focused their cameras on a screaming crowd of ordinary reporters, fans, and members of the public that did not necessarily appreciate Justin Bieber's talent. When Bieber arrived, the cameras wobbled and failed to get a proper glimpse of him. In this representation, he appeared to be hiding in shame, a sinner going to confession. The live telecast then repeated fragments of edited shots of police escorting a barely noticeable Bieber.

Both the unstable camera angles as well as the repeated snapshots of edited content were codes and conventions that re-constructed the reality of 'live' experiences into a highly coveted exclusivity accessible only through a tabloid media format. The narrative devices used in this format increase sensory arousal, attention, and instantaneous perception on a cognitive level, thereby enabling an understanding of the exclusivity of fame. In contrast to reports that made Bieber the object of media spectacle and attention, a subsequent report represents his ordinariness. In her report, journalist Ann Hui (2014) illustrates how Justin Bieber partied at a Toronto nightclub less than two days after the assault charge. In the report, Hui emphasises the contradiction between the extraordinariness of his infamy and the ordinariness of his casual encounters and party attire. This paradox raises questions about authenticity and fuels the ongoing public desire for the star. The maintenance of desire is also necessary for authenticating and legitimising the role that governments and media play in reporting further news on Bieber's March 2014 court case.

These news stories mark a shift away from the development of merit-based talent in national heroism and leadership to mediation on, and commodification of, unethical expressions as saleable emotions. In a Canadian context, Julie Rak (2008) explains that a celebrity's greatness can be ideologically linked to that of a nation. The fame of Canadian celebrities, then, does not necessarily refer to their talent. Instead, it reflects cherished values that authenticate the nation (Nandy, 2012). In Justin Bieber's case, meta-narratives of the nation have little to do with his musical talent. Indeed, representations of Bieber's assault charge and regulations governing his behaviour help to maintain ethical and moral boundaries that the Canadian nation aims to restore. Popular narratives surrounding his arrest have become ordinary vehicles for Canadians wishing to express their country's authenticity and morality in comparison to dominant images of crime and violence in America.

Justin Bieber's stardom relies on the contrast between ordinariness and extraordinariness in an imaginary relation to Canada. Canadian production companies and media often construct Bieber's stardom in ways that are specific to the nation. For example, a Canada.com news article titled "Justin Bieber fever threatened by cold blast of overexposure" (Harris, 2011) links his stardom to Northern frontier conditions. The article reviews the vast number of endorsement contracts that Bieber received and discusses difficulty in handling them. The article imagines this difficulty as a "cold blast of overexposure" (Harris, 2011). Here, the expression 'cold blast' conjures up images of Northern frontier-style snowstorms and wind chills. As explained in Chapter 3, ethnometeorological studies on Canadian climate show how representations of cold weather are often cultural constructs that mediate national identity in a way that mythically represents Northern endurance and strength. These ordinary frontier conditions challenged early Canadian settlers, and at least figuratively, they challenge Justin Bieber as well. This symbolic setting frames Justin Bieber's stardom as an extraordinary achievement: the taming of harsh conditions in an imagined Canadian frontier. This cultural production of stardom helps to imagine the nation as strong and extraordinary.

A *Toronto Life* magazine also illustrates expressions of Canada as a frontier nation in Bieber's stardom. The article, titled "Captain Canuck Goes Hollywood," reports on a Canadian film production that aims to cast Bieber as 'Captain Canuck' (Vaccaro, 2011a). According to the article, Bieber's role as Captain Canuck represents "an honest Mountie-turned-intelligence-agent [...who] gained his superpowers from an encounter with aliens while camping" (Ibid.). The symbolic association between Canuck and Mountie in the media representation of Justin Bieber can be read from the scholarly perspectives of Jason Dittmer and Soren Larsen (2007), as explained in Chapter 6. In their view, the word 'Canuck' referred to a national superhero in Canadian comic books and is now an informal reference to English Canadians. The imagined hero is recognised for strength, endurance, moral integrity, and controlled aggression (Dittmer & Larsen, 2007). These mythical traits of Canadianness are parallel to those of the Mountie in national discourses. Both the Canuck and Mountie emerged from an imagined Northern frontier. In the *Toronto Life* article, Bieber is associated with the "politeness" and "honesty" of a Mountie and represented as a "maple-leaf adorned superhero" (Vaccaro, 2011a).

The imagination of his 'honesty' and 'politeness' underlines a moral value that has emerged from the endurance against ordinary frontier conditions in Canada's colonial history. The official national symbols of the Mountie and maple leaf in Bieber's representation signify wilderness conditions out of which the nation-state was built, as seen in Chapters 3 and 4. A rhetorical question in the *Toronto Life* article prompts readers to further imagine and reconstruct the frontier nation: "But what Canadian super-talent has the gravitas, popularity, charm and politeness to represent the True North's true hero? [...] the name that comes to mind is none other than Justin Bieber" (Vaccaro, 2011a). The mediation of Bieber's talent as 'True North's true hero' shows how his authenticity is culturally constructed within national discourses of the North. It imagines harsh conditions against which Bieber's extraordinary heroism is established in Canada.

In addition to representing Justin Bieber as 'True North's true hero,' the *Toronto Life* article helps to imagine Bieber's fame as morally stronger than that of American stars. The article titled "Captain Canuck Goes Hollywood" suggests how Bieber may encounter imagined frontier conditions of the Wild West in Hollywood. In the film, Bieber plays the role of Captain Canuck, a role that originally represents a Mountie. Just as the Mountie represents the Northern frontier in binary relations to the Wild West, the Canuck articulates a "national identity against that of USA" (Dittmer & Larsen, 2007, p. 741) and is imagined as stronger and better than its southern counterpart. This imagination is rooted in a Canadian frontier ideology that characterises the North as a harsher place than the

American Wild West. For William Katerberg (2003), the 'North' of North America is an imagined site where a stronger colonial power conquered the West. As seen in the case of CWOF inductees, Bieber figures as a Canuck who not only goes to Hollywood but also symbolises a collective sense of national heroism that is morally superior to its American counterpart. The cinematic adaptation of the comic book and its media representations act as extratextual elements that qualify Bieber's stardom in Canada. Both the film and its media representations celebrate Bieber's talent as a set of Canadian qualities in relation to the US. These representations help to reclaim Bieber's Canadian national identity from Hollywood, since he migrated to the US for his music career. In the process, the media support an authentic and sovereign representation of the Canadian nation in relation to dominant US practices.

Media constructions of Justin Bieber's stardom also intersect with mundane and banal representations of the nation that contrast with official symbols of the Canadian frontier. In media, representations of nation-branded products and markers help to maintain Canada as Justin Bieber's homeland. The ordinariness of consuming these products helps to authenticate Justin Bieber's fame, as well as that of the Canadian nation. In a report on the press conference of *Never Say Never*, CTV described how "Canada [is] still home for Bieber" (Droganes, 2011). In this context, CTV cites Justin Bieber stating that, "I miss Tim Hortons. I miss my friends and my family and my dog Sam" (Ibid.). For Bieber, his friends, family, and pet dog represent a personal sense of belonging amidst the ordinary settings of his home and hometown. This personal and ordinary sense of belonging is appropriated by the practice of consuming Tim Hortons coffee, which constitutes a Canadian national pastime.

In contrast to official symbols, such as Mounties and the maple leaf, the symbol of Tim Hortons coffee locates a rather mundane national pastime in Justin Bieber's stardom. Tim Hortons figures as a nation-branded artefact that symbolises coffee as a natural product and unites citizens via a shared sense of authenticity of the land (Cormack, 2008). In Canada, the consumption of Tim Hortons coffee has gained nationwide popularity for two main reasons. First, the founder of Tim Hortons coffee was a famous Canadian hockey player, hockey itself being the most popular sport nationally. Tim Hortons' fame helps to celebrate hockey as a national pastime, a celebration that also honours Canada. Second, the Canadian population enjoys the ordinary, mundane pleasures of consuming coffee. The marketing of the Tim Hortons franchise as a national brand represents a liberation from the state regulation of popular culture (Ibid.). Thus, Tim Hortons brand coffee has become a popular cultural marker of the Canadian lifestyle. In this lifestyle, Canadians enjoy the natural, mundane, and ordinary pleasures of everyday life because these pleasures are more authentic than practices originating from the nation-state. These ordinary pleasures not only mediate Justin Bieber's authenticity as a real Canadian; they also mediate the Canadian nation.

The mediation of Bieber's ordinariness in a national context also surfaces in a *National Post* article. In reviewing his celebrity memoir, *First Step 2: My Story Forever* (Bieber, 2010), the article makes the following claim: "From humble beginnings in some mythical land called Canada (home of "maple syrup and Caramilk bars") to his ascent to global superstardom, Bieber exposes himself raw to the world" (Hertz, 2010). In this media report, maple syrup, like Tim Hortons coffee, represents ordinariness and authenticity, characterising the raw nature of both Justin Bieber's stardom and of the Canadian land. Maple syrup is a common natural product in Canada. As a symbol of nature, maple syrup is more authentic than the state-sanctioned emblem of the maple leaf, which is associated with bureaucratic affairs. The branding of maple syrup as a national (and natural) symbol, then, authenticates Justin Bieber and the homeland where his stardom is constructed.

In Justin Bieber's media representations, the usage of both Tim Hortons and maple syrup reinscribes a territorially bound identity via the very contrast it creates with state-regulated popular culture (Cormack, 2008). The images of these products not only help to identify and authenticate the Canadian nation as the products' place of origin, but also to authenticate the citizens who live in that nation and consume these products. As mentioned in Chapters 3 and 4, the underlying premise of associating nature with nation represents the shared quest for authenticity and spiritual belonging with a land that unifies its people (Manning, 2003). Members of the land inhabit the territory, a unit of space. As territorial space gives the impression of home, narratives conflate home and the land, providing the nation's roots and boundaries (Herb & Kaplan, 1999; Manning, 2000). In Canada, media narratives represent natural products such as Tim Hortons coffee and maple syrup to evoke images of a homeland from which the products originate. While maple syrup naturally originates in Canada, coffee plants come from elsewhere. Yet, for media and other cultural institutions, Tim Hortons coffee is as natural as maple syrup because its corporation is based in Canada. These products, through their origins, authenticate the territorially bounded Canadian nation as the homeland of its citizens.

In this national context, the CTV report and *National Post* article use Tim Hortons and maple syrup to symbolise Justin Bieber's national identification with his homeland. The article contrasts the ordinariness of Bieber's Canadian home with the extraordinariness of his "global superstardom" (Hertz, 2010). The contrast between Canada's ordinariness as 'home' and the extraordinariness of Bieber's 'global stardom' raises questions of authenticity: Is he an ordinary citizen or an extraordinary star? The ongoing desire to know the 'real' Justin Bieber helps fuel the appeal and desire that is key to his stardom. Nonetheless, the ordinariness of home — both literally and figuratively — authenticates Bieber's national self. It also authenticates the Canadian territory that is both a point of departure and return for the star.

Lisa Ray

Canada has been a site of departure and return for actor Lisa Ray through both traditional and online media practices and representations. Lisa Ray is a Canadian-born actor who, since 1986, has been famous for her modelling and acting careers in the Indian entertainment industry (Sahgal, 2009). Ray also received international acclaim for acting in Canadian films screened at the Toronto International Film Festival. Compared to media representations and fame in India, however, Canadian media payed less attention to Ray's talent. As a *Globe and Mail* report once stated, Lisa Ray "is well-known to festival fans, but an even bigger celebrity in India" (Dixon, 2009). But her talent and stardom in Canada heightened when she released her blog *Yellow Diaries,* declaring that she had multiple myeloma at the age of 37.

The release of her blog marked a turning point in the media representation of Ray's Canadian fame. In general, her blog demonstrated the presence of three variables that are central to online and offline stardom. These variables are 1.) authenticity, the degree to which the celebrity shares real-life experiences; 2.) the consistency with which a celebrity commits to posting on a regular basis; and 3.) the interaction in which the celebrity responds to fans' comments or questions (Galerman, 2009). After meeting these blogging criteria and establishing her ordinariness via her revelation about cancer, Ray's stardom in Canada rose. Although she became famous prior to the advent of the Internet, Ray's popularity heightened when she blogged about her ordinary experiences receiving cancer treatment in Canada. Traditional media then reprinted her blog entries. The ordinariness of cancer treatment contrasted with the extraordinariness of her celebrity talent abroad. In this contrast, the question of authenticity opened up different opportunities to authenticate her stardom and, by extension, authenticate Canada.

In traditional and online media, Lisa Ray's stardom often figured in Canadian discourses of public health and disability. Like Jade Goody and Christopher Reeve, Ray's life-threatening illness played a role in constructing her fame in Canada. Historically, celebrities' illness or disabilities have had a dual role in popular press. For one thing, when a public personality is ill, his or her fame is constructed as an effect of the paradox between the public (merit) and the private (struggles). Yet, in the words of Gerrard Goggin and Christopher Newell, "fame and celebrity are crucial systems in the construction of disability" (2004, p. 3). In other words, a celebrity's illness plays a role in constructing cultural understandings of disability. Goggin and Newell study the case of Christopher Reeve and explain how his fame figures in critical disability studies:

> The construction, but especially the consumption, of Reeve as disabled celebrity, is consonant with powerful cultural myths and tropes of disability. In many Western cultures, disability is predominantly understood a tragedy, something that comes from the defects and lack of our bodies, whether through accidents of birth or life. Those 'suffering' with disability, according to this cultural myth, need to come to terms with this bitter tragedy, and show courage in heroically overcoming their lot while they bide their time for the cure that will come (Goggin & Newell, 2004, p. 3).

The views of Goggin and Newell help to understand how Ray's stardom is articulated in Canadian discourses of disability/illness. Normative understandings of her cancer and her ordinary struggles provide contrasting conditions to fight it with extraordinary talent.

A *Globe and Mail* news article illustrates the contrast between the ordinariness of fighting cancer and extraordinariness of talent in Lisa Ray's stardom. The article's headline states that, "A global actor reveals her private fight: An incurable cancer, a determined spirit" (MacDonald, 2009). In this headline, the ordinary private struggle of Ray's medical treatment is contrasted with the extraordinariness of both her talent and her determination to face the illness. In this contrast, the reality of Ray's survival may entail a crisis of her authenticity that readers may seek to resolve. The article resolves the crisis in emphasising her "determined spirit" (MacDonald, 2009) — a marker of 'sincerity' that authenticates private self (Dyer, 2004, p. 30). Headlines such as "Lisa is epitome of grace under pressure: Deepa Mehta" (MidDay, 2009) shows Ray's authentic self in her extraordinary efforts to fight cancer. Compared to these extraordinary expressions, there are media reports that highlight ordinariness in her struggles. For example, a media report opens with her words, "Sometimes life drags you down from the clouds and that's good" (Dubey, 2009). Here, the title does not mention Lisa Ray and appears to compare her with ordinary people facing similar life challenges. These expressions of ordinariness contrast with her extraordinariness in other headlines such as "Ray of Light" (Dymond, 2009). In representing contrasts between ordinariness and extraordinariness, the media reports construct her authenticity. The media representations particularly frame Lisa Ray's talented 'self' and 'health' as sites of real determination and integrity in a national context.

Lisa Ray's stardom can be examined within particular national discourses that help to authenticate Canada. The national discourse around the Canadian health care system is especially significant to consider in representations of Ray's stardom. Canadian media and national organisations devoted prominent coverage to Ray's fame after she was diagnosed with cancer and the provincial health care system treated her condition. In Canada, the state and media designate free 'universal health care' as a provincial responsibility to which citizens are entitled as a basic right. As mentioned in Chapter 7, the health care system is an important component of Canada's culture and national identity that differentiates it from America (Candace Johnson Redden, 2002; Lemco, 1994). The government provides universal, guaranteed access to medically necessary health care services for all Canadians ("Canada's Health Care System," 2011).

The national role of the Canadian Stem Cell Foundation, a non-profit organisation, is important to consider in the construction of Lisa Ray's fame. The Foundation works in association with the medical care system as well as with celebrities in the context of their medical condition. The social and semiotic construction of Lisa Ray's public persona is evidenced in an online announcement from the Canadian Stem Cell Foundation. The announcement appeared below the words, "Standing Tall" and "Looking for a Hero? Celebrate Science" (Administrator, 2010). While the former referred to Canadian fire fighter Derek Punchard, the latter referred to Chris Jarvis, an Olympic rower and a member of Canada's National Rowing Team. Jarvis spoke at an event called "Celebrate Science," which advocated Canadian scientific research. Although the commentary referred to Jarvis, it acted as an intertextual reference to Lisa Ray, who also spoke at the event. Lisa Ray's presence was emphasised by the following question: "Want to meet Lisa Ray? (It's rhetorical. Who wouldn't?) Lisa Ray is an actor, model, philanthropist and writer with an international career in Canada, the US, and India" (Administrator, 2010). The question refers to her private character (invisible to the public) that is struggling with cancer. At the same time, the answer to this question reveals her public personality and a career that is famous to many audiences/fans. The paradox of Lisa Ray's private and public self in national health discourses questions her authenticity.

The tension inherent in the construction of Ray's authenticity is negotiated on the following two levels. First, on a public level, Lisa Ray's authenticity resides in the credibility and expertise of scientific discourses in Canada. In their study, Mike Goodman and Christine Barnes (2010) suggest that non-profit organisations often situate celebrities within scientific discourses that support humanitarian development. Goodwin and Barnes draw on scholar Stephen Hilgartner to argue that,

> [S]cientific credibility is an important part of the 'performance' of science, which is particularly pertinent to discussions of the growing 'expert' of the development celebrity [...]. Like science, celebrity also holds an elevated position within society - though in markedly different ways (2010, p. 7).

Although this research applied to scientific development, it is reasonable to expect that the role of celebrities should be quite similar when it comes to science in any field, including medical research. Here I take 'development' to mean more than economic development abroad; instead, I extend it to general progress in other areas, such as medical science in a national context. The para-social relationship between scientists and celebrities shares an authoritative voice that socially constructs authenticity out of credibility and expertise.

Second, on a personal front, the organisation celebrates Lisa Ray's heroic conquest of cancer. In this respect, her merit lies in her physical strength, while first-hand knowledge of her scientific treatment authenticates both her heroism as well as the national health organisation. As Goodman and Barnes indicate, first-hand knowledge of a human condition is central to constructing the authoritative and authentic voice of a celebrity. The Canadian Stem Cell Foundation celebrates Ray's heroic conquest and, in the process, celebrates itself as well. The two-way relationship resonates with the establishment of both "celebrity diplomacy and the more contemporary 'celebritisation' of development" (Goodman & Barnes, 2010, p. 4). The famous hero is thus not just Lisa Ray, but also the development of science in a national setting. Lisa Ray's public self also stands for a 'national self' that celebrates science and supports health care for thousands of Canadians.

Canadian media raised Ray's star-status after exposing her ordinary struggles with cancer (via her blog *The Yellow Diaries*), but in the process it privileged medical discourses over representations of her film performances. At that time, Lisa Ray enjoyed a red-carpet appearance at the 2009 TIFF for her performance in the film *Cooking with Stella* (2009). During the film festival, major media corporations publicised Lisa Ray's struggle with cancer. Compared to the attention media gave to medical discourses, her film received far less coverage, despite the fact that it premiered at TIFF. The dominant representation of Ray's medical condition is illustrated in the opening lines of the following *Globe and Mail* article during TIFF:

> She gives countless speeches advocating stem cell research, does
> charity work for Princess Margaret Hospital in Toronto, blogs to a
> global audience and is writing a book on her own cancer
> experience (MacDonald, 2010).

In this representation, the *Globe and Mail* frames Ray's public personality
as that of a Canadian medical science advocate, not a film star. From this
angle, Ray's stardom originates from her involvement with the scientific
progress of the Canadian nation, not from the film industry. After her
cancer diagnosis, popular media heavily focused on how Ray was
appointed as one of the Four National Ambassadors for Plan Canada's
Because I Am a Girl Child campaign. During that time, Ray also served as
a spokesperson for the National Stem Cell Week. In addition, she raised
$23,000 for Multiple Myeloma Research at Princess Margaret Hospital.
Her media representation as a National Ambassador advocating national
medical research both mediated and authenticated her identity as a
Canadian.

The material practices of Lisa Ray's charity also mediated the
authenticity of her Canadian personality. In general, celebrity endorsements
of humanitarian/charitable causes are symbols of authenticity, credibility,
and expertise (Goodman & Barnes, 2010; Hart & Tindall, 2009). As
Goodman and Barnes clarify, the "first-hand knowledge and/or the
'credentials' to be able to speak authoritatively" (2010, p. 6) through
material texts also give the impression of authenticity. The construction of
Lisa Ray's authenticity via charity occurs on two levels. First, Canadian
media construct dominant representations of Ray in primary relation to
national medical research. In the context of TIFF, media representations
establish Lisa Ray as a 'real Canadian,' advancing national campaigns,
rather than as a talented actor. Second, media help to authenticate Ray's
Canadianness on the grounds of her authority, credibility, and expertise in
charitable acts. For Laura Frances Errington Moss (2003), attributes of
Canadian national identity overlap with humanitarian values and charity. In
Canada, this moral disposition mythically emerges in the face of harsh,
Northern frontier conditions. As explained in Chapter 3, these human
attributes reinforce the moral elements of endurance. In this context, media
discourses about Lisa Ray's humanitarianism intersect with those of the
Canadian nation. Her media representation as a National Ambassador of
Because I Am a Girl Child campaign and her national medical research
advocacy mediate and authenticate her Canadian identity. Her charity's
material contributions also mediate her Canadianness as an authentic part
of her persona. These media representations help to popularise and

celebrate Lisa Ray as a heroic charity worker, as opposed to a globally recognised acting talent.

In addition to public health care and charity, national discourses of multiculturalism have also framed the representation of Lisa Ray's stardom in Canada. During the 2009 TIFF, a *Globe and Mail* online article titled "A Global Actor Reveals Her Private Fight" (MacDonald, 2009) showed a bulleted list that reflects TIFF and its multicultural relationship with Bollywood in India:

- A global actor reveals her private fight: An incurable cancer, a determined spirit

- Festival's investment in Bollywood now paying dividends

- Epidural may aid a woman's long-term health

In the article, the bulleted list exemplifies the political and economic subtext of media discourses about Lisa Ray. While the first and last points focus on public health, the second line abruptly interposes the focus with the claim, "Festival's investment in Bollywood now paying dividends" (MacDonald, 2009). This particular claim refers to the significance of multicultural investments by TIFF. The *Globe and Mail* made this claim despite the fact that her film *Cooking with Stella* was a Canadian production, not a Bollywood one. The claim thereby symbolises official multiculturalism in Canada and legitimises Ray's representation as a Canadian.

The representation of Lisa Ray's Canadian national identity in relation to multiculturalism also surfaces in an online version of *Chatelaine* magazine. In its article, "The Thoroughly Canadian charm of Lisa Ray," the magazine situates her national identity as an effect of official multiculturalism:

> Born in 1972 in the then-largely white Toronto suburb of Etobicoke, Ray exemplifies Trudeau-era multiculturalism: Her father is Bengali and her mother is Polish. She was exposed to her parents' birth cultures from the start, and rejected and chose little bits here and there from each, which was a wonderful way to grow up. She ate curry, spoke Polish to her maternal grandmother and watched movies by Federico Fellini and Satyajit Ray with her cinephile dad (Giese, 2007).

In the above media representation, 'Trudeau-era multiculturalism' locates Lisa Ray in a Canadian national context. The context specifically refers to former Canadian Prime Minister Pierre Trudeau, who passed the 1971 Multicultural Act. This legislation subjected media representation to state regulation. As a consequence, scholar Minelle Mahtani claims that, "Multicultural policy affects media representations of minorities in Canada because by law, Canadian media organisations are expected to reflect the multicultural and multiracial nature of Canada" (2001, p. 3). Although the cultural policy intends to be a symbol of diversity, representations favour English Canadian nationalism and often fail to represent the complex fabric of Canada's population (Wood & Gilbert, 2005). These preferred meanings of English Canadian nationalism are reflected in the multicultural representations of Lisa Ray in the following way.

The *Chatelaine* magazine article mediates Ray's ethnic roots in Polish and Bengali cultures as minorities in a colonialist context of a predominantly Anglophone Canada. The article emphasises the "little bits" of Ray's birth cultures in a "largely white suburb" (Giese, 2007), thereby reinforcing a core Anglophone national identity. The discursive construction of Ray's national identity reflects how multiculturalism implicitly constructs the idea of a core English Canadian culture wherein other 'bits' of cultures become 'multicultural' in relation to that unmarked (yet dominant) Anglo-Canadian core culture (Mackey, 2002; Moodleya, 1983). The article describes Ray in association with ethnic markers such as 'curry' and 'Bollywood' that standardise a South Asian ethnicity as a discursive effect of selected postcolonial practices in India. The word 'curry' appropriates the Western origin of a cuisine in British colonial India (Leong-Salobir, 2011). Moreover, the word 'Bollywood' reflects and reinforces the dominant cultural practices of North India (Mishra, 2002), a region invaded and settled by Central Asians and British colonisers. Selective ethnic markers such as 'curry' and 'Bollywood' represent Lisa Ray as a colonised 'Other,' and this practice upholds a stronger colonialist national identity in Anglophone Canada.

The use of ethnic markers in Canada contrasts with the way fans in India interpret Lisa Ray's national identity. On Ray's blog *The Yellow Diaries,* fans articulate and reproduce her national identity according to national and ethnic contexts. For example, an Indian fan named Debajyoti Dutta-Roy posts: "But, in the end, perhaps, you will always be 'Be yourself, I'm an Indian woman'..." (Ray, 2009). Similarly, another fan named Asish posts, "Hi, Thank you for the post. You are a real inspiration for me. A brave Indian woman" (Ray, 2010). In both cases, fans interpret Ray's national identity as an effect of her father's Indian culture. However, another media report cites Ray as stating, "I am not in favour of categories, rather than being called an Indian or a Canadian, I'd prefer to be called a world citizen" (PTI, 2009). Ray further expresses that, "It is funny, maintaining these dual personalities. I have two profiles - people know of a different Lisa Ray in India and here I have a separate identity as an actor" (PTI, 2009). As seen in most traditional and online media representations, however, Lisa Ray's 'separate identity as an actor' in Canada is mediated as a performer of Canadian nation values — as both a humanitarian and multicultural citizen. These representations show how media and fans resonate with existing national discourses in constructing and maintaining Ray's stardom. These representations also show that Canadian stardom mostly relies on the authenticity of a 'national self,' rather than on talent of its stars alone. The representations of the 'national self' authenticate Canadian stars and, in the process, the nation from which they emerge.

Maria Aragon

Media representations of Maria Aragon's fame provide insight into the national context of Canada. Aragon became famous after performing Lady Gaga's song *Born This Way* in a home video that her sister uploaded on YouTube. When Lady Gaga noticed the YouTube video, she shared it with over eight million Internet fans on Twitter. It was only after Lady Gaga's tweet that Maria Aragon's YouTube video went viral, racking up over 2.9 million viewers. Soon after Aragon achieved her online popularity, Lady Gaga invited her for a duet. The duet was on *Born This Way* at the Air Canada Centre in Toronto on March 3, 2011.

Like her Tweet, Lady Gaga's onstage performance acted as a text in relation to which viewers watched and interpreted Maria Aragon's YouTube video as a site of fame. The following media statements illustrate Aragon's fame in particular relation to Lady Gaga:

> Maria has become an overnight sensation on YouTube with the video of her singing *Born This Way* garnering more than 2.9 million views [...] It went viral after an enthusiastic Twitter message from Lady Gaga to her eight million followers (Wiebe, 2011).

> Lady Gaga granted a 10-year-old Winnipegger a share of her spotlight on Thursday, inviting YouTube singing sensation Maria Aragon onstage for a duet on *Born This Way* in front of a roaring crowd at the Air Canada Centre [...]. Aragon -- who shot to Internet fame after a video of her performing Gaga's outsider anthem went viral and drew more than 17 million views -- managed to remain perfectly poised throughout the performance (Patch, 2011).

The reading of Maria Aragon's YouTube video is positioned between the primary texts of Lady Gaga's tweet and her onstage performance. In this context, Maria Aragon's online fame is a cultural effect of intertextuality, whereby viewers do not read signs of her YouTube video's ordinariness in isolation. Rather, viewers read the text in paradoxical relation to the extraordinariness that is symbolised by texts of Lady Gaga's tweet and onstage performances. The intertextuality that constitutes Maria Aragon's fame demonstrates how an online fan can become a celebrity. At the same time, Aragon remains a fan even though she also became famous. As scholar Matt Hills explains, fans can "become celebrities and niche-mediated figures of recognition in their own subcultures" (2006, p. 103). This explanation applies to any online user who achieves celebrity status within a network of fans. The lack of a central Internet authority enables online fans and audiences to freely produce and circulate their selves as media texts and become celebrities like Maria Aragon.

Whether Maria Aragon is popular as an artist or fan, media often represent her talent within Canadian national discourses that help to sustain her temporary, online fame. Traditional media often depict Aragon in terms of her Canadian attributes, such as multiculturalism. A number of media reports refer to Maria Aragon as a Filipino-Canadian. For instance, a *Globe and Mail* article stated that, "the young Filipino-Canadian chanteuse gained international acclaim for her YouTube cover of Lady Gaga's *Born this Way*, which landed her plaudits from the American superstar [...]" (Chase, 2011). The *Globe and Mail* made this statement in the political context of Canadian Prime Minister Stephen Harper, who visited Maria Aragon's home during his 2011 election campaign and sang a duet with her. The report continued, stating that, "Mr. Harper, who's courting the big Filipino community in Winnipeg like every other party in the 2011 election, journeyed to Maria's home to meet her" (Ibid.). A City TV report elaborated on the ethnic context in which Maria Aragon's national identity was represented: "Reporters, campaign staff and even the Harpers were politely asked to take off their shoes inside the Filipino-Canadian family's home" (Ditchburn, 2010).

The subtext of these media reports is twofold. First, Canadian Prime Minister Stephen Harper performed an "ethnic outreach program" (MacCharle, 2011) that reflected acting "very ethnic" (Siddiqui, 2011) during his 2011 election campaign. The purpose of this performance was to win votes from ethnic communities and to support a majority government that has a minority of ethnic representatives. In this context, Prime Minister Stephen Harper singing a duet with Maria Aragon was not neutral, nor was it based on mere musical talent. Rather, the act of singing existed in a hegemonic relationship with ethnic communities that are not Anglophone Canadians.

Second, the media reports underscore that Prime Minister Stephen Harper is a Canadian while Maria Aragon is a *Filipino-Canadian*. Maria Aragon's national identity is hyphenated, and the hyphen between Filipino and Canadian signifies the social and semiotic construction of relocating Canadian citizens who are 'Other' than the dominant Anglophone Canadian population. Hyphenation is a signifying practice in which the hyphen is a national and ethnic signifier that both denies entry into the myth of the nation and locates alternative sites of belonging (Jackson & Ponic, 2001; Mackey, 2002; Manning, 2000). As scholar Eva Mackey writes, hyphens are significant within the social construction of national identities in Canada:

> Canada has a proliferation of hyphenated peoples. Many Canadians identify themselves as German-Canadian, Ukrainian-Canadian, Chinese-Canadian, Greek-Canadian, Afro-Canadian, French-Canadian, Native-Canadian, Italian-Canadian and so on. While all these hyphenated forms all have their own histories of constitution, some groups are widely considered more 'ethnic' than others. Others have the privilege of being simply 'Canadian' (Mackey, 2002, p. 20).

For Mackey, the hyphen sign marks Canadians other than White British settlers who themselves remain "unmarked, unhyphenated, and hence normative" (p. 102). From this perspective, media texts represent Maria Aragon's identity as a fragment of the complete, or core, English Canadian nation that her fame supports. In expressing Maria Aragon's national identity, the word 'Filipino' does not refer to her domestic culture alone; it also refers to the non-English ethnicity of her parents, who immigrated to Canada from the Philippines.

The expressions of national identity are not limited to mainstream Anglophone media in Canada. They overlap with mainstream media content in the Philippines. For producers and audiences in the Philippines, Maria Aragon is Filipino based on her ethnicity and the nationality of her parents. For this reason, media productions of *Manilla Bulletin Publishing Corporation*, the *Philippine Daily Inquirer*, and blogs produced in the Philippines or by Filipino diaspora communities consider Maria Aragon to be Filipino. These expressions reflect and reinforce the idea that Maria Aragon's national identity rests on more than just the territorial constructions of the nation where she resides; it also rests on her ethnic background. This ethnic background, in turn, supports Canada's official multiculturalism that contrasts with America's melting pot, as seen in Chapters 5 and 7.

In other cases, Maria Aragon's identity is represented as a Canadian whose fame is different from Hollywood constructions of stardom. In particular, her media representations reclaim Canadian national identity by 'reversing' dominant American conceptions of fame. For example, a *Globe and Mail* article reverses dominant American fame in favour of celebrating Canadian talent. The article opens with the headline: "Lady Gaga goes gaga for Canadian girl's rendition of *Born This Way*" (Staff, 2011a). Similarly, a photograph which appeared in a Winnipeg Free Press article (Patch, 2011) depicts how Lady Gaga looks up to Maria Aragon performing her song in Toronto. The headline and image mediate Aragon's talent as a discursive construction of Canadianness that sets her apart from America. The article's headline situates Aragon's talent in a Canadian context by proclaiming that, "Toronto Crowd Goes Gaga For Winnipeg Girl" (Ibid.). Here, Toronto and Winnipeg help to distinguish Maria Aragon's Canadianness from the American "Gaga" (Ibid.). The pop star's name, 'Gaga' acts as a metaphor for the dominant symbol of fame whose dominance is ironically reversed in the article's photograph. Indeed, American star Lady Gaga looks up to Canadian Maria Aragon, erasing cultural memories of Aragon's initial role as a Lady Gaga fan. This reversal reclaims Aragon's talent for Canada and mediates that talent as a performance of Canadianness in binary relations with America.

Other media representations also show how Maria Aragon's Canadian fame is expressed in the context of Hollywood. The reports illustrate the media treatment of her fame as a reclamation of Canadianness in America:

> A Canadian-grown YouTube star is getting attention for more than her vocal skills. Maria Aragon - the 10-year-old Winnipeg girl whose cover of a Lady Gaga hit earned millions of views on the popular video-sharing site - is in Los Angeles shooting a commercial for Ralph Lauren (Staff, 2011b).

> A 10-year-old Winnipeg singing sensation who has rocketed to internet fame is in California taping a segment for an upcoming episode of the Ellen DeGeneres Show [...] (CBC, 2011b).

> [...] The 10-year-old's cover of Lady Gaga's hit "Born This Way" on YouTube has been viewed more than 25 million times, and her story received international coverage, resulting in a duet with Gaga at her Toronto concert and an appearance on Ellen DeGeneres' Los Angeles-based talk show (Staff, 2011b).

As the above media texts articulate, Maria Aragon's popularity is as much based on her Canadian upbringing as it is her innate talent. Here,

'Canadian-grown' is another hyphenated national identity that contrasts with America's melting pot. The contrast is further emphasised when Aragon's photo shoot and interview with Ellen DeGeneres in Los Angeles is mentioned to symbolise 'making it' in Hollywood. In Canadian popular culture, Los Angeles is known for its cultural construction of the Hollywood stardom that dominates Canadian talent. However, Hollywood is now a site for reclaiming Canadian fame through immediate media attention. In this context, the media attention given to Aragon's talent is an 'attributed fame' of Canadian national identity that exceeds her vocal skills.

The media attention given to Maria Aragon in the US contrasts earlier fame-based practices. As seen in previous chapters, Canadians often 1.) migrated to America, 2.) became amalgamated into American popular culture and experienced an erasure of their Canadianness, and 3.) were later reclaimed as Canadians through media attention awarded at sites such as TIFF and CWOF. With the rise of reality TV and Internet, this three-step flow of reclaiming Canadian talent has collapsed into one-step, in which Canadian talent is immediately recognised in Hollywood. In this view, Aragon's immediate fame as a Canadian is intertextually contingent upon the fame of Lady Gaga and Ellen DeGeneres in Los Angeles. Los Angeles is a cultural site where the national differences between America's Hollywood and Canada are played out. In this context, Aragon is represented as an American 'Other.' In other words, media construct her stardom in binary relations with dominant American representations of fame while also reclaiming her Canadian fame in a one-step process.

Maria Aragon's talent is expressed as an urban construct of the Canadian nation. As explained in Chapters 3 and 7, an urban national identity symbolically expresses Canada as an industrial and technological nation that developed out of the colonisation of frontier regions. This urban national identity, in turn, helps to recognise Canada as a strong frontier nation within North America. Aragon is often referred to as a "Winnipeg tween" (Staff, 2011c), a point unrelated to her musical skills. Other reports identify Aragon as a "10-year-old Winnipeger" (Ditchburn, 2010), "Winnipeg's Maria Aragon,"(CBC, 2011b), and "Winnipeg's singing sensation" (CBC, 2011b). These expressions are popular ways of locating Maria Aragon's talent within an urban-Canadian national context, a status that is separate from that of a Filipino-Canadian or an American 'Other.' These urban expressions are forms of local diversity that stand in for multicultural and frontier identities and support a colonialist English Canadian identity. Representations of Maria Aragon's online fame thus reveal multiple types of Canadian national identity that intersect in different, overlapping ways.

Conclusion

The chapter began with a question exploring whether the Internet changed how Canadian stars are constructed and maintained, and it addressed the role that Internet technologies play in shaping Canada's celebrity cultures. The decentralised nature of the Internet has helped to improve the subordinate positions of Canadian talent. It has also popularised Canadian fans who admire American pop stars. Given the dominance of Hollywood stardom, the initial rise of these stars would have been difficult without the use of Internet technologies. America's Hollywood stardom and Canada's lack of a central, industrialised star system challenges fame-based practices in traditional media. The decentralised setting of the Internet enables both online users (including celebrities) and fans to participate in cultural constructions of fame in Canada. The difference between traditional offline and online practices is that there is a lack of hierarchical control in the latter, leading to more user participation and a direct, immediate construction of fame. In Canada, this immediate construction has collapsed the past three-step process of fame into a single step. The case studies of Justin Bieber and Maria Aragon exemplify how fans have become celebrities in Canada. Lisa Ray had greater recognition of her talent through the Bollywood star system…that is until she blogged about her cancer treatment in Canada. Her blog helped to authenticate her 'national self' in the context of the Canadian public health care system.

Yet, as the case studies demonstrate, traditional Canadian media recognise and legitimise online fame. In general, online celebrities are not limited to those discovered on the Internet. They include celebrities who have already gained fame in traditional, offline settings but who used Internet tools to promote their talent further. In all cases, the question of authenticity is significant to understanding their online popularity. Indeed, Internet fame is a distinct and fragile sort of celebrity, with a fleeting, ephemeral character that is extended only after it is integrated into a physical 'star system' of recording or film industries. Case studies of Justin Bieber, Lisa Ray, and Maria Aragon show how traditional media represent and popularise these stars' recording or film work. These forms of celebrity representations are important for Canada as a nation where online celebrities are constructed, distributed, and received.

The case studies in this chapter illustrated that both traditional and online media represent and sustain online Canadian celebrities within national discourses. Online celebrities' national identity is expressed in contrasting ways. At times, media producers and Internet users associate online celebrities with official national symbols. The chapter showed how Justin Bieber's stardom is articulated in relation to official symbols such as the Canadian flag, the maple leaf, and Mounties. Similarly, celebrities like Lisa Ray and Maria Aragon are represented and understood in relation to federal policies such as the Federal Multiculturalism Act. At other times, online celebrities are associated with mundane products and practices that are not sanctioned by the nation-state yet still mark Canadianness in everyday life. In representations of online celebrities, the North, Captain Canuck, maple syrup, and Tim Hortons often designate Canadianness. Some of these markers and products contrast with official symbols, as they signify everyday consumption that is free from the state bureaucracy. However, they also overlap with official symbols because they signify Canadian myths that associate the nation with the dominance of an English Canadian identity in an imagined Northern frontier.

In Canadian celebrity cultures, online users engage with texts that represent the nation in multiple ways. They accept, negotiate, or subvert the meanings of a dominant national identity. While some users accept the predominant representation of Canadianness, others, such as the cases of Lisa Ray and Maria Aragon, negotiate or subvert them. In the case study on Lisa Ray presented in this chapter, her national identity is sometimes represented as Canadian and sometimes as Indian by both traditional media and by online fans. Ray, however, is also an Internet producer of her own celebrity texts who claims to be neither Indian nor Canadian, but a world citizen.

The multiplicity of Lisa Ray's national representations overlaps with that of Maria Aragon. Media productions treat Aragon's national identity as Filipino-Canadian or Canadian. Studies show that the articulation of these multiple national identities is contingent upon national differences with America. Most reports show that Maria Aragon is treated as a Canadian in strong relation to America's Hollywood. Her fame expresses her talent as well as the performance of her Canadianness in the context of a dominant American celebrity culture. These performances help to subvert previous myths of a Canadian inferiority and resist appropriating standard notions of Hollywood fame. Other reports on Aragon's fame express her urban national identity that ideologically supports Canada as an industrial nation. The articulation of national identities is both different from, and similar to, traditional offline representations of Canadian celebrities. It is similar to offline celebrities in that discourses of online fame intersect with those of the nation. In these intersections, online celebrities' national identities originate in offline settings of national movements and their symbolic representations. Nevertheless, the articulation of national identities is different from offline representations in the sense that Internet users are able to present and reproduce texts in a setting that is distinct from traditional media. On the Internet, users can produce their own celebrity texts, thereby giving an impression of authenticity. The representations of these texts are open to higher accessibility, immediacy, non-linear communication, and interactivity with audiences and fans. These characteristics help to generate global fame while offering opportunities to explore situated experiences, as opposed to a standardised national identity.

For Canadian cultural institutions, the significance of using national symbols and markers online lies in reclaiming the national identity of international celebrities. This act of reclamation is significant now that the Internet allows fame to transcend territorial boundaries and allow celebrities such as Justin Bieber and Maria Aragon to receive contracts in Hollywood after gaining initial online fame. Although Lisa Ray did not move to the US, she was predominantly famous in India's Bollywood until traditional and online media representations of health in Canada reclaimed her Canadianness. In the historical context of Canada's identity crisis, the construction and maintenance of Canadian national symbols may prove to be of less importance in the Internet age. Nevertheless, the maintenance of territorial boundaries and the premise of a unified national identity (Eriksen, 2007; Herb & Kaplan, 1999) may still threaten the nationality of an online celebrity. In response, however, media and audiences are often able to reclaim global celebrities' Canadian national identity with the help of local symbols that characterise national territorial boundaries.

Indeed, online media discourses engage with those of the nation in offline, territorial settings. In these ways, media producers and audiences are able to mitigate or negotiate what might be perceived as global-national tensions in maintaining online territorial integrity. For example, I have shown that although Justin Bieber is a global star, Canadian media imagine and represent him in relation to the urban context of his hometown, Stratford, and national markers of Canada. This Canadian representation occurs despite the fact that, for the most part, Justin Bieber does not live in Canada. Media corporations such as CTV and the *National Post* use offline symbols and myths of the nation to produce and represent Justin Bieber as Canadian. Similar symbols and myths thrive in celebrity texts of Lisa Ray and Maria Aragon. The material production of these texts takes place in both online and offline versions of their reports. From a material and symbolic perspective, then, the texts of online celebrities intersect with offline national texts. These expressions of national identity are common within purely offline fame, but in online cases, fans play a greater role in supporting these expressions.

9 Canadian Meanings of Fame

This book set out to answer the question: how do contemporary Canadian media represent celebrities in the English Canadian context? In relation to this question, the book aimed to address how Canadian media construct national identity through representations of celebrities in popular culture. The question emerged in the context of the myth that Canada neither has celebrities nor a star system. Yet, Canada continues to produce and consume celebrities, especially in the context of Hollywood. In these productions, the national identity of celebrities is articulated in several important ways.

This concluding chapter shows how the book addressed its central question through a set of three interrelated myths: 1.) the North, 2.) the lack, and 3.) the American better 'Other.' Each of these recurring concepts is discussed in relation to the background material (Chapters 1 - 4) and the research conducted in case studies (Chapters 5 - 8). This chapter synthesises notions of national identity expressed in Canadian celebrity cultures, and highlights the Canadian meaning of fame in national contexts.

The North

Canadian fame symbolically expresses the cultural construction of the Northern frontier. As highlighted in Chapters 1 - 4, Mounties, the maple leaf, ice/snow, ice hockey, and Canucks are some of the most popular symbols of the Canadian North. While Mounties and the maple leaf are *official* symbols of the North, wilderness, frozen conditions, ice hockey, Canucks, and maple syrup are *unofficial* symbols. But whether official or unofficial, these popular Northern symbols reflect and reinforce the rhetorical practice and infrastructure of technological nationalism. The cultural content representing mythical qualities of the wild, vast, and empty spaces of the North fosters the conditions out of which the rhetorical, economic, and political use of technologies emerged and supported the nation. While technological intervention via industrialisation and natural resource exploitation has left the physical North in a critically threatened condition, this has not stopped cultural institutions from adopting romanticised images of the North that ignore reality. Indeed, this romanticised North legitimises and calls for the technological integration of Canada. This integration, however, involves heavy investments into technology and leaves limited resources and revenues for the production of domestic content in the sparse Canadian market.

Amidst these conditions the Toronto International Film Festival (TIFF), as seen in Chapter 5, imports many Hollywood films and stars, both American and Canadian, and it supports US-based runaway production facilities in Canada. Chapter 6 discussed TIFF's parallel organisation, Canada's Walk of Fame (CWOF). This is a commemorative site that constructs a collective Canadian memory through Northern resistance to Hollywood stardom, even as it emulates the Hollywood Walk of Fame. The CWOF and its media representations focus on Canadians that migrated to Hollywood and reclaims their national identity through the use of Northern symbolism. The extreme Northern conditions both challenge and motivate Canadians to reclaim the North American frontier that is dominated, culturally and economically, by the US.

In Canada, fame-based practices in reality TV programs also engage in national discourses of the North. Chapter 7 observed how fame and the North intersected on different levels. While the ice-skating rink of *Battle of the Blades* symbolised vast, empty, frozen lands, it also functioned as a new 'skill frontier' where ex-National Hockey League stars reconstructed their previous talent-based fame through figure skating in order to re-gain technological control over nature. Their sharp 'battle blades,' in addition to existing media technologies, integrate and represent the ice-skating rink as a frontier nation. The juxtaposition of the CN tower, a symbol of the technological nation, and Niagara Falls, as a symbol of nature, also reflects and reinforces the Canadian frontier in *Canadian Idol*. Even US-based media like *Hollywood Report* use rhetorical phrases such as 'The Great White North' to describe reality TV programs like *Battle of the Blades*, *Canadian Idol*, and *So You Think You Can Dance Canada* as cultural products of the Northern frontier. In Canadian fame, these symbolic expressions of the North reflect and reinforce the frontier in which it emerges, and they confirm the need for technologies to integrate the nation.

Symbols of North are not limited to celebrities constructed by traditional media. Chapter 8 demonstrated that Canadian celebrities with an online presence are also associated with the North. The case study of Justin

Bieber showed how his celebrity image is interwoven with official Northern symbols such as Mounties and the maple leaf, as well as unofficial markers of the North that include the Canuck, Tim Hortons, maple syrup, and endurance as a moral value. Similarly, the case study of Lisa Ray demonstrated how the moral values of strength and determination served as unofficial symbols of the Canadian nation that also shaped Ray's celebrity status. In this respect, her fight against cancer, in addition to her humanitarian and charitable efforts, reflects and reinforces notions of endurance that are ideologically connected to harsh, Northern frontier conditions.

The Lack

In Canadian fame, the heroic strength symbolised by the North is contrasted by inferiority in the myth of lack. Cultural productions, as discussed in Chapter 3, have supported the myth of lack in ways that provide the ideological conditions for negotiating effects of vast, empty lands and conflicting cultures across Canada. These conditions laid the foundation for Canadians to deploy technologies and build what is now called a technological nation. The rhetorical use of technologies, however, facilitates homogenous representations of an English Canadian colonialist culture, marked by disappearance and the loss of individual, local, and regional differences.

The lack of representation of homegrown stars at TIFF is an example that feeds on the rhetorical myth. Indeed, heavy investments into technology within a sparse market and a dearth of human resources do not facilitate a centralised studio and star system in Canada. At an imaginary level, this absence has grown into a myth that Canada lacks stars. Chapter 5 highlighted that Canadian stardom is characterised by an under-representation of — even a lack of reverence for — its homegrown stars. In TIFF representations, the city of Toronto and its audiences are instead named as 'stars,' but these stars lack individual talent. These stars are 'absent referents' that reflect and reinforce the myth of lack in Canada's technological nationalism.

CWOF practices and representations support the myth of lack by engaging in an existing national discourse shaped by an inferiority complex. The myth of inferiority around CWOF inductees is expressed in various ways. These expressions largely suppress or subordinate CWOF stardom in Canada. Some representations also interrogate the achieved status of CWOF inductees and, in the process, reinforce an absence of their recognition. In other cases, the inferiority complex around CWOF inductees is expressed by highlighting their unconventional practices, which do not meet dominant standards of fame in America. Although the CWOF and attendant media construct fame in a negative manner, this construction is not necessarily defamatory. Instead, as discussed in Chapter 6, CWOF and Canadian media consider this kind of 'anti-fame' to be a distinct form of popularity that is proudly Canadian.

Canadian reality TV shows both support and subvert national discourses based on the myth of lack. As Chapter 7 demonstrated, programs like *Battle of the Blades* use metaphors of the North, thereby emphasising a lack of regional/local differences across the nation. *Canadian Idol* and *So You Think You Can Dance Canada* also reinforce these differences by popularising contestants in relation to their regional and urban places of origin. These regional differences, in turn, stand in for multicultural diversity that supports a core English Canadian identity. In most cases, these constructions prioritise metanarratives of English Canada over famous peoples' actual experiences. These reality shows also undermine or reconstruct existing or potential fame in a way that reclaims past Canadian values and glosses over innate talent. Nonetheless, new performances of Canadianness create a popular recognition of Canadian fame. Evaluations by reality show judges and hosts reflect a form of disbelief in Canadian talent that is followed by a process of discovery and recognition of that talent, a talent long-buried beneath the Canadian inferiority complex. This recognition of fame is therefore a new Canadian value. The appeal of rising Canadian celebrity cultures within discourses of lack marks both continuities and shifts in the way fame has been interpreted in a national context.

The shifts and continuities in Canadian fame are also happening on the Internet. The case studies of Justin Bieber, Lisa Ray, and Maria Aragon show that talented individuals with an online presence can gain instant recognition in Canada, especially when they further engage in national discourses and/or step into Hollywood. In the past, there was a three-step process whereby most Canadian talents 1.) migrated to America due to lack of resources in Canada, 2.) became amalgamated into Hollywood's popular culture and subjected to an erasure of their Canadianness, and 3.) were later reclaimed as Canadians through media attention. This process has now been now collapsed into a single step, whereby Canadian talent is immediately recognised in Hollywood *and* Canada. This popular recognition subverts the past myth that Canada lacks stars, but it also negates Canadian cultural diversity. Indeed, stars such as Lisa Ray and Maria Aragon are represented in terms of a hyphenated national identity. This lack exists as the hyphenation signifies a core English Canadian identity while relegating ethnic cultures to the national margins. Nevertheless, these stars did not need to migrate to America to gain stardom in Canada. On the contrary, their stardom helps to subvert previous myths of an inferiority complex while still allowing them to appropriate Hollywood fame.

The American Better 'Other'

The superiority of the 'North' and the inferiority of the 'lack' function as an American 'Other' in Canadian notions of fame. The concept of Canada as an 'Other' emerges out of the rhetorical, economic, and political practices of technological nationalism and continentalism. As explained in Chapters 1 - 4, Canada's dependence on America creates a sense of American cultural imperialism that Canadian popular culture paradoxically consumes, embraces, supports, and resists. There is a recurrent representation of how Canada is *not* America. This feeds back into the notion of 'lack,' and underpins the idea that Canada is a northern nation that is *better than* America. As Chapters 3 and 4 note, the 'North' of North America (as in 'Hollywood North'), acts as a site for imagining a conquering colonial power that out-conquers America's Wild West. Most Canadian practices and representations with regard to celebrity culture establish the North as a stronger frontier and, by extension, resist the American Wild West. Similarly, when stacked up against American hegemony, the myth of lack and the Canadian feeling of inferiority do not reflect *actual* inferiority. This process instead reveals a differentiation expressed via the distinctly Canadian characteristics of unity, morality, humbleness, politeness, and all-around 'betterness' that place Canada well above the boastful gregariousness of Hollywood celebrity promotion. The strong Northern frontier and its inherent moral superiority thereby intersect with the myth of lack to offer (contradictory) national resistance to American stardom. In Canada, the notion of celebrities as American better 'Others' is indeed a myth, but it still functions to express this resistance.

The Canadian version of fame also functions as an American better 'Other' at TIFF. As observed in Chapter 5, TIFF is often represented in the context of Hollywood North. At a material level, this representation encourages the Hollywood film industry to invest in Canadian show business talent. In this respect, TIFF as Hollywood North functions as a symbolic extension of America, where Hollywood stars are celebrated and Canadian stars are underrepresented. This unequal representation demonstrates Canada's dependence on American stars, productions, and investments, thereby reinforcing the myth of lack. But this myth still serves to differentiate Canada from America. Hollywood North negotiates the 'lack' of Canadian stars by imagining them as superior to their American counterparts. As Chapters 4 and 5 reveal, the 'North' in Hollywood North symbolises the 'better' half of the North American frontier. In this context, Canadian celebrities are thus imagined as 'better' than American stars that TIFF systematically "Others."

For the CWOF, the superiority of the Northern frontier and the Canadian inferiority complex help to 'Other' America. The result is a necessary resistance, as the CWOF embraces the Hollywood Walk of Fame while it simultaneously reclaims expatriate Canadian stars. Chapter 6 explored this resistance and reclamation through the idea of the American better 'Other.' The CWOF adopts America's successful Walk of Fame model, but its representations of inductees reflect myths of Canadian inferiority. By glorifying Canadian stars as national heroes in an imagined Northern frontier that is stronger than that of America, the CWOF systematically 'Others' America, thus marking Canada's Walk of Fame as superior to the Hollywood Walk of Fame (and its attendant Wild West frontier ideology) that the CWOF nonetheless emulates.

In Canadian reality TV programs, fame-based practices often engage with a 'mosaic' of different cultural identities that differentiate Canadian diversity from America's so-called 'melting pot.' This kind of 'Othering' supports a core English Canadian identity against which minority linguistic and ethnic groups are visibly contrasted. As discussed in Chapter 7, reality TV programs popularise Quebecois contestants by emphasising their French-Canadian heritage. This national identification distinguishes Quebecois contestants from the rest of English Canada and supports a core English Canadian identity. In addition, reality shows popularise contestants in association with regional urban centres rather than rural localities. This urban-centred view helps to symbolise Canada as a technological and industrial nation that developed against the wilderness frontier. Even as the equal opportunities given to diverse groups help to (however mythically) imagine Canada as better than America's melting pot, manufactured notions of Canadian bilingualism and urban-based regionalism replace actual diversity.

The mythical qualities of being an American better 'Other' also surface in representations of online celebrities. The case studies in Chapter 8 showed three ways in which these representations highlight Canadian superiority. They include expressions of the North, multiculturalism, and subversion of American stardom. While Justin Bieber is associated with the North, Lisa Ray and Maria Aragon are represented in terms of their multiculturalism and their hyphenated national identity. In addition to these discursive practices, media explicitly represent the subversion of Hollywood fame. Chapter 8 explained how visual and written texts are used, literally and figuratively, to shift admiration from Lady Gaga to Maria Aragon. This reversal of Hollywood fame is used to reclaim Maria Aragon's talent in Canada. Her talent is thus mediated as a performance of Canadianness that is more admirable, and thus, better than American fame.

Meanings of Fame in Canada

Three interrelated concepts emerged in this book as integral to representations of Canadian fame: the North, the lack, and the American better 'Other.' Canadian media technologies disseminate these concepts.

The mythic qualities of these concepts reinforce an imagined Northern frontier that technology (the form) integrated into Canada's nation-building process. In Canadian representations of celebrities, the North and the lack help to overlook the crisis of the geographic north and the local conflicts brought on by colonialist technology in that region. Similarly, the myth of the American better 'Other' helps to overlook the heavy import of American media content. This imported content compensates for Canada's lack of economic and human resources that resulted from Canada's heavy investments in nation-building technological infrastructure. Mythical representations of the North, the lack, and the American better 'Other' (content) are discursive effects of the rhetoric of technological nationalism that have privileged technological infrastructure and its process of implementation (form). In this respect, these myths reinforce an imagined Canadian frontier that technology (form) integrated to build Canada. These myths are also used in the construction of fame to create imaginary conditions for national integration through transportation and communications technology. Canadian celebrity content thus feeds the economic, political, and technological interventions that have created and supported the nation.

At the same time, the North, the lack, and American better 'Other' (content) are the roots of the discursive rhetoric of technological nationalism that has privileged Canada's technological infrastructure and its process of implementation (form). Celebrity content is therefore both a colonialist tool and a rhetorical form of technique or technology that facilitates national integration in present times. The industrialised and mechanised form of Canadian media technologies disseminates celebrity texts in association with the North, the lack, and the American better 'Other.' These texts, in turn, create a mythical technological frontier bolstered by national rhetoric that is also mythical in its origins. In short, the representation of the North, the lack, and the American better 'Other' in celebrity texts (content) is both a cause for the mobilisation and legitimacy of technological nationalism (form) as well as an effect of that nationalism.

In Canadian celebrity cultures, the bidirectional relationship between form and content supports a sense of Canadian national ambivalence. This book has highlighted how Canada best exemplifies this ambivalence via its simultaneous embracing of, and resistance to, American celebrity content. This is a rhetorical form of nationalism. If the 'medium is the message,' an expression for which Marshall McLuhan became famous, I suggest that the celebrity message is also the medium in technological nationalism. Whether through content or form, the uses of media technology in celebrity culture enable the nation in ways that are specific to the social contexts in which they are produced. In Canada, the cultural production of celebrities (content) can determine the medium of technological nationalism, such as runaway film production facilities in Hollywood North and decentralised Internet (form). Conversely, there is ambivalence in the fact that technological nationalism can be centred on rhetorical content in addition to form. In fame, this bidirectional relationship — the way that content and form enable each other — also enables the Canadian nation. Chapter 3 explained how there is a constant ambivalence between form and content. This ambivalence is both central to the unconscious ways in which the North, the lack, and the American better 'Other' are reproduced and fundamental to the construction of the Canadian nation.

In Canada, the dominant meaning of fame becomes a set of North American values that largely emerge within national discourses. Understanding fame in Canada (or other nations for that matter) requires an understanding of the context out of which that fame is constructed, circulated, and received. Hence, there is no single Canadian celebrity culture; multiple domains of celebrity culture exist, and they all influence the ways in which fame is accepted, negotiated, or resisted. If there is a Canadian celebrity culture, it consists of multiple subcultures that exist within dominant representations of the Canadian nation. The cultural constructions of Canadian fame are underpinned by the competing dynamics of Canada's technological nationalism and the dominance of US continentalism. Canadian discourses on fame often celebrate a constructed notion of Canadianness, and promoting this Canadianness is just as important (if not more so) as supporting the talent of Canadian celebrities. The case studies in Chapters 5 - 8 showed that Canadian representation of stardom (including that of the city and audiences) mediates talent as a discursive effect of the national context in which it is produced and received. Here, the achievement of Canadian values is popularly recognised and celebrated as a form of stardom. Simultaneously, Canadian media representation of talent resembles and appropriates the Hollywood stardom that dominates cultural practices in North America. Thus, Canadian fame is a complex (often contradictory) 'North-American' mixture of Hollywood stardom and Canadian national values. It is defined by varied and multiple meanings of Canadianness.

The multiplicity of Canadian fame emerges in media representations that engage with national discourses in overlapping and contradictory ways via three interrelated concepts. In addition, celebrity texts integrate national symbols that are either official or unofficial markers of Canada. These official and unofficial symbols overlap in the sense that their rhetorical use of the North, for example, constructs Canadian nationalism. Like official symbols of the state (e.g., Mounties and the maple leaf), unofficial markers (e.g., ice hockey and Canuck) forge a territorially bound national identity that contrasts the state's vision of Canadian culture. These symbols appear in representations of Canadian celebrities. The difference lies in the extent to which celebrity representations conform to state intervention in Canadian popular culture. The use of unofficial symbols emphasises everyday pleasures that are a stark contrast to bureaucratic interventions into popular culture (e.g., Mounties at CWOF galas). In these competing national discourses, the identities of Canadian celebrities intersect in multiple overlapping and contradictory ways.

Celebrities' Canadian identities also overlap and contradict through representations of Canadian fame that emphasise mundane pleasures such as receiving star treatment in Hollywood North or casually walking on stylised maple leaves in the CWOF sidewalk. The trials and triumphs of figure-skating former hockey stars on *Battle of the Blades* also serve as unofficial representations of Northern identity produced to appeal to Canadians. The use of unofficial symbols such as the Canuck, Tim Hortons, and maple syrup signifies the everyday pleasures of being Canadian and also contests state-intervention in the construction of Canadian nationalism. In these cases, the representation of fame both engages with and contests past Canadian myths. These representations foster the discovery and promotion of new Canadian talent, a process that competes with state-sanctioned celebrations of Canadian national values. In these competing national discourses, celebrities' Canadian identities have multiple, sometimes contested, meanings.

In this book, I pointed out that both nations and celebrities share notions of authenticity. In Canada, selected images of Northern nature and its related myths authenticate celebrities, but more importantly, they serve to authenticate the national context in which they are constructed and represented. Authenticity, as explained in Chapter 1, is a quality that is central to both the appeal of the celebrity as well as the values the celebrity embodies. One of the sociological functions performed by celebrity texts is resolving ideological tensions of the nation in which they are constructed, and supporting national values. As observed in this book, celebrity texts are often constructed within national discourses to address existing problems of national identity. In Canada, these problems arise due to ideological differences within the nation and with other nations — namely America. When celebrity texts function in relation to contradictions within and between ideologies, the relationship between the celebrity and the contradictions may not necessarily be one that supports those contradictions (e.g., the North and the lack). In fact, celebrity texts can also question or subvert contradictions in order to negotiate competing ideologies. In either case, Northern nature in Canadian celebrity texts restores and popularises a sense of authenticity that is lost in the technological developments and contradictions of nation-building.

In the Canadian context, celebrities' authenticity addresses contradictions that exist within Canada's ambivalence with regard to its own national identity as well as its ideological differences with America.

The use of technology in building the Canadian nation relies on ambivalence. As explained in Chapter 3, technology is dominating when it conquers nature but facilitates freedom when nature is romanticised as sublime. These paradoxes in the use of technology, in both content and form, exist in relation to the concept of nature in Canada. Regardless of the state of nature, the actual use and function of technology in enabling nation-building remain constant.

There is neither an absolute domination nor freedom but an inherent ambivalence between the uses of technologies in building the nation. The ways in which the forms of technology are used are also partly ambivalent because their relationship with content is contingent. This ambivalence, as Chapter 3 explains, arises out of opposition between America's free market philosophy and Canada's public subsidies that support protectionist measures for cultural productions. The rhetorical use of technology in a sparse market, the lack of financial resources, and the mediation of situated experiences (including actual talent) are the driving forces behind Canada's social, economic, and political relationship with America. In expressions of the North and the myth of lack, Canadian ambivalence is expressed in terms of how it is *not* the place of American Dreams and is, therefore, an American 'Other.' In Canadian celebrity cultures, Hollywood North unfolds as an ambivalence that negotiates tensions with American cultural imperialism and homogenous representations of the nation-state. In this setting, the simultaneous celebration of Canadian stars in Hollywood and the reclamation of their Canadian identity through national symbols such as the North mark Canada's ambivalence regarding its own nationhood. The paradox within this ambivalence characterises a fame that also marks the progress and success of Canada. The nation, like celebrities, functions on the paradox that exists in its own ambivalence. The question of authenticity in both cases generates and sustains celebrities' appeal.

The layered understanding of the Canadian nation as represented through fame is further supported by various encounters that took place beyond the writing of this book. Toward the end of this book, I had the opportunity to explore and attend various national events, interview public personalities, and offer critical commentary on celebrity cultures for the Canadian magazine *StarBuzz Weekly*. This offered me several opportunities to explore the ambivalence of Canadian national identity in celebrity cultures. My encounters with film stars and critics at the Kingston Canadian Film Festival (KCFF) shed light on the global-local intersections of Canadian fame that I discussed in Chapter 7. Although the KCFF operates on a smaller scale than TIFF, its practices allow further reflections about Canadian celebrity cultures. As the name of the film festival suggests, the locality of Kingston played a role in determining national identities in Canadian popular culture. Often, national boundaries are distinguished in relation to 'the global' in international film festivals. However, as emphasised by the national film festival KCFF, Canadian nationalism is also constructed in relation to 'the local' in Canada. In my interviews with Canadian film star Nadia Litz and film critic Jason Anderson, they indicated how Kingston is an appropriate location and uniquely positioned for the Canadian Film Festival. Geographically, Kingston is located between Canada's two largest cities: English-Canadian Toronto and French-Canadian Montreal.

Historically, Kingston was also Canada's first capital, and it is geographically close to the present capital city, Ottawa. A film legacy at Queens University in Kingston also acts as a critical base for the industry. From these perspectives, the local–national dynamic of Kingston acts as a context through which the dominant Canadianness of film stars — rooted in Canadian history and geography — can be interpreted. That said, Anderson claims that the Canadian Film Festival is not just about a singular national identity: it is about every identity that Canadian films can embrace. Indeed, the expression of Canadian national identity is multifaceted in the sense that it changes yearly with the themes of Canadian productions. Nadia Litz, who attended Cannes Film Festival for her acting in the award-winning film *The Five Senses*, reveals that the KCFF is distinct in the sense that it is not simply about celebrities. Litz discloses that while Cannes is about film sales, KCFF is about peer support for the Canadian cultural industry. This differs from TIFF, which largely supports Hollywood fame and creates the conditions for standard constructions of Canadian identity. Anderson concludes that a number of independent films and actors at the festival do not focus on one national, pan-mainstream, and stereotypical Canadian identity. In screening both mainstream and independent films, the festival does not focus on a stardom that celebrates particular kind of Canadianness. For Anderson, Canadian national identity is multiple, fluid, and layered, and this is expressed in emerging practices of Canadian celebrity cultures.

The different notions of Canadian fame can further be interpreted from the perspectives of Canadian author Sharif Khan (2010). Although Khan's work looks at heroism, it overlaps with the heroic qualities and talent that characterise meritocratic fame and sheds light on its multifaceted qualities. In his critical essay, Khan observes how Canadian heroism is not singular but rather dichotomous: the Canadian government and other corporations shape its dichotomous qualities. He uses the case study of Canadian military hero Russell Williams as an example of the dual nature of fame. Williams is a former Colonel in the Canadian Forces who was arrested on charges of rape and murder in 2010. Since his arrest, Williams has been popularly characterised as a 'sociopath' (Northcott, 2011; Rankin & Contenta, 2010). This kind of popularity contradicts his former national fame, when he was awarded the highest honour as Trenton's single Olympic torchbearer. Khan points out two forms of popular recognition:

> Russell Williams looked and played the part of a shining hero who could do no wrong; a rising star soaring high on the national stage before going down in flames as perhaps the most ruthless sociopath in Canadian history (Khan, 2010).

With Khan's observation in mind, it can be argued that Williams' fame is not just contingent on his merit; rather, it is measured against Canada's moral consciousness. At first, Williams symbolised Canadian heroism due to his military exploits and his carrying of the Olympic torch. Later, he achieved greater fame via his infamy as a criminal sociopath. In both cases, his fame was contingent upon Canadian national values. In such cases, notions of meritocratic fame and talent are mediated in accordance with the national contexts in which they are produced, distributed, and received. Khan poignantly suggests that the Canadian government and other corporations are responsible for both kinds of popular statuses in Canada. He argues that institutions such as the Canadian Forces shape soldiers in a way that psychologically desensitises them to kill enemies and serve the nation. When the same psychology is applied to everyday life, however, society and popular media characterise the military as sociopathic. But this conclusion fails to acknowledge that national — and thus, ostensibly good — imperatives justify the type of military training that they criticise.

These recognitions, whether heroic or villainous, are constructed in ways that are in some way meaningful to the idea of the Canadian nation. The paradox between heroism and infamy generates questions about Williams' authenticity and, in the process, media discourse about the nation. Khan's case study of Russel Williams demonstrates how contradictions inherent within Canadian fame are not separate from national contradictions. Although this book has not considered deviant behaviour and criminal acts as characteristics of Canadian fame, it lays the groundwork for future research into that topic.

Sharif Khan's observations about Russel Williams can also be applied to the case of Jian Ghomeshi's fame in Canada. Like Williams, Ghomeshi is a former national celebrity who was arrested on charges of deviant criminal behaviour, and his fall precipitated a media spectacle not unlike the one that followed Williams' descent into national infamy. Jian Ghomeshi became famous through his popular CBC radio show Q, where he covered the arts in Canada and abroad from an intellectual — yet accessible — standpoint.

Ghomeshi's fame made him a Canadian national hero, but on October 23, 2014, the Canadian Broadcasting Corporation reported that its popular radio host had allegedly choked and beaten multiple women during several violent sexual encounters over a multi-year period. Following these allegations and the consequent loss of both his job and heretofore glowing public reputation, media across Canada propagated representations of Ghomeshi's anti-heroism. With an intellectual nod to Sharif Khan, I argue that Ghomeshi's fame was measured against Canada's moral consciousness on two levels. Before his allegation, Ghomeshi was represented as a Toronto-based public radio star who showcased Canada's cultural difference in comparison to America's scandal-driven Hollywood, which is largely operated by private enterprises. Following Ghomeshi's sexual abuse scandals, however, he became the walking embodiment of sociopathic behaviour and anti-heroism. Ghomeshi shares his infamy with another [in]famous Torontonian: former Mayor Rob Ford, who made international headlines thanks to his boorish displays of public intoxication and drug usage, misogynist statements, and alleged spousal abuse.

Whether they are committed by a radio personality or a politician, illegal and unethical acts must be reported and evaluated in their unmediated forms. The celebrity is a media text that can re-construct a persona's unmediated self and shift attention away from ordinary acts of violence in everyday life. Although Canadian media have raised the issue of feminism in relation to the Ghomeshi story by encouraging women to voice their opinions about his behaviour, the media also sensationalised and privileged both Ghomeshi and Ford by excusing them for several violent acts and giving them the benefit-of-doubt over their accusers. In many cases, journalists remain silent regarding criminals who also happen to be celebrities. Jonna Brewer, an ex-CBC host and one of Ghomehi's victims, expressed this concern:

> [...] I felt the amount of notoriety and respect [Ghomeshi] has in Canada versus me, who's essentially nobody compared to him, people will not believe my side (CBC 2010).

Star power, fuelled by media, can popularise and desensitise extraordinary figures in their everyday actions. When the same psychology is applied to them as ordinary citizens, the nation-state and media popularise them as anti-heroes. In both cases, media representations often do not sympathise with ordinary victims unless their coverage of tarnished stars can guarantee better coverage for the stars' victims *and* increase news sales. In Canada, Jian Ghomeshi publicly declared that his violent sexual acts were consensual. Although his partners may have agreed to his actions for psychological and physical pleasure, they were also silent victims who were not able to speak out until much later. The media spectacle surrounding Ghomeshi has re-constructed his persona into that of a criminal sociopath. Ironically, this scandalous position fuels his infamy, which, in turn, benefits media sales, and better sales reap national economic and political benefits. Ghomeshi's past and present fame is contingent upon Canadian national values. The dichotomy of his fame is mediated to such an extent that he is no longer remembered as a public intellectual talent. Instead, the national contexts in which he has been produced and received have transformed Ghomeshi into a sensational effect. This transformation prioritises coverage of his infamy and shifts attention away from the much-needed media literacy and sex education that would benefit his fellow citizens.

The multiplicity of Canadian fame also emerges in transnational and postcolonial contexts. The need for transnational and postcolonial readings of celebrity texts developed in response to an interview that I conducted with international actor Kabir Bedi for the Canadian entertainment magazine *StarBuzz Weekly*. In the interview, Bedi shared his first-hand experience with fame after his performance in the Canadian theatre production *TAJ*. He is already internationally famous for his acting in the James Bond film *Octopussy* and in other productions such as *The Bold and Beautiful*, the Italian series *Sandokan*, and many Bollywood films. From his experiences, Bedi was able to reflect on his fame in different national contexts, including Italian, Indian, American, and Canadian. He recalled that audiences and fans in one nation may be less familiar with his work in another:

> Fame means different things to different people. The way people receive me in different countries is in very different ways. In Europe, they know me for a series, *Sandokan*, [which was a] story of an Asian pirate, fighting for freedom against the British but falling for an English girl [...] People so identified my role that they could not imagine putting me in anything else. I had to disappear for few years and act in Hollywood. People from America know me from *Bold and Beautiful* where I did a dozen of the series. A lot of people growing up in America and the Indian diaspora knew me in that context (Bedi, 2011).

Actor Kabir Bedi's interpretation of fame can be framed in context of scholar Jo Littler's theoretical work on transnational celebrities. For Littler, celebrities can "be globalized and consumed differently in different places, their meanings shifting alongside their geographical context" (2011, p. 1). As indicated in Chapter 1, his research specifically shows "how texts can be read differently according to the national cultures they are part of, and celebrity is subject to similar cultural reframing" (Ibid.). Celebrity texts, as this book demonstrates, refer to different national cultures as well as subcultures within a particular nation, such as Canada. The national reading of Bedi's fame is observed in Canadian media representations of his performance. During the Canadian premiere of *TAJ*, Bedi's transnational fame is received in a way that is specific to a diasporic national culture. Unlike stars at TIFF and other cultural sites, Bedi's associations with Hollywood and European countries, where he is widely famous, are less represented by Canadian media. During his performance in *TAJ*, Bedi is mostly represented as an Indian film star (CBC, 2011) or a Bollywood superstar (Maga, 2011). The Canadian representation of Kabir Bedi, compared to his personal interpretation of fame, prioritises Bedi's Bollywood connections over his transnational renown. Indeed, Bedi recalls that while he makes his base in Mumbai, his work is mostly situated outside of India:

> I have become an international actor. Bollywood is a small part of my resume. Because I am from India and from Bollywood, the only Bollywood actor who went and lived abroad for many years, and made a career abroad before going back to Bollywood, it is more where I came from and where I return to (Bedi, 2011).

Although Bedi is well known in Italy and the US, the Canadian media located Bollywood as his primary site of fame and portrayed it in their representations of his work. In doing so, these media representations articulate the complex mixture of globalisation, diasporic migrations, hybridity, colonial memory, and ambivalence within the Canadian nation that combine to shape his celebrity status. The emphasis on his Bollywood celebrity, rather than his international fame, intersects with postcolonial dynamics shared by Canada and India. This intersection suggests a need for a postcolonial reading of celebrity texts in future research, which will lead to a better understanding of the cultural meanings of fame in Canada. Imperialist agendas and transnational subjectivity in post-World War II can also be expanded in this respect.

Future Research on Canadian Celebrity Cultures

While neo-colonialist and postcolonial studies of celebrities were beyond the scope of *Fame in Hollywood North*, the book provided the theories and case studies that are necessary to the study of Canadian celebrity cultures from a postcolonial angle. In concluding this book, I suggest that a postcolonial study of Canadian celebrities may shed further light on nationalist constructions of fame in Canada. In general, there has been a minor focus on postcolonial studies of celebrities. Indeed, the emphasis has instead been on the history, meaning, and functions of the Western notion of fame. Yet, as Robert Clarke explains in his book *Celebrity Colonialism,*

> [C]elebrity provides a powerful lens for examining the nexus of discourses, institutions and practices associated with the dynamics of appropriation, domination, resistance and reconciliation that characterise colonial and postcolonial cultural politics (2009, p. 4).

Future research on Canadian fame can invite a number of contexts and parallels that should be considered when studying postcolonial or ex-colonial nations. These nations include Australia, New Zealand, and India among many others. Indeed, as Canadian scholar Laura Moss indicates, a paradigm divide,

> [I]s often perceived between the "invader-settler" nations of Australia, New Zealand, and Canada, where the process of colonization was predominantly one of immigration and settlement, and those parts of the world where colonization was predominantly a process of displacement, impoverishment, sublimation, and even annihilation (2003, p. 2).

Colonialist practices in India, Pakistan, and Bangladesh reflect Moss' latter point. Yet, at the same time, Moss argues that Canada's national identity, when placed in a comparative, postcolonial framework, still relies on the emphasis placed on the "basic similarity" and/or the "wide contrasts and local differences" (p. 1) of colonial, neo-colonial, and postcolonial histories, locations, and cultures.

In studies of Canadian celebrity cultures, the growing production and representation of Bollywood celebrities in Canada are more than mere exemplars of postcolonialist traditions; it is also as a form of 'reverse colonialism.' Reverse colonialism emphasises the cultural, political, and economic influences of past colonies of Western Europe powers (Giddens, 2003). The international sale of Brazilian television programmes to Portugal, and the "emergence of a globally oriented high-tech sector India" (p. 16) with offices in the US are examples of reverse colonialism. In Canada, the emergence of Hollywood North reflects and reinforces practices of reverse colonialism. In this respect, western locations such as Vancouver reclaim an economic dominion that historically originated in Central Canada (Toronto and Montreal), in the east of the country. A glimpse into the eighteenth-century colonial history of Canada shows that Anglo-American invasions progressed east to west, from the Atlantic regions of Nova Scotia and New Brunswick to the western Prairies. Economic and political power since the Canadian Confederation of 1867 has been primarily located in Montreal and Toronto. In fact, Toronto is not only Canada's financial capital, but it has become the third-largest financial hub in North America.

Nonetheless, present-day economic forces have also moved to Vancouver on Canada's west coast, the site of origin for Hollywood North. In addition, the rise of non-Western star machineries such as the Bollywood industry in India may either challenge or support Western Eurocentric perspectives in Canadian popular culture. Quite often, media interpret the place of Indian film and star productions in Canada as 'Bollywood North' or 'Bollywood West.' These expressions are rhetorical strategies that indicate shared power dynamics between the Northern frontier of Canada and the Northern frontier of British India, both of which are former colonialist locations. These expressions also emphasise Northern locations in India where Western imperial forces invaded and settled — forces that continue to be dominant in both Indian and Canadian representations of Bollywood stars. These expressions exemplify the complex interplay of colonialism and postcolonialism, including reverse colonial discourses, practices, and events in Canadian celebrity cultures that should be investigated further. The celebration and treatment of other non-Western stars in Canada can be studied through the lens of postcolonialism as well. In doing so, conventional ascriptions of class, race, and ethnicity in colonialist practices can be critically considered and analysed in celebrity studies.

Postcolonialism offers an important theoretical framework for the future interpretation of Canadian celebrity texts. It can better illuminate the ways that Canadian celebrity texts, as cultural products of Canadian history, articulate nationalism and identity on the margins of multiple imperial locations, rather than simply Canada's Northern colonialist frontier. It will offer comparative studies of celebrities among Canadian and other ex-colonial nations and recognise the different orders, relations, and migrations of colonial subjects and agents without conflating them. This would contribute to a better understanding of how celebrities are written into negotiations or rewritings of Canadian history via the appropriation of Canada's geopolitical diversity. This would also include French-Canadian national culture and its star system, which may compete and/or overlap with discourses of English Canada. Indeed, Canada's history involves multiple layers of colonialism: the French over the native population, the 'Anglo' over the French, and America over Canada. Within English Canada, there are number of cities and towns that are participating in the rising stardom of talented individuals. These practices of stardom may or may not support imperialist ways of expressing fame and, as such, would benefit from an examination through a postcolonial lens.

A postcolonial reading of celebrity texts in Canada can also shed light on the colonial legacies of the US-Canadian relationship and identify new shifts that might change it. Laura Moss argues that a postcolonial interpretive framework can examine the "alignment of American and Canadian histories of exploitation and a subsequent erasure of the border between the countries and the specificities of their histories" (2003, p. 6). This book addressed the blurring boundaries between the US and Canada within the theoretical framework of continentalism. In this regard, Chapter 4 specifically highlighted the complex relationship between continentalism and technological nationalism, including how this relationship plays out in material and symbolic constructions of Hollywood North. These constructions partly resulted in the cultural erasing of national boundaries between the US and Canada and helped to create an ambivalent notion of Canadian national identity.

Fame in Hollywood North reiterated this point by demonstrating how Canadian reality TV shows both accept and resist American methods of popularising talent. Canadian national ambivalence recognises talent while also negotiating the tensions that arise from the combination of American cultural imperialism and homogenous representations of the Canadian nation-state. The book also addressed the past uncertainty of place that wracked generations of invaders and settlers in Canada by considering US-Canada relations primarily from the Canadian vantage point of technological nationalism. It showed how technological nationalism often injected colonialist perspectives of the frontier into Canadian celebrity productions. The book then highlighted the binary relationship between America and Canada, in which Canada is ideologically perceived as North America's better 'Other.' This binary is evident in most media representations of celebrities, and technological nationalism and continentalism offer theoretical understandings of the complex national expressions within Canadian celebrity cultures. Nonetheless, the shared colonial legacies of the USA and Canada (along with their possible associated shifts) have yet to be properly addressed. A postcolonial reading of Canadian celebrities' national identity could mark the changes and continuities of colonialist intents in both Canada and America, as well as contribute to a more equitable representation of talent in both nations.

Chapters 6, 7, and 8 of this book particularly revealed how Canada has seen an increasing shift towards an awareness of homegrown talent that extends beyond the traditional recognition of celebrities who achieved fame in America. Nonetheless, an emphasis on Hollywood stardom remains present even amidst this shift. The final sections of this book charted how Hollywood North started to transform from a service-provider that predominantly catered to the American entertainment industry into a partly Canadian film industry unto itself. Traditionally, Hollywood North has been defined as a 'locations and service industry' that facilitates American productions in Canadian settings (Gasher, 1995, 2002; Tinic, 2005). These productions are then imported back to Canada for a net profit. As a result, Canadian socio-cultural experiences of talent are deemphasised in favour of American places and celebrities. Yet, the Hollywood film industry also employed (and continues to employ) Canadian labour and talent, a practice that contributed to the increased representation of Canadian locations and talent independent of American productions.

As discussed in Chapter 5, the Rising Star Program at TIFF offers pertinent examples of the recognition of Canadian locations and talent independent from American productions. The launching of this programme marked a shift from dominant representations of Hollywood stars. In *Toronto Magazine*, cultural critic John Crossingham highlights this shift, stating how a "growing number of internationally distributed films and television programs are choosing Toronto as both a location and the story's actual setting" (2010, p. 54). Crossingham draws on Canadian films like *Scott Pilgrim vs. The World* and Canadian television series *Flashpoint* that major US network CBS purchased for prime-time viewing. These productions are not only filmed in Toronto; they also *take place* in Toronto, a departure from traditional practices that used Toronto as a stand-in for New York or Chicago. These types of productions do not alter, obscure, or remove Canadian landmarks and signifiers such as flags, mailboxes, street signs, and newspaper boxes in order to construct American cities, nor do they emphasise Northern icons such as Mounties to reclaim the Canadian frontier in North America. In this setting, the rising reputation of Canadian talent is free from dominant American influences. Canadian reality TV shows, as discussed in Chapter 7, have also displayed a new recognition of Canadian talent.

Despite these developments, however, the long shadow of American celebritydom still looms large. The opening page in an issue of the *Toronto Magazine*, for example, highlights Hollywood stars such as Jennifer Connelly, Julianne Moore, and Oprah Winfrey at the Toronto International Film Festival (TIFF). As discussed in Chapter 5, an emphasis on Hollywood is also observed in TIFF's Rising Star Program. These trends reveal Canada's continued support for, and dependence on, the Hollywood star system, even as it becomes increasingly aware of the preponderance of homegrown celebrity talent in its own national backyard.

Conclusion

In Canada, fame is largely constructed and represented within national discourses. The cultural construction of Canadian fame is contingent on particular social, political, and economic contexts but largely underpinned by the competing dynamics of Canada's technological nationalism and US-dominant continentalism. The Canadian meaning of fame can therefore be interpreted as a quintessentially North American one that is underscored by the complex interplay of Hollywood stardom and the celebration of Canadian national values. Celebrities in a Canadian context thus carry multiple meanings of fame that support national discourses. In Canadian constructions of fame, actual talent is mostly mediated through the discursive effects of the Northern frontier, the lack it creates, and the America it 'Others.' There are different national discourses in which celebrities are constructed; consequently, there is no single Canadian expression of fame.

Fame in Hollywood North pointed out the dominant representations of fame in Canada as well as the margins on which talent is expressed. While national discourses around the Northern frontier, the lack, and the American 'Other' are dominant, a new awakening towards the discovery of talent, especially from non-English speaking groups, is still marginal but nonetheless rising in Canada. Indeed, this new discovery contradicts previous Canadian myths of inferiority and activates an admiration of fame as a new Canadian value. The shifts in representational practices of fame thus intersect with national discourses that overlap and/or contradict. This book not only explored representations of particular Canadian celebrities but also the Canadian meaning of fame as understood in the industrial production of Canadian, US, and international celebrities in Canada. The expressions of national identities in these cultural productions have been the recurring theme of this book. Themes of national identities have also emerged in my personal observations as a fame critic and writer. These observations not only offer a layered understanding of the Canadian nation, but also lay the foundation to explore future shifts and continuities in the representation of actual talent in postcolonial contexts.

Bibliography

2000 The Inductees. (2008). *Canada's Walk of Fame 2008.*

2009 Tribute Show. (2009). On *The Canada Honours.* Toronto.

About Us. (2011). *Canada's Walk of Fame* Retrieved August 15, 2011, from http://www.canadaswalkoffame.com/aboutus

Adams, C. (2003). The Rape of Animals, the Butchering of Women. In S. J. Armstrong (Ed.), *The animal ethics reader.* London: Routledge.

Administrator. (2010). "September 2010." *The Canadian Stem Cell Foundation Blog.* Retrieved October 13, 2015, from http://stemcellfoundation.ca/2010/09/

Adria, M. (2010). *Technology and nationalism: Canadian social identity in the age of the Internet.* Montreal: McGill-Queen's University Press.

Alberoni, F. (1972). The Powerless 'Elite': Theory and Sociological Research on the Phenomenon of the Stars. In D. McQuail (Ed.), *Sociology of mass communications: selected readings.* Harmondsworth: Penguin.

Allan, B. (2002). The Grey Fox afoot in a modern world. In E. P. Walz (Ed.), *Canada's best features: critical essays on 15 Canadian films.* New York: Radopi.

Ames, M. M. (1993). The Canadianization of the American Fair: The Case of Expo 86. In D. H. Flaherty & F. E. Manning (Eds.), *The Beaver bites back?: American popular culture in Canada.* Montreal: McGill-Queen's Press.

Anderson, B. (1991). Imagined Communities: Reflections on the Origin and Spread of Nationalism. London: Verso.

Andres, V., & Kakoullis, A. (2011). *Press Release: Canada's Walk of Fame Festival.* Toronto: Holmes Creative Communications

Andrews, D. L., & Jackson, S. J. (Eds.). (2001). *Sports Stars: The Cultural Politics of Sporting Celebrity*. London and New York: Routledge.

Astakhov, S. (1960). Canada at the Cross-roads. *International Affairs, 11*(6), 111-112.

Atwood, M. (2004). *Survival: a thematic guide to Canadian literature*. Toronto: McClelland & Stewart.

B'béri, B., & Middlebrook, R. (2009). The Paradox of National Identity: Region, Nation, and Canadian Idol. *Canadian Journal of Communication, 34*.

Babe, R. E. (1990). *Telecommunications in Canada: Technology, Industry and Government*. Toronto: University of Toronto Press.

Baltruschat, D. (2009). Reality TV Formats: The Case of Canadian Idol. *Canadian Journal of Communication, 45*.

Bannerji, H. (2000). *The dark side of the nation: essays on multiculturalism, nationalism and gender*. Toronto: Canadian Scholars' Press.

Barney, D. D. (2005). *Communication technology*. Vancouver: UBC Press.

Bedi, K. (2011, June 23). Soho Metopolitan Hotel, Toronto. In-person interview.

Beltrán, M. C. (2002). Bronze Seduction: The Shaping of Latina Stardom in Hollywood Film and Star Publicity. The University of Texas, Austin.

Berland, J. (1988). Locating Listening: Technological Space, Popular Music, Canadian Mediations *Cultural Studies* (Vol. 2). London: Routledge.

Berland, J. (1994). On Reading 'The Weather'. *Cultural Studies, 8*(1).

Berland, J. (2006). Space at the Margins: Colonial Spatiality and Critical Theory After Innis. *Topia: Canadian Journal of Cultural Studies, 1*(55).

Berland, J. (2009). North of empire: essays on the cultural technologies of space. Durham: Duke University Press.

Berton, P. (1974). *The National Dream: Building the Impossible Railway*. Montreal: CBC.

Bhabha, H. K. (1990). Introduction: Narrating the Nation *Nation and Narration*. London: Routledge.

Bickford, P., & Letts, D. (2009). 'Ice Pilots NWT' takes flight. *Northern News Services*.

Bickley, C. (2000). Legends Get Star Treatment. *The Toronto Sun*, p. 55.

Bickley, C. (2001). Canucks who walk the walk. *Toronto Sun*.

Bieber, J. (2010). *Justin Bieber: First Step 2 Forever: My Story*. New York: HarperCollins Publishers

Billig, M. (1995). *Banal nationalism*. London: Sage Publications Ltd.

Biressi, A., & Nunn, H. (2005). *Reality TV: realism and revelation*. London: Wallflower Press.

Block, S. (2008). Idols still getting used to newfound celebrity status. *CTV.ca*.

Boberg, C. (2010). The English Language in Canada: Status, History and Comparative Analysis. Cambridge: Cambridge University Press.

Bodmer, T., Nightingale, T., & Upton, C. (2010). BC's Sunshine Coast Artist Profile of Hannah Stone, Acrylic Ink Painter. from http://www.goingcoastalmagazine.com/profile19.htm

Bodroghkozy, A. (2001). "I ... Am ... Canadian!" Examining Popular Culture in Canada: Recent Books. *Topia, 5*(Spring).

Boire, G. (2004). How Long is Your Sentence?: Classes, Pedagogies, Canadian Literatures. In Cynthia Sugars (Ed.), *Home-work: postcolonialism, pedagogy, and Canadian literature*. Ottawa: University of Ottawa Press.

Boorstin, D. J. (1962). *The Image: A Guide to Pseudo-Events in America*. New York: Athenaneum.

Bow, B. (2008). *National Identity, Regional Community, and the 'Deeper Integration' Debate in Canada*. Paper presented at the ISA's 49th Annual Convention, Bridging Multiple Divides, Hilton San Francisco, San Francisco.

Braman, S. (2006). Change of State - Information, Policy, and Power. Michigan: MIT Press.

Bräuchler, B., & Postill, J. (2010). *Theorising Media and Practice*. New York: Berghahn Books.

Brescia, M. M., & Super, J. C. (2009). *North America: an introduction*. Toronto: University of Toronto Press.

Brewer, J. (2014) "Jian Ghomeshi allegedly choked, beat N.B. woman with belt." Retrieved December 24, 2014, from http://www.cbc.ca/news/canada/new-brunswick/jian-ghomeshi-allegedly-choked-beat-n-b-woman-with-belt-1.2818879.

Brockington, D. (2008). Powerful environmentalisms: conservation, celebrity and capitalism. *Media Culture Society, 30*(4).

Buckel, B. A. (2008). Nationalism, Mass Politics, and Sport: Cold War Case Studies at Seven Degrees. Naval Postgraduate School, Monterey.

Byers, M. (2008). Canadian Idol and the Myth of National Identity *Programming reality: perspectives on English-Canadian television.*

Caldwell, J. T. (1995). Tabloid TV: Styled Live/Ontological Stripmall *Televisuality: style, crisis, and authority in American television.* Piscataway: Rutgers University Press.

Canada's Health Care System. (2011). *Health Canada.* Retrieved December 4, 2011, from http://www.hc-sc.gc.ca/hcs-sss/pubs/system-regime/2011-hcs-sss/index-eng.php

Canada's Walk of Fame 10 Years. (2008). Toronto: Universal Studios Home Entertainment.

Canada Honours. (2009). Canada's Walk of Fame.

Candace Johnson Redden. (2002). *Health care, entitlement, and citizenship.* Toronto: University of Toronto Press.

Capel, G. M. D. (2007). 'Damned If They Do And Damned If They Don't': The Inferiority Complex, Nationalism, and Maclean's Music Coverage, 1967-1995. University of Waterloo, Waterloo.

Caragata, W. (1979). *Alberta labour: a heritage untold.* Halifax: James Lorimer & Company.

Carey, J. (1989). Communication as culture: Essays on media and society. Boston: Unwin Hyman.

Carter, A. (2003). Namelessness, Irony, and National Character in Contemporary Canadian Criticism and the Critical Tradition. *Studies in Canadian Literature 28*(1).

Catt. (2008, November 20). Earl Stevenson's Blog.

Cavanagh, E. (2009). Fur Trade Colonialism: Traders and Cree at Hudson Bay, 1713-67. *Australasian Canadian Studies, 27*(1-2).

CBC. (2000a, November 10). 'Hollywood North' to Grow Again.

CBC. (2000b). Montreal Declares Itself the New 'Hollywood North'. *CBC News.*

CBC. (2006). Definition of Canadian TV under scrutiny at CRTC hearings. *CBC Arts.* Retrieved April 14, 2016, from http://www.cbc.ca/news/arts/definition-of-canadian-tv-under-scrutiny-at-crtc-hearings-1.589945

CBC. (2010a, November 19). 'Battle' rookies survive Boot Camp. Retrieved April 14, 2016, from http://www.cbc.ca/battle/2010/07/battlerookiessurvivebootcamp.html

CBC. (2010b). CBC Reveals Star Studded Battle of the Blades Cast. Retrieved November 19, 2011, from http://www.cbc.ca/revenuegroup/cbc-reveals-star-studded-battle-of-the-blades-cast.html

CBC. (2010c, November 20). Competition reignites Bure's fire.

CBC. (2010d). Season 2. On *Battle of the Blades*. Toronto.

CBC. (2010e). Week 4. On *Battle of the Blades*. Toronto.

CBC. (2011a). Harper pitches Arctic development. Retrieved November 25, 2011, from http://www.cbc.ca/news/politics/story/2011/08/24/north-harper-tour.html

CBC. (2011b). Lady Gaga Winnipeg fan to appear on Ellen. *CBC News*.

Chan, F. (2011). The International Film Festival and the Making of a National Cinema. *Screen 52*(2).

Chapeskie, A. J. (2001). Northern Homelands, Northern Frontier: Linking Culture and Economic Security in Contemporary Livelihoods in Boreal and Cold Temperate Forest Communities in Northern Canada. Minneapolis: USDA Forest Service.

Charland, M. (1986). Technological Nationalism. *Canadian Journal of Political and Social Theory, X*(1.2).

Charlesworth, H. (1935). Broadcasting in Canada. Annals of the American Academy of Political and Social Science, 177(January).

Chase, S. (2011). Harper performs campaign-trail duet with young Gaga fan. *The Globe and Mail*.

Chidley, J. (2002). Stars and bars. *Canadian Business, 75*.

Chin, D. (1997). Festivals, Markets, Critics: Notes on the State of the Art Film. *Performing Arts Journal, 19*(1).

Chu, J. M. (Writer). (2011). Justin Bieber: Never Say Never. USA.

Chung, A. (2008). Mulroney wedding a small, elegant affair. *The Toronto Star*. Retrieved from http://www.thestar.com/news/canada/chapter/527940

Cillia, R. D., Reisigl, M., & Wodak, R. (1999). The discursive construction of national identities. *Discourse and Society, 10*.

City in the Spotlight. (2006, September 7). *The Toronto Star*.

Clarkson, S. (2001). The multi-level state: Canada in the semi-periphery of both continentalism and globalization. *Review of International Political Economy, 8*(3).

Cohen, B. (1995). Technological Colonialism and the Politics of Water *Cultural Studies, 8*(1).

Collins, R. (1990). *Culture, Communication and National Identity*. Toronto: University of Toronto Press.

Corliss, R. (2006, September 11). How Toronto Attracts the Stars. *Time Canada*.

Cormack, P. (2008). 'True Stories' of Canada: Tim Hortons and the Branding of National Identity. *Cultural Sociology, 2*(3).

Corner, J., Schlesinger, P., & Silverstone, R. (1998). *International media research: a critical survey*. London: Routledge.

Costello, V. J. (1999). Interactivity and the 'Cyber-fan': An Exploration of Audience Involvement within the Electronic Fan Culture of the Internet. The University of Tennessee, Knoxville.

Cox, D., & Stellick, G. (2006). '67: The Maple Leafs, Their Sensational Victory, and the End of an Empire: John Wiley and Sons.

Craig, T. (1997). The missionary lives: a study in Canadian missionary biography and autobiography (Vol. 19). Leiden: Brill.

Cross, S. (Writer). (2009). Whip It. USA.

Crossingham, J. (2009). True North, Strong & Funny: Canada's Legacy as the World's Preeminent Nation of Comedy. *Canada's Walk of Fame 2009*.

CRTC. (1985). Canadian Radio, Television and Telecommunications Commission (CRTC). *A Broadcasting Policy Reflecting Canada's Linguistic and Cultural Diversity*. Ottawa: CRTC.

CRTC. (2002). *Support for Canadian Talent* Ottawa: Canadian Radio-television and Telecommunications Commission.

CTV. (2003). Most Memorable Canadian Idol Season 1. Retrieved November 22, 2011, from http://www.youtube.com/watch?v=XxrHveNLgFM

CTV. (2006). Idols live it up in their swank Top 10 mansion. Retrieved November 20, 2011, from http://www.ctv.ca/CTVNews/Entertainment/20060725/idol_mansion_20060725/#ixzz1eDexzZ5s

CTV. (2008a). All Canadian Idol Season 6 Auditions Retrieved November 19, 2011, from http://www.youtube.com/watch?v=7tP67pfm-NU

CTV. (2008b). Canadian Idol Season 6 Top 24 Performances - Part 3. Retrieved November 20, 2011, from http://www.youtube.com/watch?v=hYOacx8yKUM

CTV. (2008c). Canadian Idol Season 6 Top 24 Performances - Part 5. Retrieved November 20, 2011, from http://www.youtube.com/watch?v=iL0I0F4COjU

CTV. (2008d). eTalk. Toronto: CTV.

CTV. (2008e). *eTalk Wins TIFF with Most-Watched Coverage*. Toronto CTV Inc.

CTV. (2008f). Eva Avila Canadian Idol Winner. Retrieved November 20, 2011, from http://www.youtube.com/watch?v=pyPya78VZ-w

CTV. (2009a). About eTalk. Bell Media.

CTV. (2009b). eTalk. Toronto: CTV.

CTV. (2010a). Canada's unpolite, trying to win at Olympics: Colbert. Retrieved from http://www.ctv.ca/servlet/ChapterNews/story/CTVNews/20100131/col bert_canada_100131/20100131

CTV. (2010b). Season 3. On *So You Think You Can Dance Canada*. Toronto.

Cullen, J. (2003). The American dream: a short history of an idea that shaped a nation. Oxford: Oxford University Press.

Culture and National Identity. (1998). *Fraser Forum* Retrieved August 12, 2012, from http://oldfraser.lexi.net/publications/forum/1998/august/identity.html

CWOF. (2011). What Makes Canadians So Funny? Retrieved June 11, 2011, from http://www.canadaswalkoffame.com/node/1421

Czach, L. (2004). Film Festivals, Programming, and the Building of a National Cinema. *The Moving Image, 4*(1).

Czach, L. (2010). Cinephilia, Stars, and Film Festivals. *Cinema Journal, 49*(2).

Davis, C. H., & Kaye, J. (2009). International Production Outsourcing and the Development of Indigenous Film and Television Capabilities: The Case of Canada. Lanham: Rowman and Littlefield.

Dawson, M. (1998). The Mountie from Dime Novel to Disney. Toronto: Between the Lines.

Dayan, D., & Katz, E. (1992). *Media Events: The Live Broadcasting of History*. Cambridge, MA: Harvard University Press.

Derkits, R. (2004). *Lukeford.com: Public Sex, Celebrity and the Internet.* Unpublished Ph.D. Dissertation, Stanford University Stanford

Dewey, J. (1916). *Democracy and Education*. New York: MacMillan.

Ditchburn, J. (2010). Harper joins Lady Gaga superfan Maria Aragon to croon Lennon tune. *City News*.

Dittmer, J., & Larsen, S. (2007). Captain Canuck, audience response, and the project of Canadian nationalism. *Social and Cultural Geography, 8*(5).

Dixon, G. (2009). Festival's investment in Bollywood now paying dividends. *The Globe and Mail*

Donald, S., & Gammack, J. G. (2007). *Tourism and the branded city: film and identity on the Pacific Rim.* Hampshire: Ashgate Pulishing Ltd.

Dowd, A. (2010). Travel Postcard: 48 hours in post-Olympics Vancouver. *Reuters.* Retrieved from .http://www.reuters.com/chapter/idUSTRE62U1OY20100331

Doyle, J. (2011). Canada's Walk of Shame: It's your tax dollars at work. *The Globe and Mail.*

Droganes, C. (2011). 'I'm not perfect,' Bieber says on return to Canada. Retrieved December 6, 2011, from http://www.ctv.ca/CTVNews/TopStories/20110201/bieber-toronto-appearance-110201/

Druik, Z. (2006). Framing the Local - Canadian Film Policy and the Problem of Place. In G. Sherbert, A. Gerin & S. Petty (Eds.), *Canadian Cultural Poesis: Essays on Canadian Culture.* Waterloo: Wilfred Laurier Press.

Dubey, B. (2009). 'Sometimes life drags you down from the clouds & that's good'. *The Times of India*

Dubied, A., Dubbey, M., & Gorin, V. (2009). *Rumors and Subjectivity: Introducing Celebrity News.* Paper presented at the Trust, Truth and Performance: Diverse Journalisms in the 21st Century.

Dyer, R. (1991). *A Star is Born* and the Construction of Authenticity. In C. Gledhill (Ed.), *Stardom: Industry of Desire.* London: Routledge.

Dyer, R. (1998). *Stars.* Bury St. Edmunds: St. Edmundsbury Press.

Dyer, R. (2004). *Heavenly bodies: film stars and society.* London: Routledge.

Dyment, D., & Rae, B. (2010). *Doing the Continental: A New Canadian-American Relationship.* Toronto: Dundurn Press Ltd.

Dymond, G. (2009). Ray of light. *CBC News.* Retrieved December 5, 2011, from http://www.cbc.ca/arts/tiff/blog2009/2009/09/ray-of-light.html

Eade, J., & Mele, C. (2002). *Understanding the City: Contemporary and Future Perspectives.* Oxford: Blackwell Publishers Ltd.

Economic Activity Associated with the 2008-2009 Operations of TIFF. (2010). Toronto

Edwardson, R. (2003). The Many Lives of Captain Canuck: Nationalism, Culture, and the Creation of a Canadian Comic Book Superhero. *The Journal of Popular Culture 37*(2).

Edwardson, R. (2008). Reviews: The Maple Leaf Forever: A Celebration of Canadian Symbols. *The Canadian Historical Review, 89*(2).

Elash, A. (2009). *'Battle Of The Blades' Draws Huge Audience In Canada*: National Public Radio.

Ellis, J. (2007). Stars as a Cinematic Phenomenon. In S. Redmond & S. Holmes (Eds.), *Stardom and Celebrity: A Reader*. London: Sage Publications.

Eriksen, T. H. (2007). Nationalism and the Internet. *Nations and Nationalism, 13*(1).

eTalk. (2009). *Life of the Red Carpet*. Toronto: CTV.

Evans, P. (2006). Pam Walks the Walk. *The Toronto Star*.

Farquharson, V. (2004). The Wind at her Back. *National Post*.

Farquharson, V. (2005). A Street Full of Stars. *National Post*.

Ferguson, W., & Ferguson, I. (2003). *How to be a Canadian*. Madeira Park: Douglas & McIntyre.

Filion, M. (1996). Broadcasting and cultural identity: the Canadian experience. *Media Culture Society, 18*, 447.

Fixmer, A. "Canadian Television in the USA". Canadian.TV. Retrieved December 19, 2014. http://canadian.tv/videos-canadian-television-in-the-usa--[bpv4cimrYFw].cfm

Flaherty, D. H., & Manning, F. E. (Eds.). (1993). *The Beaver Bites Back? American Popular Culture in Canada*. Montreal: McGill University - Queen's University Press.

Francis, D. (1997). *National dreams: myth, memory, and Canadian history*. Vancouver: Arsenal Pulp Press.

Fremeth, H. (2006). Maple Leaves, Beavers and Satellites: Technological Nationalism as Philosophy and Theory. Paper presented at the CCA Annual Conference 2006.

Frick, J. (2004). Monday the Herald; Tuesday the Victoria: (Re)packaging and (Re)presenting the Celebrated and the Notorious on the Variety Stage. *Nineteenth Century Theatre and Film, 30* (Winter).

Frye, N. (1980). Conclusion to A Literary History of Canada *The stubborn structure: essays on criticism and society*. Methuen: Routledge.

Fulford, R. (2002). How Embarrassing. *National Post*.

Galerman, E. (2009). Celebrity Hot Spots: Engaging Fans Through Blogs. In K. S. Burns (Ed.), *Celeb 2.0: how social media foster our fascination with popular culture*. Santa Barbara: ABC-CLIO.

Gamson, J. (1994). *Claims to fame: celebrity in contemporary America*. Berkeley: University of California Press.

Garcia, P. (2008). *eTalk Wins TIFF with Most-Watched Coverage*. Toronto CTV Inc.

Gardner, J. (2000). Walk with the Stars. *Marquee, 25*.

Gasher, M. (1995). The Audiovisual Locations Industry in Canada: Considering British Columbia as Hollywood North. *Canadian Journal of Communication, 20*(2).

Gasher, M. (2002a). *Hollywood North: the feature film industry in British Columbia.* Vancouver: UBC Press.

Gasher, M. (2002b). *Hollywood North: the feature film industry in British Columbia.* Vancouver: University of British Columbia Press.

Gass-Donnelly, E. (Director). (2007). This Beautiful City Canada. [Motion Picture]. 20/40 Films: Canada.

Gatehouse, J. (2003). And the winner is ... Ben Mulroney: The ex-PM's son emerges as a star in his own right. *McLean's Magazine*

Gavey, N. (1989). Feminist Postructuralism and Discourse Analysis. *Psychology of Women Quaterly, 13*(4).

Geraghty, C. (2007). Re-examining Stardom: Questions of Texts, Bodies and Performance. In S. Redmond & S. Holmes (Eds.), *Stardom and Celebrity: A Reader*. London: Sage Publications.

Gero, M. (Director). (2007). Young People F---ing. [Motion Picture]. Copperheart Entertainment: Canada.

Giddens, A. (2003). *Runaway world: how globalization is reshaping our lives.* New York: Taylor & Francis.

Giese, R. (2007). The thoroughly Canadian charm of Lisa Ray. *Chatelaine.*

Giles, D. (2000). *Illusions of immortality: a psychology of fame and celebrity.* New York: Palgrave Macmillan.

Gill, A. (2004). Reality bites Canada. *The Globe and Mail.*

Gillmore, A. (2014) Fleeting Fame in Canada. *The Winnipeg Free Press.*

Gittings. (1998). Imaging Canada: The Singing Mountie and Other Commodifications of Nation. *Canadian Journal of Communication, 23*(4).

Gittings, C. E. (2002). Canadian national cinema: ideology, difference and representation. London: Routledge.

Goggin, G., & Newell, C. (2004). Christopher Reeve, Super Crips, and Infamous Celebrity. *M/C Journal: A Journal of Media and Culture, 7*(5).

Goodman, M., & Barnes, C. (2010). *Star/Poverty Space: The Making of the Development Celebrity.* London: Department of Geography, King's College.

Gordon, D. (2002). Celebrities take a walk on famous side. *The Toronto Star.*

Govani, S. (2009). *Boldface Names*. Scarborough: HarperCollins Canada.

Grabe, M. E., Zhou, S., Lang, A., & Bolls, D. (2000). Packaging Television News: The Effects of Tabloid on Information Processing and Evaluative Responses. *Journal of Broadcasting & Electronic Media, Fall*.

Grace, S. (2001). *Canada and the Idea of North* Montreal: McGill-Queen's Press

Grant. (1999). Canuck Walk of Fame just got a little longer. *Toronto Sun*.

Grant, G. (1965). *Lament For a Nation: The Defeat of Canadian Nationalism*. Ottawa: Carleton University Press.

Grant, G., Davis, A., & Roper, H. (2005). In A. Davis & H. Roper (Eds.), *Collected Works of George Grant: 1960 1969: Volume 3 of Collected Works of George Grant*. Toronto: University of Toronto Press.

Grossman, L. (2006). Tila Tequila. *Time*.

Guignon, C. B. (2004). *On Being Authentic*. London: Routledge.

Guilbert, G.-C. (2002). Madonna as postmodern myth: how one star's self-construction rewrites sex, gender, Hollywood, and the American dream. Jefferson: McFarland & Company, Inc.

Gupta, D., & Marchessault, J. (2007). Film Festivals as Urban Encounter and Cultural Traffic. In J. Sloan (Ed.), *Urban Enigmas: Montreal, Toronto, and the Problem of Comparing Cities* (pp. 251). Montreal: McGill-Queen's University Press.

Hansson, H., & Norberg, C. (Eds.). (2009). *Cold Matters: Cultural Perceptions of Snow, Ice, Cold*. Umeå: Umeå University and Royal Skyttean Society.

Harbord, J. (2002a). *Film Cultures*. London: Sage.

Harbord, J. (2002b). Film Festivals: Media Events and Spaces of Flow. In J. Harbord (Ed.), *Film Cultures*. London: Sage.

Harris. (1998a). But Can We Walk the Walk? *The Globe and Mail*.

Harris. (1998b). 'World-class city' gives stellar Canadians a chance to be stepped on. *The Globe and Mail*.

Harris. (2007). Photo Gallery: Toronto Film Festival 2007. *Celebrity Encounters*

Harris. (2008). Walk this way. *Toronto Sun*.

Harris. (2011). Justin Bieber fever threatened by cold blast of overexposure. Retrieved December 6, 2011, from http://www.canada.com/entertainment/Justin+Bieber+fever+threatened+cold+blast+overexposure/4144156/story.html

Hart, P., & Tindall, K. (2009). Leadership by the Famous: Celebrity as a Political Capital. In J. K. P. t. H. H. Patapan (Ed.), *Dispersed democratic leadership: origins, dynamics, and implications*. Oxford: Oxford University Press.

Hays, M. (2007). Dark shadows. *CBC*. Retrieved February 17, 2012, from http://www.cbc.ca/arts/tiff/features/tiffarcand.html

Heald, D. B. (2007). Primitive Encounters: Film and Tourism in the North American West. *The Western Historical Quarterly, 38*(1).

Helen. (2008, November 20). Earl Stevenson's Blog. http://www.ctv.ca/servlet/ChapterNews/story/CTVNews/20080728/blogs_Earl_stevenson/20080728/?s_name=idol2008

Herb, G. H., & Kaplan, D. H. (1999). Nested Identities: Nationalism, Territory, and Scale. Lanham (Maryland) and Oxford: Rowman & Littlefield.

Hertz, B. (2010, October 14). Book Review: First Step 2 Forever: My Story, by Justin Bieber. *The National Post*. Retrieved from http://arts.nationalpost.com/2010/10/14/review-justin-biebers-memoir-first-step-2-forever-my-story/

Hickey, T. (1999). Walk of Fame Inductee's Gala. *Sunday Sun*.

Hillmer, N., & Chapnick, A. (2007). Canadas of the mind: the making and unmaking of Canadian nationalisms in the twentieth century. Montreal: McGill-Queen's Press

Hills, M. (2002). *Fan Culture*. London: Routledge

Hills, M. (2006). Not Just Another Powerless Elite? When Media Fans Become Subcultural Celebrities In S. Holmes & S. Redmond (Eds.), *Framing Celebrity: New Directions in Celebrity Culture*. London: Routledge.

Hoberg, G. (2000). Canada and North American Integration. *Canadian Public Policy, 26*(August).

Holmes, S. (2004). 'But this time you choose!' Approaching the 'interactive' audience in reality TV. *International Journal of Cultural Studies, 7*(2).

Holmes, S. (2005a). 'Off-guard, Unkempt, Unready'?: Deconstructing Contemporary Celebrity in Heat Magazine. *Continuum: Journal of Media & Cultural Studies, 19* (1).

Holmes, S. (2005b). 'Starring… Dyer?': Re-visiting Star Studies and Contemporary Celebrity Culture. *Westminster Papers in Communication and Culture, 2*(2).

Home. (2011). *Canada's Walk of Fame*. Retrieved August 15, 2011, from http://www.canadaswalkoffame.com/home

Horton, D., & Wohl, R. (1997). Mass Communication and Para-Social Interaction In H. Mackay (Ed.), *Consumption and Everyday Life*. London: Sage.

Howell, C. (2001). *Blood, sweat and cheers: sport and the making of modern Canada*. Toronto: University of Toronto Press

Hudson, J. C. (2002). *Across this land: a regional geography of the United States and Canada*. Baltimore: The Johns Hopkins University Press.

Hulan, R. (2003). *Northern Experience and the Myths of Canadian Culture*. Montreal: McGill-Queen's Press

Hunt, K. (1981). The Fame Game. *Cinema Canada, October*(78).

Hutsel, C. (2002). It's Everyday Theatre Having the Stars Underfoot. *The Toronto Star*.

Ice Pilots NWT Heads To Global. (2010). Retrieved May 7, 2011, from http://www.channelcanada.com/Chapter4933.html

Ice Pilots to Film Episode in Oshkosh. (2011). *Reality TV Stars from Buffalo Airways to Bring DC-3 to AirVenture*. Retrieved July 16, 2011, from http://www.airventure.org/news/2010/100708_buffalo.html

Jackson. (2001). Gretzky Nation: Canada, Crisis, and Americanization. In D. Andrews & S. Jackson (Eds.), *Sport Stars: The Cultural Politics of Sporting Celebrity*. London: Routledge.

Jackson. (2007). Star Power? Celebrity and Politics among Anglophone Canadian Youth. *British Journal of Canadian Studies, 20*(1).

Jackson, & Ponic, P. (2001). Pride and Prejudice: Reflecting on Sport Heroes, National Identity, and Crisis in Canada. *Sport in Society, 4*(2), 43-62.

Jeffrey, L. (1996). Private Television and Cable. In M. Dorland (Ed.), *The cultural industries in Canada: problems, policies and prospects*. Toronto: James Lorimer & Company Ltd.

Jenkins, H. (2006). *Fans, Bloggers, and Gamers: Exploring Participatory Culture*. New York: New York University Press.

Jensen, J. (1992). Fandom as Pathology: The Consequences of Characterization. In L. A. Lewis (Ed.), *The Adoring Audience: Fan Culture and Popular Media*. London: Routledge.

Jett, S. C. (1997). Place-Naming, Environment, and Perception among the Canyon de Chelly Navajo of Arizona. *Professional Geographer, 49*(4).

Johnson, B. D. (2006). From Zombies to Molotov cocktails. *Maclean's*.

Jones-Imhotep, E. (2004). Nature, Technology, and Nation. *Journal of Canadian Studies, 38*(3).

Kalant, A. (2004). National Identity and the Conflict at Oka: Native Belonging and Myths of Poscolonial Nationhood in Canada. New York: Routledge

Kamakuraa, W. A., & Russell, G. J. (1993). Measuring brand value with scanner data. *International Journal of Research in Marketing, 10*(1).

Kat. (2008, November 20). Earl Stevenson's Blog. http://www.ctv.ca/servlet/ChapterNews/story/CTVNews/20080728/blogs_Earl_stevenson/20080728/?s_name=idol2008

Katerberg, W. (2003). A Northern Vision: Frontiers and the West in the Canadian and American Imagination. *American Review of Canadian Studies, 33*(4).

Kaufmann, E. (1998). "Naturalizing the Nation": The Rise of Naturalistic Nationalism in the United States and Canada: Society for Comparative Study of Society and History.

Kaufmann, E., & Zimmer, O. (1998). In Search of the Authentic Nation: Landscape and National Identity in Canada and Switzerland. *Nations and Nationalism, 4*(4).

Kim, A. (1993). The Absence of Pan-Canadian Civil Religion: Plurality, Duality, and Conflict in Symbols of Canadian Culture. *Sociology of Religion, 54*(3).

King, B. (1991). Articulating Stardom. In C. Gledhill (Ed.), *Stardom: industry of desire*. London: Routledge.

King, G. (2000). *Spectacular narratives: Hollywood in the age of the blockbuster*. London: I.B.Tauris & Co Ltd.

Koven, M. J. (2008). Film Festivals as Spaces of Meaning: Researching Festival Audiences as Producers of Meaning. *The Worcester Papers in English and Cultural Studies, 6*.

Krall, Arcand get stars on Walk of Fame. (2004). *The Toronto Star*.

Kroker, A. (1984). Technology and the Canadian Mind: Innis/McLuhan/Grant. Montreal: New World Perspectives.

Kroker, A. (2004). *The will to technology and the culture of nihilism: Heidegger, Nietzsche and Marx*. Toronto: University of Toronto Press.

Kryk, J. (2008). Decade. *Canada's Walk of Fame 1998-2008*.

Lash, R. (2010, May 28, 2010). B.C.'s outdoor spirit is captured in the province's network of spas. *Vancouver Sun*. Retrieved from http://www.canada.com/travel/outdoor+spirit+captured+province+network+spas/2445847/story.html

Lauretis, T. D., Huyssen, A., & Woodward, K. M. (1980). *The Technological Imagination: Theories and Fiction*. Madison: Coda Press.

Leach, J. (2002). Reading Canadian "Popular" Television: The Case of E.N.G. In J. Nicks & J. Sloniowski (Eds.), *Slippery Pastimes: Reading the Popular in Canadian Culture*. Waterloo: Wilfrid Laurier University Press.

Lee, S.Y., Sutherland, D., Weaver, D., & Woodley, A. (Director). (2008). Toronto Stories. [Motion Picture]. NowReel Films: Canada.

Lemco, J. (1994). *National health care: lessons for the United States and Canada*. Ann Arbor: University of Michigan Press.

Leong-Salobir, C. (2011). Food Culture in Colonial Asia: A Taste of Empire. Oxon: Routledge.

Leung, C. (2006). Northern overexposure. *Canadian Business magazine.*

Ley, D. (2003). Artists, Aestheticisation and the Field of Gentrification. *Urban Studies, 40*(12).

Lin, F. (2002). Dream Factory Redux: Mass Culture, Symbolic Sites, and Redevelopment in Hollywood. In J. Eade & C. Mele (Eds.), *Understanding the City: Contemporary and Future Perspectives*. Oxford: Blackwell.

Littler, J. (2011). Introduction: celebrity and the transnational. *Celebrity Studies, 2*(1).

Loiselle, A. (2003). "Fragments or Persistence of Visions: Continuity in Canadian Film History." In Kenneth G. Pryke & Walter C. Soderlund (Eds.) *Profiles of Canada*. Toronto: Canadian Scholars Press.

Longfellow, B. (2011). "The Red Violin, Commodity Fetishism, and Globalization. *Canadian Journal of Film Studies*. 10 2

Lorimar, R., & Gasher, M. (2001). *Mass Communication in Canada*. Don Mills: Oxford University Press.

Luven, L. V., & Walton, P. L. (1999). *Pop Can: Popular Culture*. Scarborough: Prentice Hall Canada.

Lypchuck, D. (2002). Filmmaker gets Walk of Fame star now, Oscar later. *The Toronto Star*.

MacCharle, T. (2011, April 14). Ethnic outreach efforts didn't break rules, Kenney says. *The Toronto Star* Retrieved from http://www.thestar.com/news/canada/chapter/975136--ethnic-outreach-efforts-didn-t-break-rules-kenney-says

MacDonald, G. (2009, September 14). A global actress reveals her private fight: An incurable cancer, a determined spirit. *The Globe and Mail*.

MacDonald, G. (2010). Lisa Ray emerges 'enriched' from battle with cancer. *The Globe and Mail*

Mackey, E. (2002). The House of Difference: Cultural Politics and National Identity in Canada: Cultural Politics and National Identity in Canada. Toronto: University of Toronto Press.

MacLennan, H. (1977). A society in revolt. In J. Webster (Ed.), *Voices of Canada: An Introduction to Canadian Culture*. Burlington: Association for Canadian Studies in the United States.

Magder, T., & Burston, J. (2001). Whose Hollywood? Changing Forms and Relations inside the North American Entertainment Economy. In V. Mosco & D. Schiller (Eds.), *Continental order?: integrating North America for cybercapitalism*. Lanham: Rowman & Littlefield.

Mahtani, M. (2001). Representing Minorities: Canadian Media and Minority Identities. Department of Canadian Heritage.

Manning, E. (2000). I am Canadian Identity: Territory and the Canadian National Land. *Theory & Event, 4*(4).

Manning, E. (2003). *Ephemeral Territories: Representing Nation, Home, and Identity in Canada*. Minneapolis: University of Minnesota Press.

Maple Leaf: A touch of home. (1999). *The Globe and Mail*.

Marshall, P. D. (1997). *Celebrity and Power: Fame in Contemporary Culture*. Minneapolis: University of Minnesota Press.

Marshall, P. D. (2006). New Media - New Self: The Changing Power of Celebrity. In P. D. Marshall (Ed.), *The Celebrity Culture Reader*. New York: Routledge.

Marshall, P. D. (Ed.). (2007). *The Celebrity Culture Reader*. New York and London: Routledge.

Mathews, V. (2008). Artcetera: Narrativising Gentrification in Yorkville, Toronto. *Urban Studies, 45*(13).

Mawani, R. (2007). Legalities of Nature: Law, Empire, and Wilderness Landscapes in Canada. *Social Identities, 13*(6).

Mazdon, L. (2007). Transnational 'French' Cinema: The Cannes Film Festival. *Modern & Contemporary France, 15*(1).

McCutcheon, L. E., Range, L., & Houran, J. (2002). Conceptualization and Measurement of Celebrity Worship. *The British Journal of Psychology, 93*.

McDowell, A. (2009). Canadians: We Like What the Queen Likes. *National Post*.

McGregor, G. (1985). *The Wacousta Syndrome: Explorations in the Canadian Landscape*. Toronto: University of Toronto Press.

McGregor, G. (1995). Review of David H. Flaherty and Frank E. Manning,eds., The Beaver Bites Back: American Popular Culture in Canada. *Canadian Journal of Sociology, 20.*

McLuhan, M. (1964). *Understanding Media: the Extensions of Man.* New York: McGraw-Hill.

McLuhan, M. (1989). Playboy Interview with Marshall McLuhan: A Candid Conversation with the High Priest of Popcult and Metaphysician of the Media. *Canadian Journal of Communication, 14* (Fall).

McNutt, M. (2009, November 19). So You Think You Can Dance Canada: Sugar and Spice, and Everyone's (Too) Nice. Retrieved April 17, 2016, from http://cultural-learnings.com/2009/09/02/so-you-think-you-can-dance-canada-sugar-and-spice-and-everyones-too-nice/

McPhail, T. L., & McPhail, B. M. (1990). *Communication: The Canadian Experience.* Mississauga: Copp Clark Pitman Ltd.

McRanor, G. (2010). Hedley pokes fun at fame-seekers, including themselves. *The Vancouver Sun.*

Mehta, D. (Director). (2009). Cooking With Stella. [Motion Picture]. Canada.

Micallef, S. (2008). Toronto Stories: The Film. *Spacing Toronto.*

MidDay. (2009). Lisa is epitome of grace under pressure: Deepa Mehta. Retrieved December 4, 2011, from http://www.mid-day.com/entertainment/2009/sep/160909-deepa-mehta-lisa-ray-cancer.htm

Millard, G., Riegel, S., & Wright, J. (2002). Here's Where We Get Canadian: English-Canadian Nationalism and Popular Culture. *American Review of Canadian Studies, 32*(1).

Mishra, V. (2002). *Bollywood cinema: temples of desire.* New York: Routledge.

Mlynek, A., & Pulfer, R. (2006). Canada's most powerful stars. *Canadian Business, 79,* p. 45.

Monaco, J. (1978). *Celebrity: the media as image makers.* New York: Dell Pub Co.

Moodleya, K. (1983). Canadian multiculturalism as Ideology. *Ethnic and Racial Studies, 6*(3).

Moran, J. (2010). TV formats worldwide: localizing global programs. Bristol: Intellect Books.

Moran, J. (2000). *Star Authors: Literary Celebrity in America.* London: Pluto Press.

Moss, L. (2003). *Is Canada postcolonial?: Unsettling Canadian Literature.* Waterloo: Wildred Laurier Press.

Mossberg, L., & Getz, D. (2014). Stakeholder Influences on the Ownership and Management of Festival Brands. In T. Andersson, D. Getz, and R. Mykletun (Eds.), *Festival and Event Management in Nordic Countries.* Oxon, England: Routledge

MTV. (2009). MTV- Justin Bieber artist profile. Retrieved December 6, 2011, from www.mtv.com/music/artist/bieber_justin/artist.jhtml#biographyEnd

Mudhar, R. (2010a, August 25, 2010). From mega clubs to mega culture in Entertainment District. *The Toronto Star.*

Mudhar, R. (2010b). Meet the new teams for Battle of the Blades. *The Toronto Star.*

Muhtadie, L., & Adrangi, S. (2003). Canada Salutes its Superstars. *The Globe and Mail.*

Murray, T. (2004). *Canadian National Railway.* Minneapolis: Voyageur Press.

Nakhaie, M. R., & Brym, R. J. (1999). The Political Attitude of Canadian Professors. *The Canadian Journal of Sociology 24*(3).

Nandy, S. (2011a, September 30). From Breakaway to Canada's Walk of Fame: Samita Nandy on the Fame of Russell Peters. *StarBuzz Weekly.*

Nandy, S. (2011b). The "Starbuzz" of the 2011 International Indian Academy Awards (IIFA)! *Starbuzz Weekly.*

New, W. H. (1989). *A History of Canadian Literature.* London: MacMillan Education.

Nichols, B. (1994a). Discovering Form, Inferring Meaning: New Cinemas and the Film Festival Circuit. *Film Quarterly, 47*(3).

Nichols, B. (1994b). Global Image Consumption in the Age of Late Capitalism *East-West Film Journal, 8*(1).

Nordicity (2013). "The Economic Contribution of the Film and Television Sector in Canada". Toronto: Motion Picture Association - Canada.

O'Leary, B. (1998). A Critical Overview. In J. Hall (Ed.), *The State of the Nation: Ernest Gellner and the Theory of Nationalism.* Cambridge: Cambridge University Press.

Ommundsen, W. (2004). Sex, Soap and Sainthood: Beginning to Theorize Literary Celebrity. *Jasal, 3.*

Onstad, K. (2007). Five questions for... Retrieved February 17, 2012, from http://www.cbc.ca/arts/tiff/features/tiff-5booth.html

Opinion. (2008). *Canada's Walk of Fame 2008.*

Orme, W. (2002). Aww, your own Walk of Fame. How Quaint. *The Toronto Star*.

Osborne, B. S. (2001). Landscapes, Memory, Monuments, and Commemoration: Putting Identity in Its Place. Kingston: Queen's University.

Osborne, B. S. (2006). From Native Pines to Diasporic Geese: Placing Culture, Setting Our Sites, Locating Identity in a Transnational Canada. *Canadian Journal of Communication, 31*(1).

Patch, N. (2011). Toronto crowd goes Gaga for Winnipeg girl. *Winnipeg Free Press*.

Peterson, L. (2009). Where to Spot Celebrities at the Toronto International Film Festival. *Travel Guide*.

Pevere, G. (1999). Taking a Walk on Fame's Side. *The Toronto Star*.

Pevere, G., & Dymond, G. (1996). *Mondo Canuck: A Canadian Pop Culture Odyssey*. Scarborough: Prentice Hall Canada Inc.

Playback. (2011). Four emerging Canadian actors get Hollywood coming-out party at TIFF. Retrieved September 20, 2011, from http://playbackonline.ca/2011/08/12/four-emerging-canadian-actors-get-hollywood-coming-out-party-at-tiff/

Porter, R. (2003). Scandalous Behaviour. *Ryerson Review of Journalism*, from http://www.rrj.ca/issue/2003/spring/395/

PTI. (2009, May 25). Rankings are not to be taken seriously: Lisa Ray. *Hindustan Times*. Retrieved from http://www.hindustantimes.com/StoryPage/Print/414412.aspx

Quail, C. (2008). So You Think You Can Dance, Canada?: Formatting and Canadian Reality Television. *FlowTV, 9*(2).

Quill, G. (1998). Canada Honours its Stars. *The Toronto Star*.

Quill, G. (2000). 'Walk finds down-to-earth charm. *The Toronto Star*.

Raboy, M. (1990). *Missed opportunities: the story of Canada's broadcasting policy*. Montreal: McGill-Queen's Press.

Rak, J. (2008). Canadian Idols? CBC's *The Greatest Canadians* as Celebrity History. In A. K. Zoë Druick (Ed.), *Programming reality: perspectives on English-Canadian television*. Waterloo: Wilfred Laurier University Press.

Ray, L. (2009). MM Memos and Gangajal. http://lisaraniray.wordpress.com/2010/03/14/mm-memos-and-gangajal/

Ray, L. (2010). Ever met a child philosopher? Retrieved April 17, 2016, from http://lisaraniray.wordpress.com/2010/03/11/ever-met-a-child-philosopher/

Redmond, S., & Holmes, S. (2007a). In S. Redmond & S. Holmes (Eds.), *Stardom and Celebrity: A Reader*. London: Sage Publications Ltd.

Redmond, S., & Holmes, S. (Eds.). (2007b). *Stardom and Celebrity*. London: Sage Publications.

Reynell, C. (1949). *The Economist* (Vol. 157). Charlottesville: University of Virginia.

Riendeau, R. (2007). *A brief history of Canada*. New York: Infobase Publishing.

Rifkin, J. (2005). Continentalism of a Different Stripe - The Bioregional (r)Evolutionary Movement. *The Walrus*.

Rofe, M. W., & Szili, G. (2009). Name Games 1: Place Names as Rhetorical Devices. *Landscape Research, 34*(3).

Rojek, C. (2001). *Celebrity*. London: Reaktion Books.

Rothman, J. (2004). Hollywood in wide angle: how directors view filmmaking. Lanham: Scarecrow Press, Inc.

Rumack, L. (2009). Howie Mandel. *Canada's Walk of Fame 2009*.

Russell, S. (2009). Frozen Columns in time: Folklore in the land of ice and snow. Retrieved August 22, 2011, from http://www.cbc.ca/sports/blogs/2009/01/frozen_in_time_folklore_in_the.html

Sahgal, N. (2009). Lisa Ray blogs: my bone marrow started sending messages, I have cancer. Retrieved December 1, 2011, from http://www.indianexpress.com/news/lisa-ray-blogs-my-bone-marrow-started-sending-messages-i-have-cancer/514835/

Salem, R. (2000). Seems Just Like Old Times. *The Toronto Star*.

Salem, R. (2002). Walking the Walk. *Starweek magazine*.

Salem, R. (2008). Our dance show better than U.S. version. *The Toronto Star* Retrieved November 19, 2011, from http://www.thestar.com/entertainment/chapter/547442

Sandra. (2008, November 20). Earl Stevenson's Blog. http://www.ctv.ca/servlet/ChapterNews/story/CTVNews/20080728/blogs_Earl_stevenson/20080728/?s_name=idol2008

Sarif, S. (Writer). (2007). The World Unseen. South Africa.

Saul, J. R. (1997). Reflections of a Siamese Twins: Canada at the End of the Twentieth Century. Toronto: Penguin Group.

Schafer, P. (1995). Canadian Culture: Key to Canada's Future Development. Markham: World Culture Project.

Schweitzer, M. (2010). Editorial. *Canadian Theatre Review*(141).

Shaw, H. (2009, September 18). Carpetbragging. *National Post*.

Sherbert, G., Gerin, A., & Petty, S. (Eds.). (2006). *Canadian Cultural Poesis: Essays on Canadian Culture*. Waterloo: Wilfred Laurier University Press.

Shields, R. (1992). Places on the Margin: Alternative Geographies of Modernity. London: Routledge.

Sibonney, C. (2008). Michael J. Fox, James Cameron on Canada's Walk of Fame. *Reuters* Retrieved January 10, 2012, from http://www.reuters.com/chapter/2008/09/07/us-toronto-walkoffame-idUSN0649564020080907

Siddiqui, H. (2011, April 17). Siddiqui: Tories divide and conquer. *The Toronto Star*. Retrieved April 17, 2016, from http://www.thestar.com/opinion/editorialopinion/chapter/975781--siddiqui-tories-divide-and-conquer

Slater, T. (2002). Looking at the North American City Through the Lens of Gentrification Discourse. *Urban Geography, 23*(2).

Slater, T. (2004). North American gentrification? Revanchist and emancipatory perspectives explored. *Environment and Planning A, 36.*

Smith, A. (1994). Canada-- an American nation?: essays on continentalism, identity, and the Canadian frame of mind. Montreal: McGill-Queen's Press.

Smith, B. (Writer). (2007). All Hat. [Motion Picture]. New Road Films: Canada.

Soares, J. (2008). The Cold War on Ice. *Brown Journal of World Affairs, XIV*(2).

Soumalias. (2010). Toronto: Canada's Walk of Fame.

Spaner, D. (2004). *Dreaming in the Rain: How Vancouver Became Hollywood North by Northwest.* Vancouver: Arsenal Pulp Press.

Spencer, M., & Ayscough, S. (2003). *Hollywood North: Creating The Canadian Motion Picture Industry*. Montreal: Cantos International Publishing Inc. .

Sports in the Cold War. (2007). *History and the Public.* Retrieved November 20, 2011, from http://digitalhistory.concordia.ca/courses/hist306f07/projects/jbabalis/hockey.html

Staff. (1999a). Scaling a Mountain of Talent. *The Globe and Mail.*

Staff. (1999b). Stepping Out with the Stars. *The Globe and Mail.*

Staff. (2001). Stars Immortalized on Walk of Fame. *The Globe and Mail.*

Staff. (2010a). Kitchener native makes So You Think You Can Dance Canada semifinals. *The Record.*

Staff. (2010b). Wicklund eliminated from SYTYCD Canada. *BCLocalNews.com*. Retrieved January 20, 2011, from http://www.bclocalnews.com/entertainment/102971139.html

Staff. (2011a). *The Globe and Mail* Retrieved December 4, 2011, from http://www.theglobeandmail.com/news/arts/music/lady-gaga-goes-gaga-for-canadian-girls-rendition-of-born-this-way/chapter1911824/

Staff. (2011b). Maria Aragon in Los Angeles doing photo shoot. *Brandon Sun*. Retrieved from http://www.brandonsun.com/breaking-news/Maria-Aragon-is-in-Los-Angeles-shooting-a-commercial-for-Ralph-Lauren-118579659.html

Staff. (2011c). Net sensation to meet Ellen in Hollywood. *Winnipeg Free Press*.

Star Power Recharged. (2009). *Program Guide*. Toronto: Toronto International Film Festival Inc.

Star Struck. (2002). *TV Times*.

Steed, J. (1981). Pay Television. *The Globe and Mail*, p. 7.

Stenger, J. (2001). Return to Oz: The Hollywood Redevelopment Project, or Film History as Urban Renewal. In M. Shiel & T. Fitzmaurice (Eds.), *Cinema and the City: Film and Urban Societies in a Global Context*. Oxford: Blackwell Publisher.

Stern, S. (Writer). (1955). Rebel Without a Cause. [Motion Picture]. Warner Bros: USA.

Stevenson, J. (2009). Justin Bieber hits the big time. *Toronto Sun*.

Strachan, A. (2010, September 21). Jamie Sale ready for another face-off. *Postmedia News*.

Strinati, D. (2000). The Rise of the Hollywood Studio System *An Introduction to Studying Popular Culture*. London: Routledge.

Stringer, J. (2003). Neither One Thing Nor the Other. In J. Stringer (Ed.), *Movie blockbusters*. London: Routledge.

Stringer, J. (Ed.). (2001). *Global Cities and International Film Festival Economy*. Oxford: Blackwell.

Sugars, C. C. (2004). *Home-work: postcolonialism, pedagogy, and Canadian literature*. Ottawa: University of Ottawa Press.

Sung, H. (2009, September 29). Dancing Queen Leah Miller. *Flare*

Szeman, I. (2000). The rhetoric of culture: Some notes on magazines, Canadian culture and globalization. *Journal of Canadian Studies* (Fall).

Szklarski, C. (2010, March 17). 'Battle of the Blades' heads to Sweden while Canuck version getting tweaked. *680 News*. Retrieved November 20, 2011, from http://www.680news.com/sports/chapter/36540--battle-of-the-blades-heads-to-sweden-while-canuck-version-getting-tweaked

Taverner, C. (2008). *CRTC Report Shows Broadcasters Continue to Fail Audiences.* Toronto: Alliance of Canadian Cinema, Television and Radio Artists.

Taylor, C. (1997). The Politics of Recognition. In A. Heble, D. P. Pennee & J. R. T. Struthers (Eds.), *New contexts of Canadian criticism.* Peterborough: Broadview Press.

Television viewing. (2006). Statistics Canada.

Thompson, L. (2010). Monochrome Now: Digital Black and White Cinema and the Photographic Past. Retrieved November 20, 2011, from *http://www.latrobe.edu.au/screeningthepast/29/monochrome-now.html*

TIFF. (2009). *Programme Guide.* Toronto: Toronto International Film Festival Inc.

TIFF. (2015a). TIFF History. Retrieved October 09, 2015, from tiff.net/explore/history

TIFF. (2015b). Our Story. Retrieved October 09, 2015, from tiff.net/explore/about

TIFF. (2011c). TIFF Launches Rising Stars Programme. 2011, from http://tiff.net/press/pressreleases/2011/tiff-launches-rising-stars-programme

Tinic, S. (2005). *On location: Canada's television industry in a global market.* Toronto: University of Toronto Press.

Tinic, S. (2006). Global Vistas and Local Reflections: Negotiating Place and Identity in Vancouver Television. *Television New Media, 7*(154).

Tolan, F. (2005). Situating Canada: The Shifting Perspective of the Postcolonial Other in Margaret Atwood's The Robber Bride. *American Review of Canadian Studies, 35*(3).

Toronto has Earned a New Title. (1985). *Philadelphia Inquirer*

Tse, D. (2003). Walk This Way. *The Sunday Sun.*

Tuohy, C. J. (1992). *Policy and politics in Canada: institutionalized ambivalence.* Philadelphia: Temple University Press.

Turner, G. (2004). *Understanding Celebrity.* London: Sage.

Turner, G. (2010). Approaching celebrity studies. *Celebrity Studies, 1*(1).

Tyler, I., & Bennett, B. (2010). Celebrity Chav: Fame, Femininity and Social Class. *European Journal of Cultural Studies, 13*(3).

Uher, M. (2008). *Hockey as a Metaphor for Canadian History.* Masaryk: University Brno.

Vaccaro, M. (2011a). Captain Canuck Goes Hollywood: Possible Movie in the Works, with Justin Bieber as the Red-Caped Crime Fighter. *Toronto Life*.

Vaccaro, M. (2011b). TIFF Announces Rising Star Programme to Promote Canadian Talent Abroad. Retrieved April 17, 2016, from http://www.torontolife.com/daily/hype/tiff-talk/2011/01/31/tiff-announces-rising-star-programme-to-promote-canadian-talent-abroad/

Valck, M. (2007). *Film Festivals: From European Geopolitics to Global Cinephilia*. Amsterdam: Amsterdam University Press.

Vémola, J. (2009). Reflections of Marshall McLuhan's Media Theory in the Cinematic Work of David Cronenberg and Atom Egoyan. Masaryk: University, Brno.

Vipond, M. (2000). *The Mass Media in Canada*. Toronto: James Lorimer & Company Ltd. .

VISA. (2009). Want to Feel Like You're On the A-List. *The Toronto Star*.

VISA. (2010). Film Festival Sponsorship. Retrieved June 22, 2011, from http://www.visa.ca/film/screening_tor.jsp

VISA. (2011). Film Festival Sponsorships. Retrieved December 20, 2011, from http://www.visa.ca/film/toronto.jsp

Vlessing, E. (2006). Star Treatment. *Hollywood Reporter*.

Vlessing, E. (2011). Martin Short: Nice, Not Nasty, Works When Judging TV Talent Competitions. *Hollywood Reporter*.

Wallmann, J. M. (1999). *The western: parables of the American dream*. Lubbock: Texas Tech University Press.

What does it mean to be Canadian. (2010). *The Toronto Star*. Retrieved from http://www.thestar.com/specialsections/chapter/867651--what-does-it-mean-to-be-canadian

What it Means to Them. (1999). *The Globe and Mail*.

Whyte, M. (2008). Yorkville and TIFF grew up together. *Toronto Star*.

Wiebe, L. (2011). First a tweet, now an invite. *Winnipeg Free Press*.

Wilkinson, P. (2008). *Weekend In*. Toronto: Spafax Canada Inc.

Willems-Braun, B. (1997). Buried Epistemologies: The Politics of Nature in (Post)colonial British Columbia. *Annals of the Association of American Geographers, 87*(1).

Winereserva. (Producer). (2009) Shinan Govani gossip columnist to the stars dishes wine and celebrity. *The Wine Ladies* retrieved from http://www.youtube.com/watch?v=DMHBEp4OJl8&feature=related

Wise, W. (1999). "Canadian cinema from boom to bust: the tax-shelter years". *Take One: Film & Television in Canada*, 18 Winter

Wodskou, C. (Producer). (2010). Arctic Re-Imagined. *The Current*. CBC: Canada.

Wong, L. L., & Trumper, R. (2002). Global Celebrity Atheletes and Nationalism: Futbol, Hockey, and the Representation of Nation *Journal of Sport and Social Issues, 26*(2).

Wood, P., & Gilbert, L. (2005). Multiculturalism in Canada: Accidental Discourse, Alternative Vision, Urban Practice. *International Journal of Urban and Regional Research, 29*(3).

York, L. (2002). Your Star: Pauline Johnson and the Tensions of Celebrity Discourse. *Canadian Poetry, 51*, p. 8-17.

York, L. (2007). Large Ceremonies: Literary Celebrity of Carol Shields In M. Dvořák & M. Jones (Eds.), *Carol Shields and the extra-ordinary*. Montreal: McGill-Queen's Press.

Young, D. (2001). Celine Dion, national unity and the English-language press in Canada. *Media Culture Society, 23*(5).

Zacharias, Y. (2010). Scriptwriter fails to convince candidate. *Vancouver Sun*.

Index

www.ingramcontent.com/pod-product-compliance
Lightning Source LLC
Chambersburg PA
CBHW060454290526
45791CB00001B/110